Teaching Every Child Every Day

This series focuses on important contemporary topics relevant to school-based achievement and pedagogy. Each volume focuses on a single topic, bringing together commentary from some of the most important figures contributing to the problem area. The plan at this time is for at least one of the general editors to be involved in the editing of each volume, although often in collaboration with guest editors who are exceptionally expert with respect to the topic of the volume. Those interested in serving as guest editors should contact one of the general editors with a specific proposal for a volume.

Teaching Every Child Every Day

Learning in Diverse Schools and Classrooms

Karen R. Harris

Steve Graham

University of Maryland, College Park

Donald Deshler

University of Kansas, Lawrence

EDITORS

BROOK
LINE
BOOKS

ISBN 1-57129-040-0

Library of Congress Cataloging-In-Publication Data
Teaching every child every day: learning in diverse schools and
    classrooms / Karen R. Harris, Steve Graham, Donald Deshler, editors.
        p.   cm. -- (Advances in teaching & learning)
    Includes bibliographical references and index.
    ISBN 1-57129-040-0 (pbk.)
    1. Mixed ability grouping in education--United States.
2. Multicultural education--United States.   3. Interdisciplinary
approach in education--United States.   4. Education--Social aspects-
-United States.   5. Teaching--United States.   I. Harris, Karen R.
II. Graham, Steven, 1950-   . III. Deshler, Donald D. IV. Series.
LB3061.3.T43   1998
371.2'52--dc21   97-44339
                                                               CIP

Cover design, book design and typography by Erica L. Schultz.

Printed in USA by Bang Printing, Brainerd, MN.

10 9 8 7 6 5 4 3 2 1

Published by
BROOKLINE BOOKS
P.O. Box 1047
Cambridge, Massachusetts 02238
Order toll-free: 1-800-666-BOOK

CONTENTS

Introduction

KAREN R. HARRIS & STEVE GRAHAM, University of Maryland

DONALD D. DESHLER, University of Kansas

It has become commonplace to talk about the diversity evident in our schools today. Yet the challenges faced by teachers and children, as well as by parents, administrators, and other service providers, are anything but commonplace. Technological, economic, social, and cultural changes are occurring at an accelerated and unprecedented rate not only in this country, but across the world (Bandura, 1995). In our opinion, the increasing diversity in American classrooms and the changes we face represent both a source of challenge and a resource for teaching and learning; this viewpoint permeates this book.

Our schools and classrooms are rapidly becoming more academically, culturally, linguistically, economically, and racially diverse. Policy and reform initiatives, such as detracking and inclusion of children with disabilities in neighborhood schools and general education classrooms, have also increased classroom diversity. In fact, diversity is viewed by many as "one of this nation's signature or defining characteristics ... as legitimately American as football on a fall Sunday afternoon" (Fuchs, Fuchs, Mathes, & Simmons, 1997, p. 176).

While such diversity creates challenges, it also creates opportunities to build true communities of learners, learning from and about one another. As the Carnegie Foundation (1995) described them, such communities are educationally purposeful, open, just, disciplined, caring, and celebrative (cf. Harris & Graham, 1996a). These characteristics establish a safe environment that promotes risk taking and enhances social development.

TEACHING EVERY CHILD:
USING EVERYTHING WE KNOW

Creating such communities and finding effective learning approaches for all students is not easy. This task represents one of the most significant challenges faced in our time. According to the Carnegie Foundation (1995), from 1980 to 1990, the number of children in this country with limited English proficiency increased by 26%, and the number of immigrant children increased by 24%. The percentage of minority children in our schools has grown steadily from 21% in 1970 to 40% by 1992. Alarmingly, the proportion of children living in poverty in our country is expected to rise to 26% by 2020.

By the fifth grade, it is quite common today to find a 6- or 7-year difference in abilities between the least and most capable readers in a classroom (Bond, Tinker, Wasson, & Wasson, 1989). Even among children just beginning school, the diversity in backgrounds, experiences, and abilities is striking. How do we find and use the most effective teaching and learning approaches for each and every student across every grade level—without placing our children in ability groups or tracks, practices that have been found to be damaging?

We believe that the answer to that question rests upon two powerful foundations: 1) creating effective, powerful learning communities where every child belongs and every child can be successful, and 2) empowering teachers to integrate effective instructional practices (Deshler & Schumaker, 1988, 1993; Harris & Graham, 1996b). Teachers in this country, however, are often faced with a literature or educational program that promotes extreme or singular answers to how to teach children and assess what they know, are learning, and can do (McIntyre & Pressley, 1996; Pearson, 1996). For example, they are told by some that whole language is the right way for all children, only to be told by others that it is time to "get back to basics." They are encouraged to try new approaches, but are often hesitant when this means giving up approaches that have been working for them and for their students for some time.

The diversity in today's classrooms provides us with both the drive and the opportunity to thoughtfully and purposefully integrate the many effective instructional approaches we now have at our disposal, while remaining open to the careful trial of emerging approaches to instruction and assessment. Thus, teachers do not have to choose between false dichotomies, such as whole language vs. explicit instruction in phonics and comprehension. Rather, they can meaningfully integrate these approaches. Similarly, in writing, they do not have to chose between the Writers' Workshop approach (which creates such meaningful, authentic contexts for writing) and explicit instruction in important writing strategies and skills; Writers' Workshop and development of powerful writing strategies can and do work well together (Harris & Graham, 1996c; Sexton, Harris, & Graham, in press). When educators treat competing, validated viewpoints and alternative approaches with thoughtfulness and respect, a powerful repertoire for teaching and learning can be developed.

In our view, it is also crucial to integrate the disciplines, especially to integrate literacy—learning to read and write—within the content areas. This integration, using proven instructional approaches, allows a balance between improving conceptual learning, understanding, and problem solving on the one hand, and basic competencies for literacy—including increasing fluency and automaticity of skills and strategies—on the other. This balance is maintained through a view of learning as a socially situated activity that is enhanced in functional, meaningful, and authentic contexts (cf. Hogan & Pressley, 1997).

While some have argued that the integration of approaches to teaching and learning in the classroom is necessarily impossible and dangerously unguided (cf. Edelsky, Altwerger, & Flores, 1991), the authors in this book report on teachers, schools, and communities that clearly demonstrate the possibility and power of coherent, meaningful integration. As teachers and parents have long known, no one approach suits all children equally. No single intervention or viewpoint can address the complex nature of school failure or success, or of social inequalities and inequities. An integrated instructional approach allows the combination of competing models of teaching and learning in ways that maximize the strengths of each, while addressing the weaknesses in any given model through the strengths inherent in others.

A THUMBNAIL SKETCH

What, then, does our vision of integration look like? We begin with the belief that children are inherently active, self-regulated learners who construct knowledge in developmentally appropriate ways within a social context. Children's perceptions of what they are doing and why they are doing it, and of their teacher's intentions, are critical in this integration. Those leading the way in integrative approaches have created coherent, integrated instruction based in learning communities that are purposeful, open, just, disciplined, caring, and celebrative. Ongoing assessment of children's cognitive and metacognitive abilities, skills, knowledge and prior experiences—as well as their motivational, behavioral, and social characteristics—is critical to teachers' goals and actions in these learning communities. Within authentic, meaningful contexts, students are provided whatever level of support is needed (from explicit instruction through discovery) to acquire, develop fluency in, and personalize powerful skills and strategies; and to develop conceptual learning, flexible applications, and understanding. Teachers are responsive to and plan for individual needs and differences, and students are given the time they need to attain the educational outcomes valued by their teachers, schools, families, and communities.

The integration we envision is not, and won't be, easy. Yet it can be and is being done, as can be seen in the school practices in this book.

Chapter One

In Chapter 1, we share the experiences and achievements of "Mosaic Central Elementary School," a culturally and socioeconomically diverse school of approximately 430 children located just outside Washington, D.C. Children with disabilities, including serious emotional disabilities, are also included in the school. Several core values—everyone belongs, everyone can be successful, and everyone is valued and respected—have guided the school in its adaptive, "self-renewing" efforts over the past 10 years. The efforts of teachers, parents, staff, and administrators in actualizing these values and reaching established goals are discussed in this chapter.

Chapter Two

In Chapter 2, Patricia Cunningham and Dorothy Hall describe an innovative, integrative reading instruction project that began in 1989 and has since swept across the country. Their Four Blocks framework provides children with a variety of avenues to becoming literate, by dividing primary-grade language arts time among four blocks: Guided Reading, Self-Selected Reading, Writing, and Working with Words. Instruction within each block is multilevel to meet the diverse needs of children with a wide range of literacy levels, and the approach is flexible to meet the unique teaching styles of individual teachers. Cunningham and Hall eloquently describe the experiences of both children and teachers with their Four Blocks approach, and illustrate the many variations possible within each block. They describe how teachers have embraced this framework and made it their own, and how children have thrived with this approach. They conclude their chapter by sharing the voices of children, parents, and teachers who have found that the Four Blocks approach helps children enjoy school more and find success.

Chapter Three

Chapter 3 takes us into Linda Bender's classroom to observe how eight enduring principles formed the foundation for a motivating and engaging context for learning. During a 16-week unit, we follow the progress of two students from her class—Armando, a Hispanic boy, and Denisha, an African-American girl—as they raise monarch larvae as part of a study of ecological systems. Linda Bender is a participating teacher in project CORI (Concept-Oriented Reading Instruction), an outstanding example of the integration of literacy skill development within the content areas. John Guthrie, the originator of the CORI model, and Kathleen Cox explain how the principles behind CORI accommodate diverse students. As they share the impressive accomplishments in Linda's classroom, they provide a step-by-step plan teachers can follow to implement CORI in their own classrooms. The flexible design of this plan accommodates the individual needs and strengths of both teachers and students.

Chapter Four

In Chapter 4, Karen Harris, Tanya Schmidt, and Steve Graham describe an integrative approach to writing instruction for students with diverse abilities and backgrounds in the elementary and middle grades. It allows all students to profit from the authentic, meaningful approach to writing inherent in writers' workshop, but also provides them with the opportunities needed to develop powerful composition strategies. This model, known as Self-Regulated Strategy Development (SRSD), is based on over 15 years of work and research with teachers and their students—both those who enjoy writing and those who struggle with the writing process. Within the Writers' Workshop structure, each student can be offered the level of instruction necessary—from discovery through explicit strategies instruction—to come to own important writing strategies and self-regulate their use. The SRSD model also focuses on students' attitudes, beliefs, and emotions about writing, recognizing the importance of helping struggling writers to develop positive attitudes about writing and themselves as writers. The authors of this chapter take us to two classrooms. In the first, students develop an effective strategy for writing opinion essays. In the second, students expand on what they know about planning and writing stories. Students in both class-rooms (as in over 20 empirical studies) exhibit significant improve-ments in their quality of writing, knowledge of writing, approach to writing, and self-efficacy.

Chapter Five

In Chapter 5, Marjorie Montague traces the forces behind reform in mathematics teaching and learning—including the increasing diver-sity in our schools, changing expectations regarding the nation's work force, and technological advances. Mathematics reform has resulted in changes in mathematics content, pedagogy, learning experiences, time allocation, and assessment. Learning experiences increasingly focus on communicating about mathematics, solving problems cooperatively, using manipulatives to enhance conceptual learning, and incorporating calculators and other technology. Prin-ciples that can guide mathematics teachers in meeting the needs of diverse learners are presented and illustrated, as we learn about Mr. Hunt's sixth-grade class. Mr. Hunt's school has adopted an approach termed *curriculum-centered collaborative consultation.* In this model, the curriculum rather than the student becomes the source of the identified problem, and a collaborative team (including general, special, and bilingual education teachers) works together on assess-ment, intervention, and evaluation.

Chapter Six

In Chapter 6, Russell Gersten, Scott Baker, and Susan Marks address teaching students with limited English proficiency. Federal policy currently requires schools to provide these learners with instruction that promotes English language acquisition, and instruction that enables meaningful access to the school's curriculum. Their framework of language, learning, and cultural principles allows a flexibility in instructional procedures that is especially important because of the considerable variability in these students' knowledge of and facility with English. To illustrate each principle, they provide examples taken from their work in schools and classrooms and the experiences of children and teachers.

The authors discuss the critical roles of parents, guardians, and community members, as well as the need for teachers to have opportunities to collaborate and share ideas. They focus on creating long-term goals and planning for students and schools, as opposed to "putting out fires" from situation to situation.

Taken together, the chapters in this book strongly address the challenges we face in today's diverse neighborhoods, schools, and classrooms, as well as the opportunities our diversity provides. The schools, teachers, administrators, families, and communities drawn on provide examples of effective integration of what we know about achieving success for all students, illustrating what can be and is being done. It is our hope that this book will help promote continued efforts to put into practice our knowledge of what works with diverse learners.

REFERENCES

Bandura, A. (Ed.) (1995). *Self-efficacy in changing societies*. New York: Cambridge University Press.

Bond, G.L., Tinker, M.A., Wasson, B.B., & Wasson, J.B. (1989). *Reading difficulties: Their diagnosis and correction* (6th ed.). Englewood Cliffs, NJ: Prentice Hall.

Carnegie Foundation (1995). *Draft: Report of the Carnegie Task Force on learning in the primary grades*. New York: Author.

Deshler, D.D., & Schumaker, J.B. (1988). An instructional model for teaching students how to learn. In J.L. Graden, J.E. Zins, & M.J. Curtis (Eds.), *Alternative education delivery systems: Enhancing instructional options for all students* (pp. 391-411). Washington, DC: National Association of School Psychologists.

Deshler, D.D., & Schumaker, J.B. (1993). Strategy mastery by at-risk students: Not a simple matter. *Elementary School Journal, 94*(2), 153-167.

Edelsky, C., Altwerger, B., & Flores, B. (1991). *Whole language: What's the difference?* Portsmouth, NH: Heinemann.

Fuchs, D., Fuchs, L.S., Mathes, P.G., & Simmons, D.C. (1997). Peer-assisted learning strategies: Making classrooms more responsive to diversity. *American Educational Research Journal, 34*(1), 174-206.

Harris, K.R., & Graham, S. (1996a). Memo to constructivists: Skills count, too. *Educational Leadership, 53*(5), 26-29.

Harris, K.R., & Graham, S. (1996b). *Making the writing process work: Strategies for composition and self-regulation* (2nd ed.). Cambridge: Brookline Books.

Harris, K.R., & Graham, S. (1996c). Teaching writing strategies within the context of a whole language class. In E. McIntyre & M. Pressley (Eds.), *Balanced instruction: Strategies and skills in whole language* (pp. 155-175).

Hogan, K., & Pressley, M. (Eds.). (1997). *Scaffolding student learning: Instructional approaches & issues.* Cambridge: Brookline Books.

McIntyre, E., & Pressley, M. (Eds.). (1996). *Balanced instruction: Strategies and skills in whole language.* Norwood, MA: Christopher-Gordon Publishers.

Pearson, P.D. (1996). Foreword. In E. McIntyre & M. Pressley (Eds.), *Balanced instruction: Strategies and skills in whole language* (pp. xv-xvii). Norwood, MA: Christopher-Gordon Publishers.

Sexton, M., Harris, K.R., & Graham, S. (in press). The effects of Self-Regulated Strategy Development on essay writing and attributions of students with LD in a process writing setting. *Exceptional Children.*

CHAPTER ONE

Self-Renewal: One School's Approach to Meeting the Challenge of Student Diversity

STEVE GRAHAM & KAREN R. HARRIS,
University of Maryland

The process of schooling has become increasingly complex during the last two decades. The typical American school has become more diverse, serving children differing in their academic, economic, linguistic, racial, and ethnic backgrounds. This includes children who do not speak English or have not yet mastered its spoken and written forms; children who come from different cultures and traditions; children who are new to the United States, either legally or illegally; children who live in poverty, as well as those who enjoy the economic benefits of the American dream; children with disabilities, including those who are challenged physically, cognitively, behaviorally, or socially; and children who are gifted, as well as those who struggle to learn.

Many educators have viewed this increasing diversity as an opportunity to build not only better schools, but a better society—one where individual differences are accepted and valued. This is not an easy task; it requires vision, commitment, and time to achieve. This is the story of how one school is working to meet the challenge of diversity, and in the process is becoming a better school.

The Cast

The chief characters in this story are the teachers and students of Mosaic Central Elementary School.[1] Mosaic Central is located outside of the "Beltway" surrounding Washington, D.C. It is situated in a mostly middle-class neighborhood of small brick houses, but includes children from an adjoining neighborhood with houses priced in the $250,000 to $300,000 range, as well as children from a nearby apartment complex that includes federally subsidized units.

Approximately 430 children attend Mosaic Central. There are three kindergarten and three first-grade classes. For older students, there are two classes at each grade level, as well as two combination classes: one for second- and third-graders, and one for fourth- and fifth-graders. The school also contains two classes for students with serious emotional disturbance (SED)—one at the primary and the other at the intermediate level—and a Head Start Learning Center that provides services for up to 14 children; on average, 4 of these children have special needs.

The school's population is culturally diverse, with children from 28 foreign countries. Some of these students are recent immigrants to the United States, coming primarily from countries in South and Central America, Africa, and Asia. Others are children of personnel in the Brazilian Navy who are stationed in Washington, D.C. Many of these children (about 50) either have just begun or are in the process of learning English.

The ethnic make-up of the school is varied. No single ethnic group is populous enough to form a majority. Thirty-eight percent of the children are white, 32% are black, 16% are Hispanic, and 14% are Asian.

A considerable proportion of the children attending the school qualify for a free or reduced-price school lunch. During the last 4 years, this proportion has climbed from 1 in every 5 students to 2 in

---

[1] This is not the real name of the school, nor were real names used for any teachers, parents, or children.

every 5. The school receives monies from Title 1 which pay for part-time Title 1 assistants and a Title 1 teacher specialist who works in the school one day a week.

The school district also provides the school with a full-time English as a Second Language (ESL) teacher, a half-time ESL support teacher, a half-time Quality Integrated Education (QIE) teacher, and a half-time teacher for disadvantaged students. These teachers are provided to schools with diverse student populations, high mobility rates, and a high percentage of students who receive free or reduced-price meals. In addition, the school employs a media specialist, a half-time reading specialist, a counselor, a special education resource room teacher, and a speech pathologist (3 days a week).

WHO ARE WE? WHAT IS OUR PURPOSE?

The last 10 years have witnessed considerable change at Mosaic Central, first in the diversity of students, and then in the ways the school has changed to meet the needs of these students. In many ways, Mosaic Central fits Peter Senge's (1990) description of a "learning organization." He contends that organizations need to be like living organisms, able to learn and change. Instead of retaining unproductive routines, successful organizations adapt to changing conditions. Adaptive organizations collectively and continually "enhance their capacity to create things they really want to create" (O'Neil, 1995, p. 20).

Joyce, Wolf, and Calhoun (1993) referred to adaptive schools as "self-renewing." According to Garmston and Wellman (1995), self-renewing schools continually ask themselves two questions: *Who are we?* and *What is our purpose?*

At Mosaic Central and other schools within the district, this process of self-reflection is facilitated through the development of a School Improvement Management Plan. Each school evaluates the working environment, the needs of the student population, the effectiveness of instructional programs, responsiveness to student diversity, and linkages between the school and the community.

One outcome of this evaluation is that each school collectively establishes goals and actions for making changes and improvements. This allows the school to adapt in an organized and purposeful manner to changing circumstances. The process of self-reflection may also help schools strengthen, refine, or identify core values. Decisions about what to do and how to do it typically involve discussions about values.

At Mosaic Central, several core values provide the foundation for a shared vision of what the school is trying to accomplish in meeting the needs of its diverse student population. The teachers and staff we interviewed are committed to creating a school where respect for human differences and caring for others is valued. They want to create a school where every child belongs and every child is successful.

Mission statements such as these are not new or uncommon (Hargreaves, 1995). They are, however, not always successful. They may not be accepted by the staff. They may become so fixed and rigid that they are unresponsive to changing needs. They may become insipid and vacuous when methods for accomplishing them are never devised or implemented.

These conditions are not evident at Mosaic Central. As in other self-renewing schools (Sagor, 1995), all faculty and staff members— from the principal to the secretaries—have a similar picture of what the school is trying to accomplish. This picture is not static, as the staff members are engaged in an ongoing process of review, adjusting their programs and priorities to the changing needs of their clients—the families and students they serve. Congruence among visions, values, and goals is also evident, as faculty members work together to develop and test their ideas on how to build a school where all belong and all are successful. The cooperative efforts of faculty are further boosted by the efforts of individual staff members, who make their own unique and individualistic contributions to the overall effort.

We begin our examination of how Mosaic Central works to meet the challenge of diversity by examining the combined and individual efforts of the staff to actualize three values: *everyone belongs, everyone can be successful,* and *everyone is respected and valued.* In each case, individual as well as cooperative staff efforts are highlighted. These examples do not provide a full catalogue of all of the school's efforts, but feature some of their more prominent endeavors.

EVERYONE BELONGS

Feeling Welcome

An essential ingredient in developing a sense of belonging is making people feel welcome—from the moment they enter the school. The school is well-kept and attractive, with children's schoolwork and art projects decorating the halls and classroom walls. The main office is located just inside the entrance and arranged so that there are no barriers or counters between staff and incoming children or parents. According to a survey conducted by the county school system, 99% of parents with children at Mosaic Central indicated that they felt "welcomed" when they walked into the main office. This was due, in large part, to the two secretaries, who are friendly and courteous to adults and children alike. To the delight of many preschool children visiting the school for the first time, the secretaries keep a drawer full of candy and other treats to share with them. One of the secretaries grew up in South America and speaks both Spanish and Portuguese.

This sense of welcome and warmth is not limited to the main office, but is evident throughout the school. For instance, parents are encouraged to visit the school, observe children at work, and help out as volunteers. Parents feel so comfortable with this invitation, and participate so freely, that Mosaic Central received a volunteer award from the State Department of Education. Teachers, too, view the school as a warm and friendly place. In one survey, the staff indicated that the greatest thing about Mosaic Central was that the school felt like a family.

Welcome clubs and buddies. The school's emphasis on creating a welcoming atmosphere is further illustrated by the process for introducing new students to the school. Because the school has a high mobility rate, there are many new students moving to Mosaic Central throughout the year. The process of welcoming new students typically begins with a meeting, during which the principal shares the school's philosophy and answers parents' and children's questions. While parents fill out the enrollment forms, the school counselor takes the new student on a tour of the school. During the tour, she takes some time to get acquainted with the child. She explains that she works with all of the children in the school, and that her job is to "help children be successful in school and feel good about themselves." She encourages new students to come and see her if they have anything they want to talk about, indicating that if she is not immediately available, they can leave a note (a self-referral system), and she will come and get them from their classrooms as soon as possible.

The day before the new student arrives to start school, the child's teacher sets up a desk with needed books and materials and informs the class that there will be a new student starting tomorrow. Two children in the class form a "welcome club" to greet the new child. Welcome clubs make sure new students have someone to show them around, sit with them at lunch, and play with them at recess.

When a new student does not speak English, he or she is paired with an English-speaking buddy—if possible, someone in the class who also speaks the child's native language. The "buddy" serves as a friend and translator, helping the new child learn what he or she needs to do. In some instances, the buddy also acts as a tutor, helping the new student understand material presented in class and complete homework assignments. For example, one pair of students called each other every night at 5:30 and worked on their homework together over the phone.

Buddies are often other children who have had "buddies" themselves. As the ESL teacher explained, "It's very easy for them, because they have been through the same thing." Some children will tell her, "I just did this ... I know what to tell him." In the upcoming academic year, the ESL teacher hopes to develop a buddy system for families, so that parents who do not speak English will have a family from the school to help them make the transition to living in a new environment.

Another way the school tries to extend a sense of welcome to students and their families is through an open house, held each year the day before school begins. This provides an initial opportunity for new students (not starting midyear) and their families to learn more about the school, meet the staff, and make new friends. It gives old students a chance to get a look at their new teachers and get reacquainted with their former classmates. To make it easier for families to attend the open house, bus transportation is provided.

All Kids Belong

Another important ingredient in developing a sense of belonging is acceptance. When children are excluded from learning with other children because they have special needs or know little English, they may not perceive themselves as equal or valued members of the school community. In an effort to develop a more inclusive school, the staff at Mosaic Central has devoted considerable energy to redesigning the school's organizational structure so that children with special needs are educated with their normally achieving peers. As the principal noted, one reason for undertaking this reorganization was to communicate the message "All kids belong."

The school's effort to develop a more inclusive school is visible at 9:30 every morning, when the first-graders get their reading folders and line up at their classroom doors, ready to go see their reading teachers. This parade includes first-grade children who have special needs and children who know little English. Their destination is one of five classrooms: the classroom of the reading specialist, of the special education resource room teacher, or of one of the three first-grade teachers.

Each of the first-grade teachers works with approximately 15 students, while the reading specialist and the resource room teacher each work with about 10 to 12 children. Neither the reading specialist nor the resource room teacher is identified as a specialist. Instead, each operates as just another one of the first-grade reading teachers. Their classrooms include students with and without special needs, as well as children who have not yet mastered English. Similarly, the reading classes of the first-grade teachers contain students with and without special needs, as well as those with limited English.

This scenario is repeated later in the day for all of the students in both the second and third grades. A somewhat similar structure is in place for students in the fourth and fifth grades in the areas of reading and math, with other specialists in the school—such as the Quality Integrated Education teacher mentioned earlier—as teachers.

Children with serious emotional disturbance (SED). Not everyone in the two classes for students with serious emotional disturbance (SED) goes outside of these classrooms for instruction in reading and mathematics. Students who are not yet ready to make this transition receive instruction in these areas from their special education teacher. The goal, however, is to mainstream each child as soon as possible. This process is facilitated by assigning an aide to work with the classroom teacher whenever a child with SED is initially integrated into a new class.

Another effort designed to integrate students with SED more fully into the mainstream of the school involved reorganizing social studies and science instruction in two classes: the fourth- and fifth-grade combination class, and the intermediate-level class for students with SED. The grade 4/5 combination class is staffed by a teacher with experience and certification in both general and special education. Her class was limited to approximately 20 students. These students and those in the intermediate class for students with SED were regrouped into two classes: a fourth-grade and a fifth-grade class. The special education teacher teaches science and social studies to the fourth-graders, while the teacher from the grade 4/5 combination class teaches these subjects to the fifth-graders. Each teacher is assigned an instructional aide to assist in this process. Students in these two reorganized classes attend lunch and recess together. The children with SED may also be mainstreamed for physical education, music, and art. A similar structure is in place for the primary-level class for students with SED and the grade 2/3 combination class.

Children with limited English proficiency. The school's approach to educating students with limited English proficiency also involves mainstreaming. The basic philosophy of the ESL teacher is that "mainstreaming these children from the first moment they walk in the door is vital." She indicated that what they learn in the general classroom and on the playground is a critical part of learning English. This is not to say that she believes that simply immersing these children in an English-speaking environment is enough. Rather, she believes that they should be kept in the classroom, and receive strong support from her.

This support includes helping children learn not only English, but the academic language of school as well. Students with limited English proficiency typically visit the ESL teacher's room for 30 minutes to an hour, three or four times a week. During that time they work on projects that supplement what they are studying in their general classes. The ESL teacher also works directly in several general classes, and hopes to do this even more in the future.

Although Mosaic Central is not a full-inclusion school, one where all students receive all of their education in the general classroom (Vergason & Anderegg, 1997), it has steadily and systematically become more inclusive each year. Students with learning disabilities and attention deficit disorders receive most of their education with their general classroom peers. In the past several years, the school has also fully mainstreamed children with hearing impairments, spina bifida, and muscular dystrophy. As the principal indicated, this effort to be more inclusive has helped reduce the stigma associated with special education. For example, most children simply do not know that the resource room teacher is a special education teacher, as she works directly in the general classroom and with general education students in her own classroom.

The school's approach to mainstreaming students with serious emotional disturbance has been more cautious. This is not surprising, since teachers are often more hesitant to include children with behavioral difficulties in their classrooms (Kauffman & Pullen, 1996). Nevertheless, every child with SED at Mosaic Central is mainstreamed for part of the day, and some students with SED receive the majority of their academic instruction with their general education peers.

Although students with limited English proficiency receive most of their instruction within the general classroom, they are typically pulled out for ESL services for 2 to 4 hours a week. A goal of the ESL teacher is to provide more of her services directly in the general classroom. Consequently, she is trying to connect with teachers who are interested in having ESL services provided within the context of their classroom.

Treat Each Other In A Caring Way

The development of a sense of belonging is also dependent on establishing conditions in which everyone feels safe and the rules are clear, fair, and applied equally to all (Marzano, 1992). This is a major priority of the staff at Mosaic Central. As the school counselor put it, "We make sure that all children know that we treat each other in a caring way, in a respectful way."

A cat and a star. Starting in kindergarten, children are introduced to the "I Care" cat, who presents six basic concepts for working and playing cooperatively with others. These include listening to each other; using your hands for helping, not hurting; caring about each other's feelings; using language that is respectful; and taking responsibility for your own behavior. To reinforce the use of these rules, they are reviewed at the start of each new year and posted on a chart in each classroom. Teachers and support staff throughout the school praise children when they see them using the I Care rules.

In addition, children are introduced to a problem-solving method for resolving conflicts. As with the I Care rules, conflict resolution is introduced in kindergarten, reviewed each year, and used throughout the school. The staff at Mosaic Central created its own version of conflict resolution, using the mnemonic "STAR" to help children remember the steps in the process. The steps of the STAR method are presented in Table 1-1 below. There are five ground rules for STAR:

- Face the person talking to you;
- Listen without interrupting;
- Use I Care language;
- Tell the truth;
- Agree to work to solve the problem.

The STAR steps and ground rules are introduced in kindergarten and reviewed in later grades; the process is modeled and children practice using the procedures via role playing. Role-playing activities are carefully selected to involve the types of conflicts children experience. For example, a scenario often used with kindergarten children is resolving the conflict that arises when two children want to sit in the same seat on the bus. Solutions that students work on developing to resolve conflicts include sharing or taking turns, compromising, postponing a decision until you are more in control, flipping a coin or using luck as a way to decide, and getting help from others. The school counselor plans to have the welcome club members help introduce both the I Care rules and the STAR steps to new students.

To facilitate the use of the STAR steps, the school counselor has developed a "Conflict Resolution Agreement" worksheet on which

---

Table 1-1. "STAR" steps to conflict resolution.

S—STATE the Problem and Your Feelings

T—THINK of Solutions

A—AGREE on a Plan

R—Be RESPONSIBLE for Your Plan

students can work out an agreement in writing. When a written agreement is appropriate, the parties involved in the conflict take the worksheet to the "peace table" or "peace corner" and sign a statement saying that they agree to abide by the ground rules. Each party then states in writing his or her feelings and "take" on the problem. The students then work together to develop possible solutions and agree on a plan; they indicate their willingness to be responsible for carrying out the plan by signing their names to the agreement. This process provides a formal counterpoint to the informal, verbal approach to resolving conflicts.

There is a press for all of the staff to use and reinforce the I Care rules and STAR steps. According to the principal, the school as a whole "wanted to be on the same page in terms of discipline issues and expectations for kids and staff." This means, he explained, that if a child is running in the hall, a "building service worker is just as responsible as I am to redirect the child." Similarly, all teachers and classroom aides are responsible not only for the children in their own classes, but for any child in the school.

Every day and crises too. To further ensure that all staff are "on the same page," Mosaic Central has developed a school-wide discipline policy that includes a school philosophy statement on discipline; expectations for students, teachers, and parents; processes for resolving conflicts (including the STAR steps); a hierarchy of consequences for dealing with inappropriate behavior (ranging from a warning, such as establishing eye contact, to expulsion from school); due process procedures for students or parents to appeal a disciplinary action; and a comprehensive behavior management plan. All students and parents are asked to read the policy and sign it.

The comprehensive behavior management (CBM) plan was implemented one year ago. The CBM plan establishes five school rules that every child is expected to follow and all staff are expected to enforce. The rules and example situations to which they apply are presented in Table 1-2. There is some overlap between the school rules and the I Care rules.

Table 1-2. School rules and example situations
to which they apply.

Rules	Examples
FOLLOW DIRECTIONS	Hall Conduct
	Cafeteria Behavior
BE WHERE YOU BELONG	Tardiness
	Playground/Recess
KEEP HANDS, FEET, AND OBJECTS TO SELF	Violating Personal Space
	Fighting
TREAT OTHERS WITH RESPECT	Verbal Abuse
	Intimidation
TAKE CARE OF THE SCHOOL AND MAKE IT SAFE	Vandalism
	Dangerous Weapons

The development of the rules required that the staff agree on their expectations for student conduct. For example, what does it mean when you expect children to walk quietly in the hall? For some teachers, that might mean being silent; for others it might mean talking softly. As one teacher noted, the major goal of the CBM plan was to "make sure that we are all, as staff members, saying the same thing to children at the same time."

To help children better understand the school rules, skits and role playing at school-wide assemblies were used to introduce and discuss expectations for children's behavior. It was stressed that the rules were designed to ensure the rights and safety of each person in the school.

In addition to the school rules, the CBM plan includes a continuum of behavior management interventions for addressing problem behaviors. The techniques range from less intensive interventions, such as warning or self-monitoring, to more intensive interventions, such as time out. The goal in implementing these procedures is for the staff to work as a team and utilize the least intensive interventions possible to help students control their behavior.

The CBM plan facilitated the process of mainstreaming children with specific emotional difficulties. Initially 12 staff members participated in 5 days of in-service activities to learn how to use the behavior management interventions. They then spent 15 hours teaching the rest of the staff these procedures. Parents were invited to learn these procedures as well. Throughout the year, the staff met to refine and review the use of these procedures. As one member of the faculty indicated, "People felt empowered." In the past, "I didn't know what to do if a child with SED was having trouble ... maybe I'll get hurt, or they'll get hurt." The CBM management plan provides teachers with the knowledge and tools to deal more effectively with students who experience behavioral difficulties. In addition, the principal indicated that the staff members were "now more willing to step in ... [and] help each other" when dealing with a difficult situation.

The school also developed a crisis intervention team designed to respond immediately to situations that may pose a threat to the safety of children or staff. The team includes the school counselor, the principal, the head of building maintenance, the reading specialist, a general class teacher, and the resource room teacher. For the most part, these are staff members who can quickly leave what they are doing in order to respond to a crisis situation. For example, if a child is attempting to leave the building without permission, one or more team members are contacted and come immediately to provide assistance.

A central tenet in the school-wide discipline policy developed by the Mosaic Central staff is that "school should be a place in which children learn in an atmosphere of security and a feeling of well being." The I Care rules, STAR steps, CBM plan, and crisis intervention team provide different but complementary mechanisms for meeting this objective, by creating a safe and predictable environment where children are expected and encouraged to treat each other with respect and caring.

EVERYONE CAN BE SUCCESSFUL

"Everyone can be successful." "We work for every child's success." "We believe in kids." "We want to maximize what they do here." Faculty comments such as these reflect a commitment to creating a school where every child is successful. These pronouncements are not simply empty statements; the staff of Mosaic Central has invested considerable energy and time in creating new programs and reworking methods of delivering instruction.

The Fuel That Runs The Engine

A major goal of the faculty at Mosaic Central last year was to integrate technology into the curriculum. Mosaic Central had just become a Global Access school, and teachers were interested in making technology a more integral part of their instruction. To facilitate this process, teachers participated in in-service activities designed to help them become more familiar with using technology as a tool for teaching. For example, one third-grade class that was planning a trip to the Kennedy Center used a CD-ROM program to do research on the composers they were going to hear. As they developed their individual reports, they used programs such as KID PICS to develop slides and pictures to enhance their presentations.

This year, the school is working on improving the reading programs at the school. Several years ago the focus was on mathematics, and before that it was on the development of the conflict resolution program. These decisions are fueled by the process of setting reasonable and attainable goals as well as developing (and revising when necessary) strategies and plans for achieving these objectives.

Taking Care Of Business

As the school works to renew and improve itself, it has not lost sight of the needs of children who are most likely to struggle academically.

In some instances, individuals work alone or form "natural collaborations" with others to improve instruction for those who struggle academically. In other instances, this effort involves the energies of the entire organization. Empowering individuals to seek out better solutions is a key element in the process of continuous improvement, one that is characteristic of self-renewing schools (Sagor, 1995).

Desk fairies. One example of a teacher's individual efforts to address the needs of students who struggle academically was the creation of desk fairies. The resource room teacher noticed that some children's desks were so messy that they had a great deal of difficulty finding anything. During class, these children often had trouble starting an assignment or making a transition to a new task, because they could not find the needed materials in their desk. Their search for materials often distracted both the teacher and their peers. Many of the students with disorganized desks had special needs or were struggling academically. To help change this situation, the resource room teacher visited students' classes after school hours and left a note and a treat from "the desk fairy" in desks that were clean—rewarding both the target students and others.

Plugging into the curriculum. The ESL teacher's desire to integrate English learning with the general classroom curriculum provides another example of an individual's efforts to develop a better solution. Teachers at Mosaic Central work together when planning a unit, so that the unit cuts across disciplines and content areas. Although the primary goal of ESL instruction is English proficiency, the ESL teacher also wanted to reinforce and extend what students were learning in their classroom units. To achieve this aim, she decided to "plug into the curriculum."

This process can be illustrated by examining how the ESL teacher "plugged into" a third-grade social studies unit. Last year, the third-grade teachers taught a unit on Ghana. The teachers introduced the unit during social studies, and integrated it into other areas of the curriculum, including mathematics, art, reading, and so forth. To complement and extend what was happening in the third-grade classrooms, the ESL teacher located a book about an Ashanti legend. With the children in her third-grade group, she used the book as a springboard for learning English *and* learning more about the country of Ghana.

After reading the book aloud in English with the ESL teacher, the class completed a number of activities based on events and concepts presented in the book. For example, in the story that they read, objects talked to people. Students were asked to write in English (with help from the teacher) a story of their own featuring talking objects. The class also developed a play based on the story, and performed it for the rest of the third-grade classes, answering questions afterwards about the story and about Ghana.

The ESL teacher and a student teacher in her classroom also arranged a special event on Ghana. A woman who had been in Ghana with the Peace Corps spent 2 hours with the third-graders, teaching them about the culture. This presentation included popular foods from the country as well as a fashion show of traditional dress with the teachers as models. Once the special event was over, the volunteer spent an additional 45 minutes with the children in the ESL group, sharing pictures and personal stories about her experiences there.

To show their appreciation, the students wrote letters of thanks to the volunteer. They then evaluated the experience, thinking about what they learned, enjoyed, and did (see Table 1-3, p. 18). To end the experience, they threw a Ghana party where they ate foods that were presented in the book they read, such as sweet potatoes and squash.

The communication book. Providing an effective program for a child who is not doing well in school is a collaborative effort, requiring frequent communication among teachers and with the family. However, as many teachers have commented (cf. Graham, Hudson, Burdg, & Carpenter, 1980), finding the time to get together to communicate is often difficult. At Mosaic Central, several teachers worked together to solve this problem, developing a "low-tech" solution—the communication book.

Table 1-3. Student evaluation of the Ghana activities in the ESL classroom.

WHAT WE LEARNED	Eat with your right hand
	Kids don't have many toys
	They make their own toys and instruments
	People make their own houses
	Houses are small
	They don't wear many clothes
	Make bags with goat skins
	No water; get it from the river
WHY WE ENJOYED IT	The game: fun, like checkers, but different
	Costumes: funny, cool, fun to look at
	Questions: lots of points, interesting
	Hut: made of grass
WHAT WE DID	Answered questions
	Looked at pictures
	Played a game
	Sat on a special pillow
	Listened to music
	Played a drum and learned how to use it as a phone
	Explained costumes

The communication book is simply a folder that the child carries to classes, in which each teacher records what is worked on that day. This ensures that each of the child's teachers knows what the others are doing, and allows them to reinforce each other's efforts. For example, if a teacher indicates that a particular student learned three new words that day, the speech teacher may decide to use those words during her lesson.

At the end of the day, the child takes the communication book home. Parents can see what their child is doing at school and check to see if there is anything special that a teacher wants them to know. Likewise, parents or guardians are encouraged to write back to school, responding to teacher queries or concerns and sharing information and concerns of their own. For instance, if the homework is too hard one night or takes too long, the parent can let the teachers know.

Team teaching. The idea for the communication book developed when a small group of teachers worked together to solve a specific problem. Another example of teachers forming partnerships to achieve a common goal involved a team teaching arrangement between the resource room teacher and teachers in the fourth and fifth grades. For part of the year, the resource room teacher acts as a second teacher in the classroom during Writer's Workshop (Atwell, 1987). Sometimes she works with small groups of students to reinforce the processes and skills emphasized during the general classroom teacher's mini-lessons. At other times, she leads the class and the general teacher works with a small group of students. This arrangement allows the teachers to devote extra attention to specific students in the classroom, including those with special needs.

One outcome of this collaboration is that the resource teacher is often invited into classrooms to teach writing strategies to students. This includes strategies for planning and writing both stories (Danoff, Harris, & Graham, 1993; Harris & Graham, 1993) and reports (Graham & Harris, 1996a). This instruction is particularly beneficial for students who struggle with writing, as they often use minimal planning, revising, and other self-regulation procedures when composing (Graham & Harris, 1996b; McCutchen, 1988). However, learning these strategies is also beneficial to the other children in the classroom (Danoff et al., 1993), as it makes more explicit the processes underlying good writing (Graham & Harris, 1994; Harris & Graham, 1994).

Class placement and educational management. The school has also developed a variety of formal structures to address the needs of children who are experiencing difficulty. Before school begins in the fall, the roster for each class is developed, with special attention given to students who have difficulty with learning or self-control. Factors such as teaching style, the composition of the class, and the characteristics of the child are all considered in class placement decisions.

At the end of the first month of school, the class lists are reviewed by each teacher and the school's educational management team. The team includes the principal, the school counselor, the reading specialist, the speech pathologist, and the resource room teacher. The classroom teacher and the team discuss the progress of each child in the classroom. When there is a concern, the group may spend some time developing a plan for "turning things around," or may schedule another session for more extended discussion and planning. Once a plan is in place, it is monitored by the teacher and the team to see if additional modifications are necessary or if applications for additional services, such as special education, are needed. In February, the team meets again with each teacher to repeat this process for every child in the class.

In addition to these semi-annual meetings with each teacher, the educational management team meets weekly with teachers to monitor plans already in place and to discuss new concerns. Before teachers make a formal referral to the team, they meet with the child's parents to discuss the situation and develop a record of the types of strategies used to address the problem. Parents are invited (in writing and over the phone) to attend the team meeting. The parent(s), the teacher, and the team discuss what is happening and what can be done to ensure that the child is successful. The emphasis is on developing a plan in which all of the parties work together.

Supplementary courses. The faculty at Mosaic Central also offer a number of special programs and academic courses for children in need of additional academic instruction. For instance, during the school year there is a 4-week course for parents and their children called "Family Math." At each weekly meeting, children and parents play math games designed to support concepts presented in class, and parents learn tips for teaching math to their child at home.

Special courses are not just limited to the school year, but are offered in the summer as well. Math Power is a 3-week summer course funded by the school district for students with poor grades in math. This course provides a preview of the mathematical concepts to be covered in the upcoming year. Last summer, the school also offered a writing program for first- through fourth-grade children most in need of additional writing instruction. The staff raised the money to fund this course through donations and by sponsoring a special event, a dinner and dance for adults. The theme for the writing course was the Summer Olympics, which were in progress at that time. Students learned strategies for planning and revising, as well as how to use technology to develop and publish their written products. Over the 2-week period, they wrote in their journals, developed stories and poems, learned how to type, and designed and advertised a carnival that was performed for students in the Math Power program.

Gifted Students

Mosaic Central does not have a special program for children who are gifted, nor does the school district provide a staff position for this purpose. The school has addressed these students' special needs, at least in part, through their reorganization efforts in math and reading and the use of open-ended and advanced projects. As we noted earlier, students are regrouped for reading and mathematics, allowing teachers to adapt instruction to students who are more proficient in these areas. Furthermore, projects in science and social studies are "open-ended," allowing for a broad range of possible responses and products. The media specialist also works with small groups of advanced students on research-based projects.

Meeting the needs of gifted children is an area in need of additional development, both at Mosaic Central and in the school system as a whole. Much more of the available attention and resources is devoted to helping children who find school challenging than to nourishing the potential of those who are gifted.

EVERYONE IS RESPECTED AND VALUED

One approach for helping students learn to respect and value themselves and others is to create an empowering school culture. Increasing inclusion (and reducing labeling), setting high expectations, creating a safe and caring environment, and providing students with the tools needed to resolve conflicts are all important in creating such a culture (Banks, 1995). The efforts of the Mosaic Central staff to actualize each of these goals were described earlier. We would like to note that the school's efforts to realize the values of belonging, success, respect, and individual worth *are not isolated events;* they involve interdependent and overlapping actions. For example, programs and activities designed to increase students' academic performance were expected to have a corresponding impact on perceptions of personal worth, as self-efficacy is enhanced when students are successful academically (Schunk, 1989).

The staff at Mosaic Central believes that the development of an environment where everyone is respected and valued is a collective effort, involving not only teachers and students, but also parents and others from the community. Like other changes at the school, these efforts involve the actions of individuals, the combined energies of several collaborators, and the efforts of the entire school—as well as the contributions of many individuals from the community.

Learning About Themselves

Throughout the school year, the school counselor facilitates small-group counseling for students dealing with similar issues. Group counseling has involved a wide range of topics, including attention deficit/hyperactivity disorders, alcohol and substance abuse, and separation and divorce. The counselor initiates these groups by consulting with classroom teachers and sending a letter home to the parents of each child in the school, asking them if they are interested in having their child participate in a particular group. If the parents indicate an interest, the counselor calls them to make sure that the group is appropriate and to discuss any concerns or suggestions the parents may have.

One goal of these groups is to help children better understand, respect, and value their own unique abilities. Another goal is to help them develop coping strategies. In the group for children with attention deficit/hyperactivity disorders, for example, the counselor asked children to consider what the term "attention deficit disorder" meant to them, how they saw themselves in relation to this term, and how they felt about it. Using material developed specifically for children, she then helped them sharpen and expand their understanding of the concept, with an eye toward reconsidering their initial conceptualizations and reactions. Next, the children identified their own particular strengths and considered how they could take advantage of them. Each child also identified goals to work on, and the group generated strategies for accomplishing those goals, role-playing the suggested strategies when appropriate. After trying out specific strategies in the classroom, the group reconvened to talk about their efforts.

Learning About Others

Learning about different cultures and other aspects of diversity is an essential ingredient in learning to respect and value diversity (Banks, 1995). One way that students at Mosaic Central learn about the value of cultural diversity is through the integration of multicultural content in the curriculum. Information about different cultures as well as the contributions made by individuals from diverse backgrounds are common ingredients in the school curriculum. Diversity-focused activities range from the development of specific units on multicultural topics, such as the one on Ghana examined earlier, to daily "magical moments" emphasizing the contributions of people from diverse backgrounds. Important multicultural events and activities are announced on a bulletin board in the hallway, and walls in and around the classrooms are decorated with artifacts, posters, and other material representative of the cultures and people being studied.

Students also learn about other cultures and people from their classmates, parents, and other adults in the community. Parents are encouraged and invited to share information about their culture in the classroom. In some instances, the presentation may involve a parent and a child. For instance, the mother of a student with spina bifida approached the school about making a presentation to her child's class. The mother and child subsequently presented information on spina bifida to the class, explaining why his legs worked differently, how his wheelchair worked, and that his condition was not communicable.

International Night. One highly visible school celebration of cultural diversity is International Night. This is a collective effort involving students, teachers, parents, the PTA, and others from the community. It is held at the end of March and is very popular, attracting about 500 people each year.

The primary goals of International Night are for each child to reflect on his or her own cultural background and to become more familiar with the heritages of classmates. In preparation for International Night, each class holds discussions about why they celebrate the event and the importance of valuing cultural diversity. In one fourth-grade classroom last year, for example, the children initiated a conversation about how some kids might not understand why or how other children were different. They also discussed how various television programs promoted cultural and racial stereotypes. They ended their conversation by considering what *they* could do to make a difference.

Preparation for International Night includes a school-wide project. One year, children and their parents decorated dolls to represent their specific cultural heritage. The dolls were approximately 2 feet tall, made of heavy paper, and constructed so that they held hands. Four hundred dolls were hung outside classes, holding hands up and down the hallways. The next year, students constructed banners and hung them from their lockers. This past year, they made shoebox dioramas.

In preparation for last year's International Night, students and teachers also developed centers to represent specific cultures on different continents. Each grade level was responsible for a specific continent (e.g., the third grade focused on Africa). Each center was located in a different part of the school and included crafts, foods, clothing, music, and other artifacts for the cultures represented. This year, the school plans to integrate technology and child-developed products that provide additional information about the countries and cultures at each center.

On International Night, parents and children are encouraged to wear costumes that reflect their heritage. Visitors wander from one center to the next, sampling food, listening to music, and examining the displays. At some centers, musicians play and participants are invited to dance. A special program is offered each year, highlighting dancers, story tellers, or other artists from a specific culture. At the end of the night, the children gather together and sing. The music teacher teaches and directs songs from the featured culture, often in the native language of that culture.

SELF-RENEWAL AT MOSAIC CENTRAL

The primary catalyst for the changes that have occurred at Mosaic Central during the last 10 years is the faculty at the school. Although the school system has encouraged the process of self-renewal through mechanisms like the School Improvement Management Plan, it is the vision and the energy of those who work at Mosaic Central that have made these changes possible.

A key figure in the school's efforts to respond to changing conditions, while maintaining a focus on improving existing services, is the principal. She has played a pivotal role in the faculty's development of core values and a shared vision. The current emphasis on inclusion, for example, is very important to the principal; her background is in special education, and she has been intimately involved in encouraging and shaping its evolution in the school.

Although the principal is actively involved in molding and

shepherding the process of school change, individual teachers are encouraged to implement their own ideas and programs. In some instances, teachers' efforts are aimed at achieving common school goals, such as inclusion. In other instances, teachers have tackled more personal goals, such as implementing a mathematics program based on constructivistic principles in their classroom. Thus, even though the principal and faculty are bound by a shared vision of what the school is trying to accomplish, a single prescription for accomplishing these values is not imposed. Furthermore, the shared vision is not so tightly woven that other goals, more personal and individual ones, are lost in the process.

Ultimately, the changes at Mosaic Central are a direct result of the energy and hard work of the teachers and other staff members. They are the ones who took up the shared vision and gave it substance. This is not to say that their work or the principal's work is done. They continue to review and renew their purpose, sharpening and extending their goals and the procedures for achieving them.

Adaptability

One factor that has facilitated the process of change at Mosaic Central is the adaptability of the staff in assuming new roles and responsibilities. The success of some changes, such as regrouping for reading and math, required the staff to conduct business in a new or different way. The attainment of other goals, such as inclusion, necessitated even greater shifts in what some teachers did on a daily basis.

The resource room teacher, for instance, initially provided "pull-out" services to students with special needs. Children would leave their general classrooms and come to work with her for short periods of time during the week. As the school moved to provide more inclusive services for children with special needs, the requirements of her job became more diverse. She was no longer tied to the resource room or to working just with students with special needs. More and more, she worked directly in the general classroom, either teaching the whole class or providing small-group or individual support to students experiencing difficulty, including students with special needs. Her work in the resource room also changed, as she became another one of the primary-grade reading teachers, teaching students with and without special needs in her own classroom.

The resource room teacher was not the only one affected by the increased emphasis on inclusion. The general classroom teachers made a variety of adjustments as well. These included changes such as team problem-solving, team teaching with the resource room teacher, and greater responsibility for the education and welfare of students with special needs.

The success of renewal efforts, such as inclusion and many of the other changes initiated at Mosaic Central, depend not only on the general support of the faculty members, but on their willingness to redefine their jobs. Sometimes this requires relatively minor adaptations. At other times it requires greater flexibility, as in the case of the resource room teacher. As she indicated, her instructional role "is different every year ... I have never had two years where it was the same."

Preparation

The changes initiated by Mosaic Central did not just happen; they were the result of planning and preparation. One provision particularly evident in most school-wide changes was extensive in-service training. This occurred for programs such as conflict resolution and the comprehensive behavior management project, as well as for actions designed to improve reading, mathematics, and the integration of technology into the curriculum.

The school primarily uses two types of in-service training to facilitate the attainment of school-wide projects and goals. One model involves outside specialists who provide instruction and consultation to the faculty. For example, to advance the goal of technology integration, a specialist was employed to help faculty members update their technology skills. Initially, the specialist offered weekly after-school training sessions on faculty-selected topics, such as using electronic mail or a Quick Take camera. This format was soon replaced by group and individual instruction and consultation sessions offered each week during school hours. During these sessions, for instance, teachers might meet with the specialist to learn about specific hardware or software they hoped to use in an upcoming unit.

The second model of in-service training involves teachers teaching each other. This model, too, was applied to technology integration. Last year, five teachers attended an institute on technology offered by the school system. They are currently in the process of teaching their co-workers the skills and knowledge they acquired.

It is important to note that planning and preparation are not limited to school-wide efforts and goals; they are equally important for efforts to support smaller groups, and even individual students. For example, upon learning that one of the children in the school had a severe hearing loss, a specialist provided in-service training to the child's teachers and other staff members, addressing questions about the child's disability and effective methods for teaching her. This seminar provided the staff with crucial information about the nature of the student's difficulties and the suggested approaches for dealing with them.

Community and Family Involvement

The parents of students have also been instrumental in shaping and supporting the process of change at Mosaic Central. Values such as respect and individual worth, for instance, are strengthened by inviting parents into classrooms to share information about their cultures and by involving the PTA and other parents in International Night. The school has further attempted to increase parental participation through special programs such as Family Math, and by promoting better communication through weekly newsletters and special projects such as the communication book. Parental participation increases the likelihood of attaining the value that everyone can be successful, as parental involvement in children's education is related to academic success (Roesener, 1995).

Over the years, the school has offered a number of special programs and classes for parents. These include workshops on special topics, such as helping with homework, dealing with attention deficit/hyperactivity disorders, using technology, implementing conflict resolution, and locating community resources. Perhaps even more importantly, many of the staff at Mosaic Central provide a "helping hand" during times of crisis. This includes charitable activities ranging from locating clothing and furniture for families in need to providing day care for a parent with cancer. As one teacher indicated, these activities are "crucial to this community feeling the way they do about this school."

In addition to parental support, the school also receives considerable support from the local community. Three connections with the community are particularly noteworthy. First, the school has formed a partnership with a local business, a banking company. Employees in the company volunteer to work once a week at the school, each with an individual child. They act as tutors and role models. Prior to meeting with their assigned children, volunteers learn basic behavior management techniques and explore with a faculty member the types of things they and the child might do together. The volunteers are typically paired with children who are experiencing academic difficulty in school. The school tries to pair each volunteer with a student from a similar cultural background; although this is not always possible, it does occur quite frequently, as the volunteers are racially and culturally diverse.

Second, volunteers are also drawn from the local high school to serve as tutors and mentors to individual or small groups of children. Third, senior citizens from a nearby assisted-living facility serve as "reading buddies" to children in the primary grades.

THE QUEST GOES ON

Our portrait of Mosaic Central is not complete. Nor is it ever likely to be, as long as the school continues the process of self-renewal. By constantly reviewing and reshaping their purpose, faculty members increase their ability to predict and adjust to new challenges and changing times.

We realize that some might quibble with the direction or types of changes made at Mosaic Central. For example, critics might contend that the school should fully include all students with special needs, or that a different approach to educating children who speak little or no English should be applied. However, the changes made by Mosaic Central are based on their understanding of the children, their parents, and the community, as well as the faculty members' vision of what their school might become. In many ways, they have realized this vision. We look forward to observing how the staff at Mosaic Central continues to learn and respond adaptively to changing conditions, and how their vision evolves over time.

REFERENCES

Atwell, N. (1987). *In the middle: Reading, writing, and learning from adolescents.* Portsmouth, NH: Heinemann.

Banks, J. (1995). *Handbook of research on multicultural education.* New York: Simon & Schuster.

Danoff, B., Harris, K.R., & Graham, S. (1993). Incorporating strategy instruction within the writing process in the regular classroom: Effects on the writing of students with and without learning disabilities. *Journal of Reading Behavior, 25,* 295-322.

Garmston, R., & Wellman, B. (1995). Adaptive schools in a quantum universe. *Educational LEadership, 52,* 6-12.

Graham, S., & Harris, K.R. (1996a). Teaching writing strategies within the context of a whole language class. In E. McIntyre & M. Pressley (Eds.), *Balanced instruction: Strategies and skills in whole language* (pp. 155-175). Norwood, MA: Christopher-Gordon.

Graham, S., & Harris, K.R. (1996b). Self-regulation and strategy instruction for students who find writing and learning challenging. In M. Levy & S. Ransdell (Eds.), *The science of writing* (pp. 347-360). Mahway, NJ: Erlbaum.

Graham, S., & Harris, K.R. (1994). Implications of constructivism for teaching writing to students with special needs. *Journal of Special Education, 28,* 275-289.

Graham, S. Hudson, F., Burdg, N., & Carpenter, D. (1980). Educational personnel's perceptions of mainstreaming and resource room effectiveness. *Psychology in the Schools, 17,* 129-134.

Hargreaves, A. (1995). Renewal in the age of paradox. *Educational Leadership, 52,* 14-19.

Harris, K.R., & Graham, S. (1994). Constructivism: Principles, paradigms, and integration. *Journal of Special Education, 28,* 233-247.

Harris, K.R., & Graham, S. (1993). Cognitive strategy instruction and whole language: A case study. *Remedial and Special Education, 14,* 30-34.

Joyce, B., Wolf, J., & Calhoun, E. (1993). *The self-renewing school.* Alexandria, VA: Association for Supervision and Curriculum Development.

Kauffman, J., & Pullen, P. (1996). Eight myths about special education. *Focus on Exceptional Children, 28,* 1-12.

Marzano, R. (1992). *A different kind of classroom: Teaching with dimensions of learning.* Alexandria, VA: Association for Supervision and Curriculum Development.

McCutchen, D. (1988). "Functional automaticity" in children's writing. *Written Communication, 5,* 306-324.

O'Neil, J. (1995). On schools as learning organizations: A conversation with Peter Senge. *Educational Leadership, 52,* 20-23.

Roesener, L. (1995). Changing the culture at Beacon Hill. *Educational Leadership, 52,* 28-32.

Sagor, R. (1995). Overcoming the one-solution syndrome. *Educational Leadership, 52,* 24-27.

Schunk, D. (1989). Social cognitive theory and self-regulated learning. In B. Zimmerman & D. Schunk (Eds.), *Self-regulated learning and academic achievement* (pp. 83-110). New York: Springer-Verlag.

Senge, P. (1990). *The fifth discipline: The art and practice of the learning organization.* New York: Doubleday.

Vergason, G., & Anderegg, M. (1997). *Dictionary of special education and rehabilitation* (4th ed.). Denver, CO: Love Publishers.

CHAPTER TWO

The Four Blocks: A Balanced Framework for Literacy in Primary Classrooms

PATRICIA M. CUNNINGHAM & DOROTHY P. HALL

Each year, six million children begin school in our public schools. Many of these children can be immediately identified as "at-risk"—the currently popular descriptor for those children who will not learn to read and write well enough to achieve a basic level of literacy and a high school diploma. The number of children at risk varies from community to community and state to state. Nationwide, NAEP results suggest that more than one third of all 9-year-olds cannot read at the "basic" level. For African Americans, 61% fail to achieve this basic level (Mullis & Jenkins, 1990).

These statistics have held fairly constant despite decades of expensive attempts to "fix" the problem. Federal fix-ups have generally included a variety of pull-out remediation programs, which have spawned huge bureaucracies and have not succeeded in eliminating the risk for very many children. State and local fix-ups often consist of regulations that prohibit children being promoted unless they obtain certain test scores, with the result that huge numbers of children are retained. Shepard and Smith (1990) reviewed decades of research on retention. Their data show that retained children perform more poorly when they advance to the next grade than they would if they had been promoted without repeating a grade, and that almost any alternative is more effective than retention. Their data also suggest that "transition" classes that cause the children in them to spend another year in the primary grades have the same ill effects as retention.

Within individual schools or classrooms, in addition to federally provided remediation and state or locally mandated retention, teachers usually try to meet the needs of at-risk children by putting them in a "bottom" reading group and pacing their instruction more slowly. The data on bottom groups does not hold out much hope that this solution will ultimately solve the problem. Children who are placed in the bottom group in first grade generally remain there throughout their elementary school career and almost never learn to read and write up to grade-level standards (Allington, 1983; Allington, 1991).

Against this backdrop, we have the peculiarly American phenomenon of the "pendulum swing": various approaches to reading come in and out of fashion. Eight years ago, when we began this endeavor, literature-based reading instruction (commonly referred to as "whole language") was the recommended approach. Today, this approach is losing favor, and school boards are mandating phonics approaches and purchasing spelling books. The search for the "best" way to teach reading overlooks the reality of individual differences. Children do not all learn in the same way; consequently, approaches with particular emphases are apt to help some children learn to read, but leave others behind. When the pendulum swings again, the next approach may pick up some of those who weren't faring too well under the previous emphasis, but lose some who were. Thirty years ago, first-grade studies carried out to determine the best approach concluded that the teacher was more important than the method, but that in general, combination approaches worked better than any single approach (Bond & Dykstra, 1967).

This chapter describes the development of a *balanced* framework for beginning reading instruction. Our first goal in developing this framework was to find a way to combine the major approaches to reading instruction, thereby avoiding the pendulum swing between trendy approaches. The second goal was to meet the needs of children with a wide range of entering literacy levels without putting them in ability groups.

The project began in the fall of 1989 in one first-grade classroom (Cunningham, Hall, & Defee, 1991; Hall, Prevatte, & Cunningham, 1995) This classroom was one of four first-grade classrooms in a large suburban school to which children from the inner city were bussed. The class contained 26 children, half boys and half girls, 26% African-American. The instructor was an experienced teacher who agreed to work with us to try to come up with a "do-able" classroom framework for meeting the two goals: providing non-ability-grouped instruction that met the needs of children with a wide range of entering literacy levels, and providing children with daily instruction incorporating several reading approaches. During this first year, we developed an instructional framework and assessment procedures. At the end of the year, our success propelled us to involve other first-grade teachers at three schools. We refined the framework to accommodate the teaching styles of 16 unique first-grade teachers.

In the third year of the program, we continued to work with first-grade teachers and children and expanded the program to the second grade. From the fourth year on, we have worked with numerous school districts throughout the country to implement this balanced framework in hundreds of first and second grades. We have also worked with some teachers in upper elementary grades to modify the framework for grades 3-5, and with some kindergarten teachers in developing a kindergarten program consistent with our framework.

THE INSTRUCTIONAL FRAMEWORK

The instructional framework is the heart of our program. The basic notions of this framework are quite simple, but its implementation is complex. There is a lot of variation depending on how early or late in the year it is and whether the framework is being carried out in first or second grade. There is also much variation attributed to the individual teaching style of the teacher and the particular make-up of the class being taught. In this section we will describe the components of instruction and provide some sense of the variety which allows their implementation in a wide range of classrooms.

In order to meet the goal of providing children with a variety of avenues to becoming literate, instructional time is divided fairly evenly between the four major historical approaches to reading instruction. The 2¼–2½ hours allotted to Language Arts is divided among four blocks: Guided Reading, Self-Selected Reading, Writers' Workshop, and Working with Words, each of which gets 30–40 minutes.

To meet our second goal of providing for a wide range of literacy levels without ability grouping, we make the instruction within each block as multilevel as possible. For each block, we will briefly describe some of the formats, materials, cooperative arrangements, etc., that we use to attain the goal of multilevel instruction.

Guided Reading

In our first several years, we referred to Guided Reading time as the Basal Block, because at that time the basal reader drove our instruction. In recent years, teachers have branched out to use other materials in addition to or instead of the adopted basal reader. Depending on the time of year, the needs of the class, and the personality of the teacher, Guided Reading lessons are carried out with the basal currently adopted system-wide, basal readers from previously adopted series, multiple copies of trade books or books from Wright, Rigby, or Troll, articles from *My Weekly Reader* or similar magazines, big books, or combinations of these materials. The purposes of Guided Reading are to expose children to a wide range of literature, teach them comprehension, and teach them how to read using materials that become increasingly harder. The block usually begins with a discussion led by the teacher to build or review any background knowledge necessary to read the selection. Comprehension strategies are also taught and practiced during this block. The reading is done in a variety of small-group, partner, and individual formats. After the reading is completed, the whole class is called together to discuss the selection and practice strategies. This block sometimes includes writing in response to reading.

Making the Guided Reading block multilevel. Guided Reading is the hardest block to make multilevel. Any selection is going to be too hard for some children and too easy for others. We don't worry anymore about those children for whom grade-level Guided Reading material is too easy, because the other three blocks provide many beyond-grade-level opportunities. In addition, our end-of-year results indicate that students who begin the first grade with high literacy levels read well above grade level by the end of the year.

We do worry, however, about those students for whom grade-level selections are too hard. To make this block meet the needs of children who read below grade level, teachers make a variety of adaptations. Guided Reading time is not spent on grade-level material all week. Rather, teachers choose two selections—one grade-level and one easier—to read each week. Each selection is read several times, each time for a different purpose in a different format. Rereading enables children who couldn't read the selection fluently the first time to achieve fluency by the last reading. Children who need help are not left to read by themselves; they are supported in a variety of ways. Most teachers use reading partners and teach children how to help their partners rather than do all their reading for them. While some children read the selection by themselves and others read with partners, teachers usually meet with small groups of children. These teacher-supported small groups change on a daily basis and do not include only the low readers.

In addition to the daily Guided Reading block in which all children are included, many teachers schedule a 10-minute easy reading support group in which very easy books are read and reread. This group of five to six children changes daily. All children are included at least one day each week. Children who need easy reading are included more often, but not every day. One way or another, we try to assure that every child has some Guided Reading instruction in material at or below instructional level several days each week. (For other ways to manage the various reading levels of children during Guided Reading, see Cunningham & Allington, 1994.)

Self-Selected Reading

Historically called *individualized reading* or *personalized reading* (Veatch, 1959), Self-Selected Reading time is now labeled "Reader's Workshop" by many teachers (Routman, 1995). Regardless of what it is called, Self-Selected Reading is that part of a balanced literacy program when children get to choose what they want to read and what parts of their reading they want to respond to. Opportunities are provided for children to share and respond to what is read. Teachers hold individual conferences with children about their books.

In our classrooms, the Self-Selected Reading block includes (and usually begins with) teacher read-aloud. The teacher reads to the children from a wide range of literature. Next, children read "on their own level" from a variety of books the teacher has gathered together and keeps on a book shelf or (more popularly) in dishpans or buckets. The teacher's selections for the classroom library include books on themes the class is studying, easy and hard library books, old favorites, and new, often easy or predictable books. Every effort is made to have the widest possible range of genres and levels. While the children read, the teacher holds conferences with and takes anecdotal records on several children each day. The block usually ends with with one or two children sharing their books with the class in a "reader's chair" format.

Making the Self-Selected Reading block multilevel. Self-Selected Reading is, by definition, multilevel, since children choose what they want to read. However, these choices can be limited by what reading materials are available and how willing and able children are to read from the available resources. Fielding and Roller (1992) sum up the problem many struggling readers have with Self-Selected Reading:

While most of the children are quiet, engaged, and reading during
independent reading times, there are always a few children who are
not. They are picking up spilled crayons, sweeping up shavings from
the pencil sharpener, making trips to the water fountain, walking
back and forth alongside bookcases, opening and closing books, and
gazing at pictures. (p. 678)

The article goes on to indicate that many of the children who "wander
round" during Self-Selected Reading time are the ones whose reading
ability is limited, and concludes that:

Either they do not know how to find a book that they can read, or
there is no book available that they can read, or they do not want to
read the books they can read. These children remind us of Groucho
Marx: They refuse to become a member of any club that will accept
them. In book terms, they cannot read the books they want to read
and they do not want to read the books they can read. (p. 679)

Fielding and Roller go on to make excellent and practical suggestions about how to support children in reading books they want to
read that would be too difficult without support, as well as how to
make the reading of easy books both enjoyable and socially acceptable. These suggestions include:

- helping children determine when a book is just right;
- encouraging children to read books that the teacher has read
  aloud;
- encouraging children to read with a friend and to do repeated
  readings of books they enjoy;
- modeling the enjoyment to be found in easier books;
- setting up programs in which children read to younger
  children and thus have a real purpose for engaging easy books;
- making lots of informational picture books available.

Although they do not use the term, following their suggestions would make the Self-Selected Reading time more multilevel. We have incorporated many of their ideas in our Self-Selected Reading block, and we also steer our more advanced readers toward books that challenge them.

Writing

The writing block is carried out in "Writers' Workshop" fashion (Calkins, 1994; Graves, 1995; Routman, 1995). It begins with a 10-minute mini-lesson. The teacher sits at the overhead projector or with a large piece of chart paper. The teacher writes and models all the things writers do (although not all on any one day!). The teacher thinks aloud, deciding what to write about, and then writes. While writing, the teacher models looking at the Word Wall for a troublesome word, as well as inventing the spelling of a few big words. The teacher also makes a few mistakes relating to the items currently on the class's Editor's Checklist. When the piece is finished (or during the following day's mini-lesson), the children help the teacher edit the piece for the items on the checklist. Next, the children go on to their own writing. They are at all different stages of the writing process— finishing a story, starting a new story, editing, illustrating, etc. While the children write, the teacher holds conferences with individuals who are getting ready to publish. From three to five pieces, they choose one to make into a book. This piece is edited with the teacher's help, and the child proceeds to the publishing table where he or she will copy the edited piece and illustrate the book. This block ends with "Author's Chair," in which several students each day share work in progress or their published book.

Making the Writing block multilevel. Writing is the most multilevel block because it is not limited by the availability or acceptability of appropriate books. If teachers allow children to choose their own topics, accept whatever level of first-draft writing each child can accomplish, and allow them to work on their pieces as many days as are needed, all children can succeed in writing. One of the major tenets of process writing is that children should choose their own topic. When children decide what they will write about, they write about something of particular interest to them and consequently something that they know about. While this statement may seem to belabor the obvious, *it is a crucial component in making process writing multilevel.* When everyone writes about the same topic, the different levels of children's knowledge and writing ability become painfully obvious.

In one of our classrooms, recently, two boys followed each other in the Author's Chair. Todd, a very advanced writer, read a book he had authored titled *Rocks.* His 16-page book contained illustrations and detailed descriptions of metamorphic, igneous and sedimentary rocks. The next author was Joey, one of the struggling readers and writers in the classroom. He proudly read his eight-page illustrated book titled *My New Bike.* Listening to the two boys read, the difference in their literacy levels was striking. Later, several of the children were individually asked what they liked about the two pieces and how they were different. The children replied that "Todd wrote about rocks and Joey wrote about his bike." Opinions about the pieces were divided, but most children seemed to prefer the bike piece to the rock piece—bikes being of greater interest than rocks to most young children!

In addition to teacher acceptance, having children choose their own topics, and not expecting finished pieces each day, Writer's Workshops include two teaching opportunities that promote the multilevelness of process writing: mini-lessons and publishing conferences. In mini-lessons, the teacher writes and the children get to watch her thinking. In these daily short lessons, teachers show all aspects of the writing process. They model topic selection, planning, writing, revising, and editing, and they write on a variety of topics in a variety of different forms. Some days they write short pieces. Other days, they begin a piece that takes several days to complete. When doing a longer piece, they model how to reread what you wrote previously in order to pick up your train of thought and continue writing. The mini-lesson contributes to making process writing multilevel when the teacher includes all different facets of the writing process, writes on a variety of topics in a variety of forms, and intentionally writes some shorter, easier pieces and some longer, more involved pieces.

Another opportunity for meeting the various needs and literacy levels of children comes in the publishing conference. In some classrooms, as children develop in their writing, they do some peer revising/editing and then come to the teacher "editor-in-chief" for some final revising/editing before publishing. As teachers help children publish the piece they have chosen, they have the opportunity to truly "individualize" their teaching. Looking at the writing of a child usually reveals both what the child needs to move forward and what the child is ready to understand. The editing conference provides the "teachable moment" in which both advanced and struggling writers can be nudged forward in their literacy development.

Finally, writing is multilevel because for some children, writing is their best avenue to becoming readers. Decades ago, Russell Stauffer (1970) advocated language experience as an approach to teaching reading in which children found success because they could both read their own words (language) and comprehend their own experiences. When children who are struggling with reading write about their own experiences and then read it back (even if no one else can read it!), they are using their own language and experiences to become readers. Often children who struggle with even the simplest material during Guided Reading can read everything in their writing notebook or folder. When children are writing, some are really working on becoming better writers; others are engaging in the same activity, but for them, writing is how they figure out reading.

Working with Words

In the Working with Words block, children learn to read and spell high-frequency words and learn the patterns that allow them to decode and spell lots of words.

Word Wall. The first 10 minutes of this block are usually given to reviewing the Word Wall words. Word Wall is a display of high-frequency words, posted above or below an alphabet. The words are written with thick black marker on colored paper and are arranged alphabetically by first letter only. The teacher adds 5 words a week until there are 110-120 words on the wall. Students practice new and old words daily by looking at them, saying them, clapping or snapping the letters, writing the words on paper, and self-correcting the words with the teacher.

Practice with the high-frequency words on the wall takes the first 10 minutes of the Words block every day. The remaining 15-25 minutes of Words time is given to an activity that helps children learn to decode and spell. Different activities are used on different days. Three of the most popular activities are described below.

Rounding up the Rhymes. This Words-block activity follows up the reading of a selection during Guided Reading or a book the teacher has read aloud at the beginning of Self-Selected Reading. Here is an example using the timeless book *In a People House* (LeSieg, 1972).

The first (and often second) reading of any text should be focused on meaning and enjoyment. When reading *In A People House,* there is lots to think about and enjoy. As the mouse shows the bird what is in a people house, children encounter wonderful "Seussian" language and pictures. Mundane things such as bottles, brooms and pillows come to life as the bird and the mouse juggle them, fly them, and fight with them!

Returning to the book during the Words block, we draw the children's attention to the rhyming words. As we read each page or two, we encourage the children to chime in and try to hear the rhymes they are saying. As children tell us the rhyming words, we write them on index cards and put them in a pocket chart. Here are the rhyming pairs rounded up from the first several pages:

mouse	chairs	brooms	thread	door	pails
house	stairs	rooms	bed	more	nails
				floor	

Next, we remind children that words that rhyme usually have the same spelling pattern, and that the spelling pattern in a short word includes all the letters beginning with the first vowel and going to the end of the word. Children then come and underline the spelling patterns in each set of rhymes and decide whether or not they are the same. In this example, all the rhymes have the same spelling patterns except *thread* and *bed*. We explain that words that rhyme usually have the same spelling pattern, but that sometimes there is another spelling pattern. Because we want rhymes with the same spelling pattern, we discard *thread* and *bed*. We also discard *more,* keeping the other two rhymes *door* and *floor*. We now have in our pocket chart five sets of words that rhyme and have the same spelling pattern:

| h<u>ouse</u> | ch<u>airs</u> | br<u>ooms</u> | d<u>oor</u> | p<u>ails</u> |
| m<u>ouse</u> | st<u>airs</u> | r<u>ooms</u> | fl<u>oor</u> | n<u>ails</u> |

The final part of this activity is to use these words to read and write some other words. This is the transfer step and is critical to the success of this activity for children who "only learn what we teach." We begin the transfer part of this activity by telling children something like,

> You know that when you are reading books and writing stories, there are many words you have never seen before. You have to figure them out. One way many people figure out how to read and spell new words is to see if they already know any rhyming words or words that have the same spelling pattern. I am going to write some words and you can see which words with the same spelling pattern will help you read them. Then, we are going to try to spell some words by deciding if they rhyme with any of the words in our pocket chart.

Here are the words rounded up from *In a People House,* along with the new words read and spelled based on their rhymes and spelling patterns at the conclusion of this activity.

house	chairs	brooms	door	pails
mouse	stairs	rooms	floor	nails
blouse	pairs	zooms	poor	snails

Making Words. Making Words (Cunningham & Cunningham, 1992; Cunningham & Hall, 1994) is an active, hands-on, manipulative activity in which children learn how to look for patterns in words and how changing just one letter or one letter's placement changes the whole word. The children are given the six to eight letters that will form the final word. The lesson begins with two-letter words, then builds to three-, four-, and five-letter words until the word that can be made with all the letters is made. They then sort the words according to a variety of patterns, including beginning sounds, endings, and rhymes, and use the words sorted to read and spell words with similar patterns.

In one lesson, the children had the letters *i, u, n, p, r,* and *t.* Following the instructions of the teacher, the children made the following words: *it, in, pin, nip, rip, run, runt, punt, trip, turn, print, turnip.* (The word *turnip* was chosen because the children had read the story "The Great Big Enormous Turnip" during the Guided Reading block. The last word made is the "secret word," because it always uses all the letters and children delight in trying to figure out what the secret word can be.)

When all the words have been made, the teacher leads the children to sort them out, first for beginning letters, and then for rhyming words. The rhyming words from this lesson were:

in	nip	runt
pin	rip	punt
	turnip	

Following the same procedure used in the transfer step of Rounding up the Rhymes, the teacher helped them to see that these rhyming words would help them read and spell other rhyming words they might encounter in their reading or need to spell while writing. In this lesson, the transfer words were *stunt, trip, spin,* and *chip.*

Guess the Covered Word. Guess the Covered Word is another popular Words-block activity. Its purpose is to help children practice the important strategy of cross-checking meaning with letter-sound information. For this activity, the teacher writes four or five sentences on the board, covering a word in each sentence with two sticky notes. Children read each sentence and then make several guesses for the word. There are generally many words that will fit the context, and the teacher points out that lots and lots of words are possibilities when you can't see any of the letters. Next, the teacher takes off the first sticky note, which always covers all the letters up to the vowel. Guesses that don't begin with these letters are erased, and new guesses which both fit the meaning and start with all the right beginning letters are made. When all the guesses which fit both the meaning and the beginning sounds have been written, the whole word is revealed. Most teachers trim or tear their sticky notes to cover the exact length of the word, so that children also become sensitive to word length.

Making the Words block multilevel. If you watched children doing the daily Word Wall practice, you would assume that they are all learning the same thing—how to spell words. But what they are doing externally may not reveal what they are processing internally. Since the new words added to the wall each week are usually chosen from high-frequency words read in selections during Guided Reading the previous week, most of the children have learned to read them before they become Word Wall words. During the daily Word Wall practice, the children who have already learned to read them are now learning to spell them. However, the other children, who were also introduced to these words last week in their Guided Reading but who require lots of practice with words, have probably not yet learned to read them. Thus, as the children engage in their daily Word Wall practice, some children are learning to spell the words and others are learning to read them. Simultaneously, everyone is practicing handwriting as they write and check the words.

Making Words lessons are multilevel in a number of ways. Each lesson begins with short easy words and progresses to some medium-sized and big words. Every Making Words lesson ends with the teacher asking, "Has anyone figured out the word we can make if we use all our letters?" Figuring out the secret word in the limited time available is a challenge to even our most advanced readers. Making Words engages even children with very limited literacy, who enjoy manipulating the letters and making the words even if they don't get them completely made until they are demonstrated with the big pocket chart letters. Ending each lesson by sorting the words into patterns, and then using those patterns to read and spell some new words, helps children of all levels see how you can use the patterns you see in words to read and spell other words.

During Rounding up the Rhymes, some children are still developing their phonemic awareness as they decide which words rhyme, and are learning that rhyming words usually—but not always—have the same spelling pattern. As they use the rounded-up words to read and spell new words, children who need it are getting practice with beginning letter substitution. Children who already have well-developed phonemic awareness and beginning letter knowledge are practicing the important strategy of using known words to decode and spell unknown rhyming words. Guess the Covered Word lessons provide review for beginning letter sounds for those who still need it. The most sophisticated readers are consolidating the important strategy of using meaning, all the beginning letters, and word length as cues to the identification of an unknown word.

VARIATIONS WITHIN THE BLOCKS

In the previous section, we have tried to provide a sense of what is the same across all our four-blocks classrooms. Since teachers in these classrooms share the belief that all children don't learn in the same way, they divide their time fairly equally between the four major approaches to teaching reading, and they include each block each day. They also believe that the differences in literacy levels among the children have not been well addressed by the traditional three-group solution. Within each block, teachers devise ways to make their instruction as multilevel as possible using a variety of whole-class, small-group, partner, and individual formats.

Once these basic principles are in place, however, the instruction in these classrooms looks very different depending on the materials used, the personality of the teacher, the school and school district policies and curricula, and other variables. There are also great differences depending on the grade and time of year. Instruction within the four-blocks framework in October of first grade looks very different from four-block instruction in May of second grade. It is not possible here to describe for you all the variations and changes teachers make as they progress through the years, but we would like to point out a few so that you will get a vision of this framework as not a rigid steel skeleton but a dynamic, fluid, flexible scaffold.

Variations within Guided Reading

Walk in and out of four-blocks classrooms' Guided Reading blocks, and you will see a great variety of materials and formats. Early in the first grade, most of our Guided Reading time is spent in shared reading of predictable books. *Brown Bear, Mrs. Wishy Washy,* and *Hattie the Hen* are common visitors, and the children and teacher read together in a variety of choral, echo and other shared-reading formats. Comprehension activities often include "doing the book," in which some children are given roles and become the characters as the rest of the children read the book. Little books based on the big books are read and reread with partners, then individually or in small groups. Class books and take-home books patterned on the big book are often constructed in shared writing activities. Often the big books read during Guided Reading are chosen because they fit a theme or unit the class is studying, and Guided Reading time flows seamlessly into other unit-oriented activities. Follow-up activities for the book and the theme often occupy some of the afternoon time.

As the year goes on, the shared reading of big books continues to be a part of Guided Reading—often providing the easier reading half of the grade-level and easier reading we try to provide each week. Other books, not big and not predictable, are added. These books might be part of a basal series, or they might be multiple copies of trade books. The emphasis shifts from reading together to reading with partners or alone. Instead of first reading the selection to the children, teachers often take children on a "picture walk" through the book—leading the children to name the things in the pictures and to make predictions, and pointing out a few critical vocabulary words students might have difficulty with as they attempt to read the selection. Children then attempt to read the selection individually, with a partner, or in a small flexible group with the teacher or another helper. The class reconvenes, discusses the selection, and then reads it chorally or in some other whole-class format (not round-robin reading, however!). Comprehension strategies are taught and prac-ticed. Predictions made before reading are checked. Story maps and webs are completed.

The next reading of the selection might include a writing activity. This writing activity, too, is done by some children individually, some with partners, and others in a group guided by an adult. Often another reading is done as an acting-out of the selection, with various children playing different parts as the rest of the class reads or tells the story.

One Guided Reading variation used when most children read at second-grade level or higher is what we call "Book Club" groups. The teacher selects three or four books related by author, genre, topic, or theme. Whenever possible, in choosing the three or four books, we include one that is easier than grade level and one that is harder. After reading aloud the first chapter of each book to the children or previewing the pictures with them, the teacher has children indicate their first and second choices for which book they would like to read. If children who are struggling choose the easier book as either of their choices, they are put in the group which will read this book (and likewise with the more advanced readers and the harder book). Once book club groups are formed, they meet regularly to read and discuss the book. The teacher rotates through the groups, giving guidance, support, and encouragement. Each day the groups report to the whole class what has happened in their book so far.

Variations Within Self-Selected Reading

Self-Selected Reading probably varies less across classrooms, grade levels, and time of year than any other block. Still, there are some differences you would notice if you came to visit during this block. Perhaps the most noticeable difference between classrooms is where the children are during this time. In some classrooms, the children are at their desks, and they read from crates of books which rotate from table to table. Each crate contains a wide range of levels and types of books, and children choose books from the crate at their table. Classrooms that use the crate system usually also have a reserved book shelf. A child who is reading a book from a particular crate (which will be moving on) can reserve that book by putting a special reserved book marker in it and placing the book on the reserve shelf. Children love having favorite books on reserve for themselves!

In other classrooms, you will see children reading at a variety of places. In addition to a reading center, many classrooms have a big-book center, a magazine center, a class-authored-book center, a science center including informational books on the current science topic, a center full of books by a particular author being studied, a taped-book listening center, and sometimes even a computer center with a book on CD. At Self-Selected Reading time, children go to these centers. In some classrooms, they rotate through the centers on different days and in other classrooms they choose which center they want to go to.

In still other classrooms, both the crate and the center variations are combined. On Monday, the boys read from the rotating crates of books at their tables, while the girls read in centers. On Tuesday, it would be the boys' turn to go to centers while the girls remain at their seats. This variation is particularly helpful in small classrooms where there are not many spaces for centers and where children would be crowded together at their tables if they were all reading there together.

Young children tend to "vocalize" as they read. We teach them to use "quiet voices," but it is still not a silent time! Everyone's concentration is improved when there is as much distance between children as possible.

Regardless of where the children are, classrooms with successful Self-Selected Reading time all rigorously enforce the "No Wandering" rule. Once you get to your spot, you stay there! In fact, in many classrooms, when children wander from their centers or do not appear to be using the books there, they are sent back to their tables. After a few times, children seldom need to be sent back. What boy (or girl) wants to lose the every-other-day center privilege and go back to the table where just the girls (or boys) are?

Another variation you would see during the Self-Selected Reading block has to do with *how* children read books. A phenomenon commonly observed in homes where 4-year-olds have books and someone to read those books to them is what we call "pretend reading." Young children want to do all the things big people can do. Just as they pretend to cook, to drive, or to be the mommy or the daddy, they pretend they can read. They do this pretend reading to a younger child or to a stuffed animal, using a book which they have insisted on having read to them over and over until they can "read" it themselves from memory. (In fact, this insistence on having a favorite book read hundreds of times is probably motivated by the child's desire to learn to read.)

Another way young children read books is by "reading the pictures." This is usually done with an informational picture book on a topic of great interest to the child. The parent and the child have probably looked at "the airplane book" or "the dinosaurs book" hundreds of times, spending more time talking about the pictures than actually reading the words. In fact, some of these books have wonderful pictures and lots of sophisticated text, and parents don't read the text at all; they just lead the child to talk about the pictures.

We teach our early first-graders that there are three ways to read. You can "pretend read" by telling the story of a familiar story book. You can "picture read" by looking at a book about real things with lots of pictures and talking about all the things you see in the pictures. Or you can read by reading all the words. Early in the year, we model all types of reading for the children. Then we look at books as a class and decide how they (at their current level) would probably read each book. The teacher gives suggestions like the following:

> *The Gingerbread Man* is a book you could pretend read because you know the story so well. Let's practice how you might pretend read it if you choose it for self-selected reading time.
>
> How would you read this book about trucks? It's got lots and lots of words in little tiny print but you could read it by picture reading. Let's practice picture reading.
>
> Now, here is an alphabet book. You see just one word and it goes with the picture. You can probably read this book by reading the words.

Once children know that there are three ways to read books, no child ever says, "I can't read yet!"

Finally, there are some variations in how children share books. Once the Self-Selected Reading block gets up and running and children know where they are supposed to be and how they are supposed to read during this time, teachers usually spend their time holding individual conferences with children. Most teachers designate the children as Monday, Tuesday, Wednesday, etc., and then hold a conference with them on their day, spending 3 or 4 minutes with each child. Children know that on their day, they should bring one book which they have selected to share with the teacher. They read a few pages to the teacher (in whichever of the three ways is appropriate for that book) and discuss the book and why they chose it. Thus, each child gets a short but dependable conference time with the teacher each week to share what they like about books.

It is also important that children get to share books with each other. In some classrooms, the Self-Selected Reading block ends with a "Reader's Chair" in which one or two children each day get to do a book talk. They show a favorite book, read or tell a little about the book, and then try to "sell" this book to the rest of the class. Their selling techniques appear to be quite effective since these books are usually quickly seen in the hands of many of their classmates.

Other teachers have "reading parties" one afternoon every two or three weeks. Children's names are pulled from a jar and they form groups of three or four in which everyone gets to share a favorite book. Reading parties, like other parties, often include refreshments such as popcorn or cookies. Children develop all kinds of tasty associations with books and sharing books!

Still other teachers arrange outings for their children to read to younger children in the school. Each child selects a favorite book and then reads it to a younger reading buddy.

Variations within Writing

Depending on the time of year and the grade level, there are many variations in the Writing block. Early in the first grade, our writing block begins with what we call *"driting."* As with reading, if you observe those lucky preschool children who have materials to write with and on, and encouragement from parents, they pretend they can write. They do this by combining drawing with some circle/line letter-like forms, and gradually some letters, a few words (sometimes copied from a book, sign, or calendar), and often a few numbers put in where they "look good." The child then proceeds to "read" what he or she has written, usually to the delight of the parents of this precocious four-year old.

Believing that we must begin where children are, and knowing that many of our first-graders have not done this "driting" at home, we begin our first-grade Writing block with driting. For the mini-lesson, the teacher places a large sheet of drawing paper on the board and then, using crayons, draws a picture and writes a few words to go with the picture. She tells the class what she is doing:

Each day at this time, I am going to draw and write something I want to tell you. Today I am drawing a pizza because today is Thursday and on Thursday night, we don't cook at my house. We go out to eat, and each week, we all take turns picking the restaurant. This Thursday is David's night to pick and I know we will be going to Pizza Hut.

As the teacher says this, she is drawing a pizza and writing the words PIZZA HUT. In the Writing mini-lesson, we try to model a type of writing which most of our children can achieve. Next, the teacher gives everyone a piece of drawing paper and gives the following instructions:

Use your crayons to draw something you want to tell us. You can write some words too, like I wrote PIZZA HUT, but you don't have to. Draw and write in whatever way you would like so that you can tell us what you want to tell us. It doesn't have to be about food. It can be about a pet, or what you like to do, or baseball or anything that you want to tell. I am going to give you ten minutes to draw and write and then we will all make a circle and tell about our driting.

As the children draw and write, the teacher goes around and encourages them, responding enthusiastically to whatever they are creating. At the end of 10 minutes, the teacher says,

Let's all get in a circle now and anyone who wants to can tell us about their driting. If you have more details you want to add, you can do that later when you have a few minutes of spare time. It doesn't have to be finished for you to tell us about it.

The teacher and children then spend 10-15 minutes letting volunteers show and tell about their driting.

When we work with teachers, they always ask an unanswerable question: "How long do you stay in the driting stage?" In some classrooms, where most children have been writing in kindergarten or at home, our Writing block looks like that described above for only a few days. In other first grades, the children have had few experiences with print, and driting remains the Writing block variation for several weeks. To answer the question of when to move to the next stage, you have to look at what the children are producing. Each day, when the teacher is doing the driting mini-lesson, she both draws and writes. Usually, early in the year, most of the children just draw. But, as time passes, more and more children will spontaneously start adding words to their drawings. Remember—there are three other blocks going on. Words are being added daily to the Word Wall. Children are learning about letters and sounds as they make words, round up rhymes, guess covered words, and do other Words-block activities; they are participating in daily Guided Reading time, and reading in whatever way they can during Self-Selected Reading time. All of these literacy activities will naturally increase children's tendency, as well as their ability, to incorporate words into their driting.

When almost all the children are using both words and drawing in their driting, it is time to move to the next stage. In most classrooms, that move is signaled by a new kind of paper, which has drawing space on the upper half and a few writing lines on the bottom half. Thus, we often call this stage the "half-and-half" stage. When the teacher decides to move on to this stage, she begins her mini-lesson by putting a piece of half-and-half paper on the board (or a half-and-half transparency on the overhead). She says something like,

> You are learning to read and write so many words that starting today
> we are going to use this writing and drawing paper for our writing.
> You will still write and draw what you want to tell us, but you can do
> your writing here and use your pencil, and then you can draw your
> picture here with your crayons.

The teacher then models this procedure. She writes a simple sentence or two (but no more), modeling how to look at the word wall for words you know are there and how to phonetically "stretch out" the other words to invent-spell them. Then she draws a picture that goes with the writing.

Next, the children do their writing, and if the move was timed correctly, most children write a few sentences. The teacher goes around and encourages the students. If asked to spell a word, she does not spell it, but rather helps the child stretch the word out and get down some letters. After 10-15 minutes, the children form a circle and share their creations just as they did in the driting stage. The teacher responds positively to what each child tells, including those few children who only have a picture! In a few weeks, with the help of the Word Wall and other words around the room, and with the teacher to help them stretch out words, even the struggling children will generally write a sentence or two to go with their pictures.

The next move is from the half-and-half stage to the stage in which children are writing on their own without teacher encouragement/stretching out words. The teacher can then spend the 15-20 minutes when the children are writing to help individual children revise, edit and publish pieces. This is also the time when we begin to use the Author's Chair procedure, in which the Monday children share on Monday one piece they have written since the previous Monday, the Tuesday children on Tuesday, etc.

There are some variations in the revising/editing/publishing stage, too. In most classrooms, teachers let children choose a piece to publish when they have completed three or four good first drafts. (Of course, "good" is a relative term that varies from child to child!) When the child has the required number of first drafts, he or she chooses one to publish and then chooses a friend to help with the revising and editing. Once this is done, the child signs up for a conference with the teacher, who helps the writer get the piece into publishable form. At this point, we fix all spelling and tidy the piece up mechanically, because we want a published piece that everyone else can read easily—and of which the child will be proud. There are variations in the publication form, too, including individual books; pieces copied, illustrated and displayed on a class author board; class books; pieces typed and illustrated using a computer publishing program; and even some class-created Web pages.

While many teachers find this pick-a-piece-out-of-every-three-or-four procedure quite workable, other teachers prefer to divide the class into thirds—including one of their most fluent and one of their least fluent writers in each third—and work with one group each week. In week 1, children in the first third edit and publish a piece, while the other two groups work on as many first drafts as they can in a week. In week 2, the students in the first third go back to first drafting while the teacher works with the second third on editing and publishing. In week 3, the students in the final third (who have been producing first drafts for 2 weeks and will have a lot to choose from) get to publish a piece. Week 4 finds the first third back in the revising/editing/publishing stage.

Regardless of how the revising/editing/publishing process is structured, it is important that children spend most of their writing time doing the hard but important work of first drafting; that during this first drafting they use the Word Wall and other room resources to spell words and stretch out the spelling of longer words; and that their published pieces be good, readable-by-others products of which they can be proud. In classrooms in which the writing block is a daily part of the classroom reading-language arts routine, all children learn to write—and many children do most of their "learning to read" work during the writing time.

Variations Within the Words Block

Word Walls. Come to visit during the daily Words block and you will see the children spending the first 10 minutes practicing Word Wall words. Each day the teacher calls out five words which the children clap and cheer for (in a rhythmic fashion), write and then check, focusing also on the handwriting of the words as they check them. What varies between classes here is the choice of words.

Most first-grade teachers begin their Word Wall with the names of the children, adding one each day rather than five each week. When learning these names, the children clap and cheer them but do not usually write them, because their writing abilities are limited and instruction on letter formation is just beginning. High-frequency words are added at the rate of five per week once the names of the children are there; at this point, the students usually begin writing the words, although often on unlined paper for a while.

First-grade teachers usually choose words to add to the wall as they appear in selections during Guided Reading. Because Word Wall words are high-frequency words, they will all occur in the selections the children are reading. Teachers consult a high-frequency list and then add the highest-frequency ones from anything read during Guided Reading. There is no particular order in which to add the words, but we try not to add two in the same week that begin with the same letter. We also try to include some easier words *(me, go, in)* along with some of the trickier ones *(what, friend, there)*. Many teachers add *what, do, you, see,* and *at* after reading *Brown Bear,* which features those words prominently.

In addition to high-frequency words, many first-grade teachers like to have a word on the wall to represent each of the beginning consonant sounds, as well as the blends *sh, ch, th,* and *wh.* Figure 2-1 on the next page presents a list of 110 recommended words (Cunningham & Hall, 1997), including high-frequency words, a few words frequently written by first-graders such as *favorite, sister, brother,* and and at least one example for each beginning sound. The underlined words have a spelling pattern that will help children spell lots of rhyming words.

In the second grade, we base our word selection more on what we observe in children's writing than on what words they have read during Guided Reading. The emphasis is still on high-frequency words, but we select those that are irregularly spelled, particularly those misspelled in students' first-draft writing. Many second-grade teachers begin their word walls with the words *they, said, was, have,* and *because*—words most second-graders can read but many cannot spell. (We would not put high-frequency words that are easy to spell, such as *me, in, go,* etc., on a second-grade Word Wall unless we had second-graders who still couldn't spell them.) Hard-to-spell high-frequency words are often on the first-grade Word Wall and then put back again on the second-grade Word Wall. In schools in which children have had a Word Wall in the first grade, they often know which words are hard for them to spell and ask to have these words

Table 2-1. The first-grade Word Wall.

after	from	me	tell
all	fun	my	that
am	get	new	the
and	girl	nice	them
animal	give	night	there
are	go	no	they
at	good	not	thing
be	had	of	this
best	has	off	to
because	have	old	up
big	he	on	us
boy	her	out	very
brother	here	over	want
but	him	people	was
can	his	play	we
can't	house	pretty	went
car	how	quit	what
children	I	rain	when
come	in	ride	where
day	is	said	who
did	it	saw	why
do	jump	school	will
down	kick	see	with
eat	like	she	won't
favorite	little	sister	you
for	look	some	your
friend	made	talk	zoo
	make	teacher	

put back on their second-grade Word Wall.

Once we have displayed the hard-to-spell high-frequency words, we try to include an example word for letter combinations including *ch, sh, th, wh, qu, ph, wr, kn;* the less common *c* and *g* sounds; the most common blends: *bl, br, cl, cr, dr, fl, fr, gr, pl, pr, sk, sl, sm, sn, sp, st, tr;* and the most common vowel patterns:

crash, make, rain, played, car, saw, caught

w<u>e</u>nt, <u>ea</u>t, gr<u>ee</u>n, sist<u>er</u>, n<u>ew</u>
<u>i</u>nto, r<u>i</u>d<u>e</u>, r<u>igh</u>t, g<u>ir</u>l, th<u>i</u>ng
n<u>o</u>t, th<u>ose</u>, fl<u>oa</u>t, <u>or</u>, <u>ou</u>tside, b<u>oy</u>, sh<u>ook</u>, sch<u>ool</u>, h<u>ow</u>, sl<u>ow</u>
b<u>u</u>g, <u>use</u>, h<u>ur</u>t
wh<u>y</u>, ver<u>y</u>

Finally, if possible, we include the most commonly written contractions *(can't, didn't, don't, it's, that's, they're, won't)* and the most common homophones *(to, too, two; there, their, they're; right, write; one, won; new, knew)*; and example words ending with *-s, -ed,* and *-ing.*

Table 2-2 on the next page presents a list of 120 words (Cunningham & Hall, 1998) that includes all of the above and is a beginning point for thinking about second-grade Word Walls. Words marked with an asterisk (*) are often also included on first-grade Word Walls. The underlined words have spelling patterns that help students spell lots of rhyming words.

Other Words-block activities. Activities that occur in the 20-25 minutes of the Words block after the Word Wall also vary, depending on the needs of children, the personality of the teacher, the grade level, and the time of year. We try to make these activities as multilevel as possible; therefore, there is not as much variance across time of year and grade level as might be expected. Early in first grade, we spend a lot of time with phonemic awareness activities that help children learn to segment and blend words and to deal with the concept of rhyme—but we continue to include some work with phonemic awareness throughout first grade and into second grade, because many children require lots of varied practice with this before they truly understand it.

We use fewer letters and only one vowel in our early Making Words lessons, but even in these early lessons, we sort for patterns and use sorted rhyming words to read and spell some transfer words. As children become more sophisticated, we use more letters and two or three vowels, but we continue to make some short easy words at the beginning of each lesson. During Guess the Covered Word lessons,

Table 2-2. The second-grade Word Wall.

ˇabout	friends	or	their
*after	*girl	other	*them
again	green	our	then
*are	gym	outside	*there
beautiful	*have	*people	*they
*because	*here	phone	they're
before	*house	played	*thing
*best	*how	*pretty	those
black	hurt	*quit	*to
*boy	*I	*rain	too
brothers	into	really	trip
bug	it's	*ride	truck
*can't	joke	right	two
*car	*jump	*said	use
*caught	junk	sale	*very
*children	kicked	*saw	wanted
city	knew	*school	*was
clock	line	shook	*went
could	*little	*sister	were
crash	*made	skate	*what
crashes	mail	slow	*when
didn't	*make	small	*where
don't	many	snap	*who
drink	more	sometimes	*why
eating	name	sports	*will
every	*new	stop	*with
*favorite	*nice	tell	won
first	*not	than	*won't
float	*off	thank	write
found	one	that's	writing

we usually only cover words with single initial consonants in our first lessons, but soon we include words that begin with letter combinations such as *sh* and *br*. We never completely stop including some words with single consonants, however. Rounding up the Rhymes is an activity that can be used numerous times at grades 1 and 2. The procedures are the same, but the book from which we are working and the rhyming patterns are different each time.

Because children's decoding and spelling abilities are so varied, and because some children require much more practice than others before they can actually use their strategies to read and write words, we plan our lessons to include several different important word understandings. We also continue to use the lesson formats across both grade levels so that children have many different opportunities to see how words work.

CONNECTIONS ACROSS THE BLOCKS

So far, we have been describing the blocks as separate entities. In most primary classrooms, each has an allotted time, and you can tell by observation which block the teacher and children are in. As much as possible, however, teachers try to make connections from one block to another.

Many teachers take the approach of organizing their teaching around a theme. These teachers often select books for Guided Reading which correlate with their theme. During the writing mini-lesson when the teacher models writing, he or she often (but not every day) writes something connected to the theme. Some of the books teachers read aloud at the beginning of Self-Selected Reading and some of the books children can choose from are theme-connected. Theme words are not put on the Word Wall—which we reserve for high-frequency words and words that represent high-frequency patterns. But most teachers have a theme board or chart in addition to the word wall. This board changes with each theme and, in addition to pictures, includes theme-related words children will need as they pursue that theme. Often the secret word in a Making Words lesson is theme-connected. The sentences a teacher writes for a Guess the Covered Word lesson might also relate to the theme.

In addition to theme connections, there are other connections across the blocks. We practice Word Wall words during the Words block—but we select them only after they have been introduced in Guided Reading, and we make sure that the children know that when they are writing, they can invent-spell words as best they can *unless* the word is on the Word Wall. Word Wall words must be spelled correctly!

Rounding Up the Rhymes occurs during the Words block, but the book from which we are rounding up has usually been read by the children during Guided Reading or read aloud by the teacher to begin the Self-Selected Reading block. Sometimes, we do Guess the Covered Word activities by using sticky notes to cover one word on each page of a big book that was used during Guided Reading. We often introduce vocabulary during Guided Reading through picture walks. While reading with small groups, we coach children on how to decode words using picture, context and letter sound clues that were taught in the Words block.

In our mini-lesson at the beginning of each day's Writing time, we model how we can find words we need on the Word Wall and how to stretch out words, listening for the sounds, to spell big words not available in the room. When we are helping children edit, we praise them for their good attempts and spelling and coach them to use things they are learning during the Words block.

Most teachers who have organized their literacy activities within the four-blocks framework find that it is natural and easy to make connections across the blocks. By providing instruction in all four blocks, we provide children with many different ways to learn to read and write. Connections across the blocks help children build bridges between what they are learning.

ASSESSMENT AND EVALUATION

In the last few years, several schools and districts have attempted to evaluate the effectiveness of the four-blocks framework. We will report some data from three different sites.

Data from the Original Four-Blocks School

Clemmons Elementary School, the school in which the framework was originally implemented, is a large suburban school with a diverse student population. Some children come from homes surrounding the school; others are bussed from the inner city. In any year, 20–25% of the children qualify for free or reduced-price lunches. Approximately 25–30% of the children are African-American, Hispanic, or Asian/Pacific Island. Since the program began, the student population has remained relatively stable, with approximately 10% of the children moving in and out each year. There have been four different administrators. Approximately half of the current first- and second-grade teachers have been there for all six years. The other half, including some beginning teachers, have joined the staff more recently. All classes are heterogeneously grouped. No children are retained, and children are not referred for special classes until second grade. Thus, the population assessed each year includes all children who are in the school at the end of first and second grade. The majority of the children have had two years of multimethod, multi-level instruction, but some children who are new to the school have had one year or less.

Throughout the year, teachers conduct assessments by observing and holding conferences with children, taking running records, and looking at writing samples. At the end of the year, children are given an informal reading inventory (IRI), the Basic Reading Inventory (Johns, 1994). Instructional levels on the oral reading passages are computed using the standard procedures. An instructional level of first or second grade is considered grade level at the end of first grade, and an instructional level of second or third grade is considered grade level at the end of second grade.

Table 2-3 on the next page presents the IRI data on the reading achievement of the population of our study. IRI data is reported starting with our second year in which all first-grade teachers were involved, and continues through 5 years of first-graders and second-graders. Approximately 100–140 children in each grade are included

Table 2-3. The results from five years of four-block literacy instruction.

	Reading Levels	No.	Percent		Reading Levels	No.	Percent
Year 1 (Grade 1) 1991	Above (Gr. 3-6)	64	64%	Year 2 (Grade 2) 1992	Above (Gr. 4-6)	77	76%
	At (Gr. 1, 2)	28	28%		At (Gr. 2, 3)	24	22%
	Below (PP, P)	10	10%		Below (PP, P, 1)	2	2%
Year 2 (Grade 1) 1992	Above (Gr. 3-6)	65	61%	Year 3 (Grade 2) 1993	Above (Gr. 4-6)	74	71%
	At (Gr. 1, 2)	26	25%		At (Gr. 2, 3)	21	20%
	Below (PP, P)	14	15%		Below (PP, P, 1)	9	9%
Year 3 (Grade 1) 1993	Above (Gr. 3-6)	76	61%	Year 4 (Grade 2) 1994	Above (Gr. 4-6)	87	68%
	At (Gr. 1, 2)	28	22%		At (Gr. 2, 3)	32	25%
	Below (PP, P)	21	17%		Below (PP, P, 1)	9	7%
Year 4 (Grade 1) 1994	Above (Gr. 3-6)	59	58%	Year 5 (Grade 2) 1995	Above (Gr. 4-6)	76	76%
	At (Gr. 1, 2)	25	25%		At (Gr. 2, 3)	16	14%
	Below (PP, P)	17	17%		Below (PP, P, 1)	6	6%
Year 5 (Grade 1) 1995	Above (Gr. 3-6)	87	64%	Year 6 (Grade 2) 1996	Above (Gr. 4-6)	97	70%
	At (Gr. 1, 2)	29	22%		At (Gr. 2, 3)	31	22%
	Below (PP, P)	19	14%		Below (PP, P, 1)	10	7%

in each year's data.

Across the 5 years, instructional-level results have remained remarkably consistent. At the end of first grade, 58–64% of the children read above grade level (third grade or above); 22–28% read on grade level; 10–17% read below grade level (preprimer or primer). At the end of second grade, the number of children reading above grade level (fourth-grade level or above) increases to 68–76%. The number reading at grade level is 14–25%. The number reading below grade level drops to 2–9%, half what it was in first grade.

While we have no control group to which we can compare our results, our data was collected across 5 years and was consistent across five groups of 100–140 children. The data look remarkably similar even though half the teachers have come since the onset of the four-blocks framework and the school has had several changes in administration. Looking at these data across 5 years, the most startling (and encouraging) results relate to those children who do not read at grade level at the end of first grade. Out of 100-plus children each year, approximately one child is unable to read the IRI preprimer passage. (This child should not be considered a nonreader, however, because this child does have simple predictable books he or she can read, and can also read his/her own writing!)

Of the 10–15% of children who do not read at grade level at the end of first grade, half are reading on (or, in some cases, *above*) grade level at the end of second grade. Looking at the first-grade data, it is impossible to predict which children will make the leap. Some children who read at the preprimer level at the end of first grade read at grade level or above at the end of second grade. Others who read further along—primer level—at the end of first grade only move to first-grade level by the end of second grade.

Standardized test data on these children collected in the third, fourth and fifth grades each year indicates that 90% of the children are in the top two quartiles. Most years, there are no children whose scores fall in the bottom quartile.

Data from a Suburban School District

The original school in which the framework was implemented does not do standardized testing until the end of third grade. Thus, we had to rely on our IRI data to assess the progress of our students. While we feel that IRI data is the best indicator of individual growth in reading, standardized tests have established reliability and are not subject to individual tester bias or skill, as IRI's are. We considered the idea of administering standardized tests to all our first- and second-graders, but rejected this notion because of the time and money involved, and because we would have no comparable control group. Meanwhile, other districts heard about, observed, and implemented the framework. Many of these districts did administer standardized reading tests in the primary grades, and one district devised an evaluation model, the results of which will be reported here.

Lexington One in Lexington, South Carolina is a suburban southeastern school district with eight elementary schools, in which 25% of the children qualify for free or reduced-price lunch. During the 1995-96 school year, first-grade teachers in the district were given information about the four-blocks framework and allowed to choose whether or not they wanted to implement the framework in their classrooms. Approximately half of the teachers chose to implement the framework and were provided with several workshops, books, and collegial support throughout the year in their classrooms.

In January of 1996, 100 first-graders in classrooms using the four-blocks framework and 100 first-graders in classrooms not using the framework were randomly selected and were given the Word Recognition in Isolation and Word Recognition in Context sections of the Basic Reading Inventory (Johns, 1994). The adjusted means for both measures favored students in the four-blocks classrooms. For the word-recognition-in-context means, the differences were statistically significant. Students in the four-blocks classrooms were, on average, reading at the beginning of second-grade level. Students in the other first grades were on average at the first-grade, second-month level.

While these results were encouraging, district officials were concerned about lack of reliability on the IRI. They devised an experiment using cohort analysis and standardized test results. In May of 1996, all 557 first graders in four-blocks classrooms were administered the Metropolitan Achievement Test. Each child was matched with a first grader from the previous year (1994-95) based on their scores on the CSAB (Cognitive Skills Assessment Battery), a test of readiness given each year during the first week of school. The total reading mean score for the four-blocks first-graders was significantly better (.0001 level) than that of the previous year's matched students. In grade-equivalent terms, the average four-blocks first grader's total reading level was 2.0, while that of the 1994-95 student was 1.6.

Based on the standardized test data, school officials concluded that the four-blocks framework had been much more effective than their previous traditional ability-grouped basal instruction. They hypothesized that since students selected for the cohort group had been taught by all the first-grade teachers in the system, teacher bias based on the enthusiasm of teachers choosing to change could not have accounted for the results. Furthermore, their classroom observations suggested that teachers who implemented the four-blocks framework had not all implemented it fully or equally well. In spite of the unequal implementation, with all children in four-blocks classrooms included, they scored on average almost half a year better than the previous group.

This district then analyzed their data by dividing both groups of students into thirds according to their CSAB scores. Figure 3-1 (on the next page) demonstrates graphically that children of all ability levels profited from the multilevel four-block instruction. There was a 15-point difference in total reading scores for the lower third, a 23-point difference for the middle third, and a 28-point difference for the upper third. The district concluded that organizing in this non-ability-grouped way had profited the struggling students and had been even more successful for students who would traditionally have been placed in the top group.

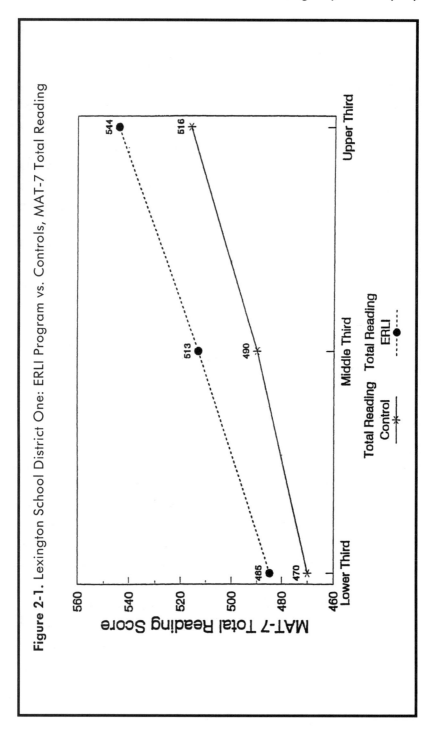

Figure 2-1. Lexington School District One: ERLI Program vs. Controls, MAT-7 Total Reading

Data from One Rural School

During the same year, a nearby school adopted the four-blocks framework and mandated its use in all first- and second-grade classrooms. Brockington Elementary School is in Florence School District Four in Timmonsville, South Carolina—a small rural district in which 84% of students qualify for free or reduced-price lunch. Based on low achievement test scores, the elementary school had been placed on the list of the state's worst schools and had tried a variety of approaches to improve reading and math test scores. During the 1991-92 school year, the school was mandated by a new superintendent to "teach the basics." A state-developed basic skills curriculum focused on "skill and drill" was implemented along with a computer-lab basic skills remediation program for Chapter 1 students. End-of-the-year achievement test scores showed no improvement. During the 1992-93 school year, teachers took a year-long graduate course on whole language. Again, the end-of-year test results failed to show improvement.

During the 1993-94 school year, another new superintendent arrived. The district continued to emphasize whole language, and teachers were trained in cooperative learning. That year's test scores showed some improvement at grades 2 and 3, but none at grade 1. During the 1994-95 school year, teachers were urged to continue to use whole language and cooperative learning; they were also trained in the Learning Styles approach of Rita Dunn. It is hard to compare test scores for this year because the state changed from the Stanford Achievement Test to the Metropolitan Achievement Test, but scores were the worst they had ever been. In grade 1, only 20% of the students scored at or above the 50th percentile on total reading. At the second-grade level, only 9% scored at or above the 50th percentile.

During the 1995-96 school year, all ten teachers—six at first grade and four at second grade—were trained in and mandated to try the four-blocks framework. (It boggles the mind to imagine how enthusiastic and confident these teachers must have been to implement one more "miracle solution"!) These teachers were given workshops, books, state-department and central office support, and other assistance. Central office and state department facilitators who visited weekly in the classrooms observed that four of the six first-grade teachers and three of the four second-grade teachers implemented the framework.

MAT total reading scores for all first and second graders in that school (including the three classes that did not really implement the framework) indicated that 30% of the first-graders and 38% of the second-graders had total reading scores at or above the 50th percentile.

The data from this school system are, of course, open to interpretation. Since different children were tested in the 1994-95 group and we have no pretest data on the 1995-96 group, we cannot be sure that the huge jump in the number of children reading at or above grade level is due to the implementation of the four-blocks framework. Having tried literally "almost everything" in the previous 5 years, however, officials in this school district are convinced that the differences are real and attributable to the balanced multilevel instruction that most of the 1995-96 first- and second-graders received on a daily basis. They are continuing implementation this year and eagerly await the results of the end-of-year testing.

THE VOICES OF CHILDREN, PARENTS, AND TEACHERS

While we are encouraged by the children's performance on our informal reading inventories and on various standardized measures, we are delighted with the reactions of the children, their parents, and the teachers. We have used a variety of measures—including observation, interviews, and surveys—to assess their level of satisfaction with the reading and writing framework.

To evaluate the reactions of children, one has only to watch them as they move through the blocks. Time and again, visitors to our classrooms have asked, "Where do you get children who behave like this? How do you get them all to do what they are supposed to do?" While all our children are not always doing what they are supposed to, this consistent reaction of visitors from all over the country indicates that our children are better behaved and more engaged than expected.

We got the first indications that discipline might improve with this framework at the end of our second year. That year, there were 16 first-grade teachers who had carried out the framework, and we were interviewing them to determine which block they liked most, least, and so on. We asked no questions about discipline, yet in talking about the framework, almost every teacher said something like:

> I don't know how this will work next year, though, because I had a much better class this year than I have had in years. Of course, I had some problem children and some who didn't move as fast as I would like, but on the whole the class was much better behaved.

Since we were carrying out the interviews with individual teachers, they could not have gotten this idea from each other—yet almost every teacher gave us the unsolicited opinion that that year's class was better behaved than most. These 16 teachers were all highly experienced and had taught in these same schools with the same populations of children for many years. When they all decided that they had "gotten better kids" that year, we began to wonder if the framework might be having some effect on discipline.

In addition to observing more engaged children, we have interviewed the children, asking the following questions:

- Which was your favorite block?
- Which block did you like the least?
- What did you like about reading and writing in your classroom?
- Are you a good reader and writer?

Some children had difficulty choosing their favorite and least favorite blocks. One child said:

> I liked them all. I like clapping the word wall words and making words
> and guessing what the covered word is and I like to write. I published
> seven books. Do you want to see them? I liked when the whole class
> read too because I like to partner read and act out the stories. I also
> like getting to choose books from the baskets and read just for fun.

Other children had clearer preferences:

- "I liked words because you got to do things. I didn't like reading from the book buckets because you had to sit in your seat too long!"
- "Writing was the best. I wrote real long books and I am one of the best writers in the room. I am going to be an author when I grow up."
- "I liked when the class read together and when I got to read with my friend but I didn't like doing the words."
- "I liked choosing my own books because I love books about animals, especially sharks and dinosaurs and other big scary animals. I like little animals too—like ants and bees. Bees are really interesting. Some people raise bees and that's their job."

Across all the children we interviewed, the four blocks got almost equal numbers of "favorite" and "least favorite" votes. This confirmed our basic premise that children come to school with their own personalities and that no single approach is ever going to be effective with all children.

When asked what they liked about reading and writing, many children expressed the following idea:

> There are lots of different things to do. The time really flies by and
> nothing lasts too long. You know what you're supposed to do when
> the block comes and you do different things in the different blocks.

Both the variety and the consistency seem to be important to children's level of satisfaction with their reading and writing. They also seem better able to tolerate a block they don't particularly like, since they know it will end soon and they will be on to something they like better.

Almost every child we interviewed believes that he or she is a good reader and writer. When asked about this, the children want to go get books they can read to you and show you the books they have authored. It appears that being able to point to books they can read and books they have written proves to them that they are good readers and writers!

Some of our most interesting information about children's reactions comes from those children who move into our schools and who have been used to a different kind of reading instruction. One such boy arrived after the Christmas break into a second-grade classroom. He was quite shy and hardly spoke, but he watched everything carefully and participated in all four blocks with the help of a buddy assigned to him by the teacher. When he had been there several days, the teacher took him aside and tried to draw him out by asking him about his old school, if he missed his friends, and so on. He said that he did, but that he had new friends, and that this school was really different. When pressed to explain the difference, he asked, "Well, when are we going to do our work?" It took the teacher a minute to realize what he meant; she then explained that in this classroom, reading and writing and working with words *was* the work. Incredulous but happy, the child explained to the teacher that in his old school they had "a whole stack of work to do every day" and sometimes he had to take it home or stay in for recess to get it all done!

The children who have been with us from the beginning see reading and writing as their work and don't know that they are missing out on worksheets—which, unfortunately, many children see as "what you do during reading and writing." While there is an occasional worksheet done during Guided Reading, it is often jointly done with a partner and then discussed and amended with the whole class. Our children spend very little of the 2–2½ hours devoted to language arts sitting at their desks completing worksheets. This may contribute both to the engagement of the children and to the better discipline universally observed and remarked upon.

This absence of worksheets leads us to a discussion of parents and parent reactions. Many parents are used to having children bring home a slew of worksheets each day. They must be assured that their children *are working* at reading and writing even though they don't see the worksheets. We explain the framework to parents through beginning-of-school meetings, newsletters, open houses, and open invitations to visit at any time. Parent volunteers come and read with children during Self-Selected Reading and help with the editing and publishing of books. We make sure that children do have things to take home, including summaries of selections read during Guided Reading, books they have read during Self-Selected Reading, books they have published, writing they have done in connection with Guided Reading, and an updated Word Wall list each week.

Parent reaction, as indicated by their unsolicited comments as well as by surveys, has been very positive. Some of them, like some of the children, like the whole framework. Other parents have specific parts they focus on. They may notice that their child is developing a love of books and wants to purchase copies of some favorite books read in school during Self-Selected Reading time. Others are "glad to know that phonics and spelling are being taught." When a school in which the framework has been in place for several years got a new administrator, the parents of the primary children were quick to let this administrator know that they didn't want any changes in the reading program!

Teachers—who are widely criticized for not being willing to try anything new—have embraced the framework and have made it their own. These teachers will tell you that they like some blocks better than others. (Teachers, too, have individual differences!) They continue teaching each block each day, however, because they see children for whom each block is critical, and they are convinced that if they left any block out, some children would not learn to read.

Some teachers who have taught for dozens of years have found themselves experiencing renewed satisfaction and success. One teacher first used the four-blocks framework in what was going to be her last year of teaching before retiring. She went on to teach for 4 more years, saying, "I can't quit now. It's finally working the way I thought it would work!" Another teacher who heard about the framework at a meeting just a year ago was outraged to learn that "This has been going on for 6 years and this is the first I've heard of it!"

The last 8 years have been exciting and satisfying years for us. We have seen the four-blocks framework implemented in hundreds of classrooms in diverse settings, with varied populations of children. This framework is based on research, but it proposes few revolutionary ideas. It provides teachers a way to implement a balanced program and more nearly meet the needs of children with a wide range of levels who do not all learn in the same way. Both teachers and children find that the framework helps them enjoy school more and find success.

REFERENCES

Allington, R.L. (1983). The reading instruction provided readers of differing reading ability. *Elementary School Journal, 83,* 549-559.

Allington, R.L. (1991). Effective literacy instruction for at-risk children. In M. Knapp & P. Shields (Eds.), *Better schooling for the children of poverty: Alternatives to conventional wisdom* (pp. 9-30). Berkeley, CA: McCutchan.

Bond, G.L., & Dykstra, R. (1967). The cooperative research program in first-grade reading instruction. *Reading Research Quarterly, 2,* 5-142.

Calkins, L.M. (1994). *The art of teaching writing* (2nd ed.). Portsmouth, NH: Heinemann.

Cunningham, P.M., & Allington, R.L. (1994). *Classrooms that work: They can all read and write.* New York: Harper Collins.

Cunningham, P.M., & Cunningham, J.W. (1992). Making Words: Enhancing the invented spelling-decoding connection. *The Reading Teacher, 46,* 106-115.

Cunningham, P.M., & Hall, D.P. (1994) *Making words.* Carthage, IL: Good Apple.

Cunningham, P.M., & Hall, D.P. (1997). *Month-by-month phonics for first grade.* Greensboro, NC: Carson-Dellosa.

Cunningham, P.M., & Hall, D.P. (1998). *Month-by-month phonics for second grade.* Greensboro, NC: Carson-Dellosa.

Cunningham, P.M., Hall, D.P., & Defee, M. (1991). Nonability grouped, multilevel instruction: A year in a first-grade classroom. *The Reading Teacher, 44,* 566-571.

Fielding, L., & Roller, C. (1992). Making difficult books accessible and easy books acceptable. *The Reading Teacher, 45,* 678-685.

Graves, D.H. (1995). *A fresh look at writing.* Portsmouth, NH: Heinemann.

Hall, D.P., Prevatte, C., & Cunningham, P.M. (1995) Eliminating ability grouping and reducing failure in the primary grades. In R.L. Allington & S. Walmsley (Eds.), *No quick fix* (pp. 137-158). New York: Teachers College Press.

Johns, J.L. (1994) *Basic reading inventory* (5th ed.). Dubuque, IA: Kendall Hunt.

LeSieg, T. (1972). *In a people house.* New York: Random House.

Mullis, I.V.S., & Jenkins, L.B. (1990). *The reading report card: 1971-88.* Washington, DC: U.S. Department of Education.

Routman, R. (1995) *Transitions.* Portsmouth, NH: Heinemann.

Shepard, L.A., & Smith, M.L. (1990). Synthesis of research on grade retention. *Educational Leadership, 47,* 84-88.

Stauffer, R.G. (1970). *The language-experience approach to the teaching of reading.* New York: Harper & Row.

Veatch, J. (1959). *Individualizing your reading program.* NY: Putnam.

CHAPTER THREE

Portrait of an Engaging Classroom: Principles of Concept-Oriented Reading Instruction for Diverse Students

JOHN T. GUTHRIE & KATHLEEN E. COX, National Reading Research Center, University of Maryland—College Park

WHAT IS AN ENGAGING CLASSROOM?

Linda Bender's* class is a kaleidoscope of diversity—home to 27 students of various cultures, experiences, learning styles and abilities. On one autumn day, Denisha and Armando, two of her students, were brimming with excitement. While Armando recorded some observations of his team's chrysalis, he exclaimed, "It won't be long now!" Denisha, his teammate, expressed concern, "But we have so much more to figure out before our chrysalis emerges into a butterfly!" With that, Armando directed his team to the classroom library

---

* Lois Bennett is the teacher who is described in this chapter as Linda Bender. Lois has taught the intermediate grades in Prince George's County, Maryland, for 23 years. She is now the 5th-grade teacher at Catherine T. Reed Elementary School. She is pursuing a master's degree in education with a special interest in curriculum. We appreciate her extensive collaboration in this case study.

and announced, "Come on, we have lots of work to do!"

This exchange between Armando and Denisha typifies the self-motivated learning that teachers, administrators, and researchers alike yearn to witness. Curiously, this seemed to be a daily occurrence in Mrs. Bender's class. When asked, Mrs. Bender attributed her students' self-initiated engagement to a pedagogy that fostered student exploration with scientific concepts and multiple types of literature.

Since 1938, Dewey directed teachers not to concentrate on passing fads and fancies of education, but rather to focus on enduring *principles* to create a motivating and engaging context for learning. Furthermore, Dewey eschewed external motivational programs in favor of instructional techniques that harness children's own internal motivations to learn.

> It is part of the educator's responsibility to see equally two things: First, that the problem grows out of the conditions of the experience being had in the present, and that it is within the capacity of students: and, secondly, that it is such that it arouses in the learner an active quest for information and for production of new ideas. The new facts and new ideas thus obtained become the ground for further experiences in which new problems are presented. The process is a continual spiral. (Dewey, 1938, p. 79)

Most teachers agree that an emphasis on algorithmic applications in an inauthentic environment with a lack of social interaction defeats the very educational objectives that we seek to promote. However, in our daily lives as educators, it is often unclear how exactly to create the conditions for students to become self-regulated, intrinsically motivated, engaged, critical thinkers. Moreover, because we are so overwhelmed by fleeting trends, we become perplexed about which principles will transform our classrooms into literate communities filled with active learners.

In this chapter, we portray the classroom of Linda Bender, a fifth-grade teacher who tailored her instructional objectives to align with eight essential organizing principles. Not only are these principles enduring; they also created a learning atmosphere that allowed her to attend to the diverse needs of each student in her class.

The eight principles creating the context for success in her classroom are:

1. organizing content around a *conceptual theme* that serves as a beacon to guide and sustain the literacy and science learning;
2. stimulating students' natural inquisitiveness through the *observation* of real-world events;
3. providing a wide array of *interesting texts* to captivate students during their informational pursuit;
4. supporting students' understanding and their search for the answers to their own distinctive questions while urging them to assume *self-direction* for their learning;
5. pressing students to be *strategic* in their quest for information;
6. advocating for a *collaborative community* among students;
7. allowing students to *express* and represent their new ideas in personal and meaningful ways; and
8. providing *coherence* through an integration of the disciplines.

We describe this principle-based union between scientific concepts and strategic literacy learning as Concept-Oriented Reading Instruction (CORI).

Linda Bender reported that when she started to fully embrace the CORI principles, a metamorphosis began to occur. Each student in her class began assuming responsibility for his or her own learning with intentional and self-motivated scholarship. Her class evolved into a thinking classroom.

In order to provide an in-depth look at what each principle involves, all the student data and teacher discourse we illustrate in this chapter was drawn from one aspect of a 16-week study of ecological systems: raising monarch larvae in the classroom. Our goal was to provide our readers with enough details about the CORI principles that teachers could actualize these methods in their classrooms.

To explain the essence of the CORI principles, we have divided the chapter into eight sections, one for each principle. Further, we divided each principle into four components. First, we define the principle and explain how educational research supports that principle. Second, we present interviews reflecting Mrs. Bender's personal goals in implementing the principle. Third, we demonstrate specific instructional discourse that exemplifies the principle. In these sections, we followed the progress of two students—Armando, a Hispanic boy, and Denisha, an African-American girl—who were randomly selected from Mrs. Bender's diverse group of students. Finally, we provide a step-by-step plan teachers can follow to implement each CORI principle in their classrooms. At the end of the chapter, we explain how CORI succeeds in teaching diverse classrooms.

CONCEPTUAL THEMES

Setting Goals for Learning with Conceptual Themes

To fully understand CORI is to see it as a conceptually centered framework that inspires the entire process of learning. The conceptual theme provides the breadth to embrace two or more disciplines, while providing sufficient depth to increase students' cognitive skills. The attainment of a conceptual goal is the "driving question" of instruction (Blumenfeld et al., 1991). To this end, the teacher derives all instructional objectives from a substantial scientific concept. Each classroom activity is directed toward the complete understanding of the conceptual theme. Our principle for Conceptual Themes in CORI is that *instruction is organized around broad interdisciplinary themes, in which content areas such as English/language arts, science, and history are taught simultaneously.*

A conceptual theme is a general idea that stands at the center of a subject area, like "adaptation" in life science. Learning about the theme includes gaining an organized collection of specific factual information. It also involves understanding the relationships among facts, and the broad principles (such as a food chain) that embrace a wide array of facts and relations (Alexander, Kulikowich, & Jetton, 1994). Literary as well as informational reading can enhance students' understanding of a conceptual theme (Hartman & Allison, 1996). When students appreciate the flight of a butterfly across the continent after reading a poem, they expand their understanding of the butterfly as an organism, and of migration as a concept. There are multiple avenues, both literary and scientific, to understanding concepts.

Organizing instruction around conceptual themes is both old and new. Nature investigations in which students studied a river with all its life-forms, history, mythology and political impact were prominent in England 100 years ago. In the present day, many educators are advocating integrated instruction. For example, the book *Coherent Curriculum* (Beane, 1995) emphasized linking students' learning of literature in English/language arts classes with the study of history, combining science and math more fully, and merging the fine arts into all subject matters. Some progressive teaching programs have even integrated *all* the subjects—including English, science, math, history, and fine arts—by teaching broad units on environmental studies, or using a single theme to understand multiple disciplines (Stephenson & Carr, 1993). Integrated teaching helps students gain cognitive and metacognitive strategies because it helps them see the roles and benefits of using strategies to gain understanding across different contexts and settings (Lipson, Valencia, Wixson, & Peters, 1993). Conceptual themes can link classroom instruction to out-of-school experiences more fully than traditional curricula.

Mrs. Bender's Vision of Her Conceptual Theme

"The broader concepts of adaptation and ecological systems are drawn into the students' conceptual understandings. We constantly revisit our broad themes to guide our inquiry and form connections with them throughout the year. Here, we use scientific themes as the center of literacy activities. For example, the students observe the life cycle of a caterpillar. At the same time, they read about metamorphosis and migration.

"The students quickly find out that the monarch butterfly is one of the

*few butterflies that migrate. The students can't actually 'observe' migra-
tion, but they are reading about it and making connections between what
they observe directly and what will happen to this butterfly when it leaves
the school grounds. It's the broader picture—what they cannot see—that's
important.*

*"There was something on TV about the demise of millions of monarch
butterflies. Many of my students couldn't wait to tell me about the
newscast. They remembered that because of the deforestation going on in
Mexico, the microclimate was interrupted. The students understood that
the monarch butterflies were frozen and more and more were being killed
because of the deforestation. That certainly is literacy—to comprehend
something read, connect it with a conception of why these events are
happening, and then to realize that this destruction is actually occurring
in Mexico!"*

Conceptual Themes in the Classroom

This autumn, Mrs. Bender chose the life sciences concept of ecological systems and interactions. She selected ecology because, coupled
with her enjoyment of the subject, it is a theme about which she has
a significant amount of knowledge. The chart in Table 3-1 (p. 83)
depicts Mrs. Bender's objectives for learning this concept.

The conceptual theme not only launched the learning process,
but also provided a gateway for each of the principles (observing,
collaborating, personalizing, learning strategies) to evolve. In this
sense, the conceptual theme drove the learning—that is, the sole
purpose for executing any principle was to *learn the concept*. For
example, when the study began, Mrs. Bender hung a poster on the
front wall. She explained that soon this would become a concept map
filled with information. She wrote the words "ecological systems" in
the middle of the poster. As her students acquired information and as
their knowledge deepened, they added facts, modified links, and
expanded the once empty space into a myriad of ideas. The concept
map was literally constructed with students' continual growth and
reorganization of their conceptual knowledge. In turn, the students

Table 3-1. Mrs. Bender's Objectives. (Conceptual Theme: Ecological Systems and Interactions.)

Scientific Content Objectives	Scientific Process Objectives	Reading Objectives	Writing Objectives
• describe how living and non-living things interact in an ecosystem	• conduct investigations using the scientific method	• demonstrate understanding of literary elements such as characters, plot, theme, mood, settings, and figurative language	• demonstrate prewriting strategies such as brainstorming, webbing, discussion, and drawing
• describe the principles of energy transfer in an ecosystem	• identify variables of study	• preview texts, graphics, pictures, headings, and subheadings	• communicate ideas, knowledge, and feelings
• demonstrate understanding of the nature of cycles in an ecosystem	• determine ways to control and manipulate identified variables	• demonstrate use of resource reading, identify genres of books	• employ drafting, revising, proofreading, and editing skills
• describe the primary features and locations of major biomes	• keep a journal to collect, organize, and record direct observations and other essential data	• activate prior knowledge and topic familiarity	• consult with peers and teachers about drafts and other writing
• identify plants and animals from each biome	• analyze data using appropriate resources (lab equipment, computer programs, etc.)	• locate and define specialized vocabulary	• write to inform, persuade, and express personal ideas
• classify animals as vertebrates or invertebrates	• construct visual representations of data (e.g., charts, graphs, models)	• adjust the pace of reading	• write journal entries
• describe how climate affects growth of plants and animals	• draw conclusions based on observations and data analysis	• locate table of contents, index, and references	• publish and share writing with others
• demonstrate understanding of our responsibility to protect the habitats, plants, and animals that comprise those ecosystems	• integrate information from data and textual sources to interpret and explain scientific phenomena	• summarize information from main ideas and details, demonstrate note-taking and paraphrasing skills	• interpret information from reading to extend understandings and reflect on personal knowledge

used it as a constant resource and evaluation of their efforts.

To support her students' deep understanding of ecological systems, Mrs. Bender used observation activities to spark student interest. Her students collected specimens, examined models, and used their senses to explore all the uncharted vistas of their world. Mrs. Bender's classroom embodied the qualities of a discovery museum that vitalized her students. The countertops were overflowing with collections of creatures, such as a fish aquarium, a salamander tank, terrariums containing monarch larvae, a "cricket condominium," various bug collections, and a large rattlesnake preserved in formaldehyde. Outside the window, birds fluttered around bird feeders. Additionally, the classroom was filled with various types of lab equipment, computers, and field guides to drive students to discovery. Observation served as an invitation for students to wonder and ask questions.

It was at this juncture that strategy development became the link between curiosity and knowledge acquisition. Without crucial reading strategies, such as how to use a table of contents or how to find the main idea of a book, students' once self-directed learning can come to a halt. Without strategic knowledge, students may become overwhelmed and choose to forgo their "great search." In Mrs. Bender's class, strategy instruction—which we will describe in a later section—arrived right on time. Students' "need to know" determined the type and amount of strategy instruction they received.

Next, students began to discuss their questions and check the accuracy of each other's facts. They pressed each other for explanations and verified their hypotheses and comprehension. For example, on one day, Armando and Denisha discussed the main idea and supporting details of a chapter when they finished reading. Armando said that he thought that the main idea was that butterflies fly from one generation to another. The group agreed but quickly realized that they needed to back up their idea with details.

STUDENT: The topic should be that they fly from south to north instead of generation to generation because we need to be more clear here.

ARMANDO: I'll erase that on my paper.

STUDENT: We need to support this with details.

DENISHA: We can look back in the book to find out the states it flies through.

Finally, each student acquired expertise in his or her own topical area—derived, of course, from the conceptual theme. Their observations, strategic searches, and collaborative efforts all helped to legitimize their personal learning processes. Now, they wanted to tell the world what they learned in their own personal way! Some students made a formal presentation to their classmates; others created artifacts or published books.

Steps in Creating a Conceptual Theme

For teachers who want to use a conceptual theme in teaching, we recommend the following steps.

1. Look at the science curriculum and goals of the district.
2. Choose a scientifically significant theme.
3. Select a comprehensive theme that embraces interdisciplinary connections, including literacy, science, and fine arts.
4. Make the conceptual theme focused enough to be understandable to students, but broad enough to embrace many activities.
5. Find a theme that you enjoy.
6. Construct a concept that will interest students.
7. Choose a conceptual theme that can offer simple and low-cost real-world interactions.
8. Select a theme that lends itself to a diverse selection of books, genres, and multimedia sources.
9. Develop a theme that lends itself to participation by all students.
10. Choose a theme that offers opportunities for a wide variety of self-expressions (e.g., writing, model building, or acting).

OBSERVING AND INTERACTING WITH THE REAL WORLD

Igniting Curiosity with Real-World Connections

Dewey (1913) proposed that building student interest is an important goal for education. In addition, researchers emphasize the importance of authenticity and meaningfulness in learning activities (e.g., Blumenfeld, 1992). Observation entices students to become interested by allowing them to be actively involved in an authentic and meaningful way.

Our principle for real-world experience is that *students interact with concrete objects, events and settings by using their senses—sight, hearing, touch, or smell—and by recording their experiences through writing, drawing, or photographing.* Students in Mrs. Bender's class began their literacy experiences by observing and interacting with the natural world. Whether it was chasing a cricket around the schoolyard, sketching the features of a caterpillar, or planting milkweed as a food source for butterflies, the students became captivated with their surroundings. In this sense, observation served two purposes.

First, observation sparked student curiosity and initial fascination with tangible objects. Students' senses were activated and their attention was so directed that they became one with the activity. Some researchers have termed this type of interest *situational interest* (Schraw, Bruning, & Svoboda, 1995). While we believe situational interest is important for initial engagement with an activity, it may also lead to students' development of long-term personal interests. Moreover, these personal interests can evolve into self-directed learning.

A second benefit of observing and interacting with the real world is that students spontaneously ask questions. Establishing a purpose for reading or writing is the first step in most language arts teaching (Paris, Wasik, & Turner, 1991). However, it is a challenge to help students establish long-term purposes that are personally significant. Interacting with the real-world creates opportunities for students to have experiences they can share, think about, and use as a basis for further learning. When students confront a real-world object (such as a lizard or a fossil) or a historical artifact (such as an arrowhead), they ask questions about its physical structures and its origins. These questions of what, how and why lead students to find and use resources for gaining an understanding and an explanation of what they have seen (Linn & Muilenburg, 1996).

Mrs. Bender's Perspective On Her Observation Goals

"Instead of just reading about something in a book, my students are active participants. They're immersed in the topic. I don't think there's anything more powerful than that to keep them interested. There are so many students who have almost no experiences with the kinds of things that we've observed. They have this experience where they are actually watching this creature grow every day. They are seeing its body features and watching the life cycle up close. They are asking questions—and then they are reading about these very things in the book! They see a picture of pupa formation in the book and they say, 'Oh, look, this is just like what we saw!' That's what's in their boxes. Next they notice that the markings on the monarch in their picture are not exactly the same as what they have seen up close in their box, and that makes them ask more questions. There are a lot of pieces in the process ... the connection between what they observe and what they cannot actually see ... the books fill the gaps."

Real-World Interaction in the Classroom

When students begin experiencing the world in their own personal way, their experiences are exceptional and unique. Observation of real-world objects sets the stage for self-direction and personal ownership. What lies before them is not just a chrysalis—it's *their* chrysalis. Because students actually "own" it, they want to know everything there is to know about it. If they want to know, they will persist in their struggle to know. In wonderment, students start to generate questions. Armando asked, "How will I know if my butterfly is male or female?" Denisha wanted to know how her butterfly would protect itself from other creatures. She also wondered if her butterfly was afraid of heights.

Mrs. Bender capitalized on her students' curiosity and asked them to write out their questions on large strips of paper. Together the students constructed a life-sized KWL (what I *know*, what I *want* to know, what I have *learned)* poster. This activity kindled the interplay between their interests and their prior knowledge about butterflies. Students started to proudly announce, "I know they lay eggs," "I know they live outside," and "I know they like to hide a lot." Then they began to question: "How do they born their babies?" "What do they do all day?" "Where do they fly?" "Do they have families?" "What do they eat?" "How do they talk?"

Mrs. Bender's students were indeed researchers and scientists. They advanced from initial observations to bona fide participation in the scientific community as they tagged their butterflies for the "Monarch Watch Research Program." Mrs. Bender reminded the students, "We have to be very exact about the information that we record for our fellow researchers at the Monarch Watch Program. We will record the tag number for each butterfly, the gender, the date, our location, and we will get the specific weather information from the weather station at the library. The librarian will show you how to read the computerized weather print-out so that we can accurately record and monitor our data."

Mrs. Bender provides models and scaffolds. Some students may not be aware that they have an important question to ask. This is when teacher modeling and scaffolding becomes critical. Students' personal questions are rewarded when their search delivers an answer to their question.

One morning, students were anxiously filling out their "larva log," noting physical and behavioral changes in their teams' specimen. Some teams' butterflies had emerged, while other teams were still waiting patiently. Mrs. Bender provided scaffolds to help students determine how to make their observations.

MRS. B.: OK, let's talk about measuring today. We concluded the other day that we should not take our chrysalides out and measure them because our handling might disturb their processes. So, how do you think we should measure them?

STUDENT: We could put the ruler against the container and measure that way.

MRS. B.: That is a good idea. Do you think we should use centimeters or millimeters?

STUDENT: I think millimeters.

MRS. B.: Why?

STUDENT: It will really show the changes.

MRS. B.: OK then, besides changes in length or width, what other changes might we want to write about today?

STUDENT: Behavior changes.

MRS. B.: *(writing student responses on the board)* OK, anything else that might have changed?

STUDENT: Color.

STUDENT: Physical characteristics.

When the students exhausted their thoughts about what changes might have occurred, the observations began. Mrs. Bender reminded students that if they needed to make close-up observations, they could use their magnifying equipment.

Mrs. Bender explained that observational events were important to revisit during all aspects of the study, so that students could transfer and apply their knowledge. On this day, when students were independently researching to find the answers to their questions, Mrs. Bender provided a scaffold for their observation.

MRS. B.: Students, come here! *(Students gather around a terrarium.)* This morning we thought that very soon some of our chrysalides would start changing, they would darken—and look at this! What color is it?

STUDENT: It's black!

MRS. B.: Yes, it looks black, and if you look very closely...

DENISHA: You can start to see the wings!

MRS. B.: Yes, you can see the wings through it. Now the reason I think this is important for Team One—this is their box, right?

STUDENT: Yes.

MRS. B.: Team One, you should put this very close to you so that you can glance at it periodically, because *(excited)* you don't often get to actually see, completely from start to finish, the butterfly hatch from the chrysalis. But what do we know from our reading about how this will look when it does happen?

STUDENT: It will start to crack

MRS. B.: It will start to crack; it will split at the bottom and will start to look as if it is unzipping. The chrysalis is becoming transparent. It is not that green, milky color any more. Now we will put this here so that you can peek over every so often, and if you see the butterfly emerging we are going to stop what we are doing and watch, because it is not usual for us to see this. Did any of the other teams record any changes from your observations this morning?

STUDENT: Yes, ours is turning a darker color too!

MRS. B.: Well, it looks like we might start to see some changes today.

Twenty minutes later a student noticed that the butterfly emerged.

STUDENT: Look, look *(holding up a box)*. Look here, it must have just come out! Look at the wings, they are crumbled and let...

STUDENT: It is so small.

MRS. B.: Yes, it might have been a small caterpillar. Let's put the box here so that you can all see it. Remember, it is very important that the butterfly not be knocked off its perch, because what can happen?

STUDENT: It could break a wing.

Mrs. Bender walked around the class showing all the students the box and asking questions like, "What is the difference between the way the wings look now and how they might look in a few hours?" The students were responding excitedly.

Observation activities in Mrs. Bender's class. In Mrs. Bender's class, students participated in a wide variety of observational activities and real-world interactions. For example, students participated in the following events:

Data Collection
- observed a wildlife habitat area
- listed and justified the components of habitats
- wrote about their observations in journals (e.g., *I think, I wonder, I saw, I want to know*)
- used field guides to identify animals and plants in the schoolyard
- planted milkweed in the schoolyard
- observed milkweed throughout the seasons
- raised monarch larvae in class
- took daily notes in an observational "larva log," noting all physical and behavioral changes of their specimen during the study
- wrote scientific summaries of data on a weekly basis
- generated hypotheses about their specimens based on evidence from reading
- sketched each phase of transformation with detail
- completed self-evaluation forms about observational techniques, interpretation, and conceptual understanding of data and hypothesis formation

Data Analysis
- constructed a data table of the phases of metamorphosis
- constructed a data table depicting the average rate of growth per day for their specimen
- computed the class's average rate of growth during each stage of metamorphosis
- graphed the growth change over each phase of study
- looked for outliers in the graphs

Experimenting

- searched for crickets in different locations outside the school building
- tallied the number of crickets found in each location (e.g., hillside, woods, soccer field)
- constructed a frequency chart
- drew conclusions about the results (e.g., noting physical and climate differences of each location and hypothesizing why more or fewer were found in each location)
- searched for information and gathered supporting evidence for their hypotheses
- experimented with different types of foods, charting which types crickets prefer and hypothesizing about why
- investigated acids (using cabbage juice) to analyze the effects of acid rain on wildlife
- classified animal bones

Steps in Guiding Real-World Interactions

1. Choose interactions that are relevant to the conceptual theme.
2. Choose interactions that are exciting and that activate students' senses.
3. Choose interactions that are easy for students to perform in or out of school.
4. Find real-world interactions that can be imported into the classroom (e.g., ant home, terrarium, plant growth, rock collection).
5. Ask students to brainstorm possible points of focus in their observing.
6. Help students to remember background experiences relevant to the observation.
7. Encourage students to think of questions, write them down, share them, and publicly display them.
8. Provide guidance for observations (e.g., charts, organized journals, time sequences) and data collection (e.g., size,

shape, texture).

9. Help students to be comprehensive in their observing.
10. Give students options about how, what, and when to observe.
11. Conduct observations both independently and cooperatively.
12. Enable students to extend their observing over multiple occasions.
13. Help students to have command of tools for recording (e.g., drawing, taping, photographing).
14. Help students to take ownership of their observations (e.g., having one's own cricket).

AIDING LEARNING WITH INTERESTING TEXTS

Interest Provokes Effort and Learning

Our principle for this section is that *teachers provide a variety of informational resources, such as expository books, references, and electronic data bases—as well as literary resources, such as novels, folktales, and poetry—on a wide range of difficulty.* In CORI, students are provided with books in a wide variety of levels, genres, and cultures. Providing students with a wide array of interesting books is important for three reasons: (1) to increase student effort in reading, (2) to aid in their comprehension, and (3) to provide students with choices about their reading materials.

First, research on interest indicates that the interestingness of tasks and materials is highly correlated with the amount of effort and time students invest in a task (Renninger, Hidi, & Krapp, 1992). Second, interesting books help students to understand what they read. Using texts of varying degrees of individual interest, as ranked by fifth-graders, Schiefele (1991) found that high-interest reading material was related to deeper levels of comprehension. Similarly, Anderson, Shirey, Wilson, and Fielding (1987) reported that student interest in reading materials is an important determinant of comprehension and retention of information.

Third, not only does interest in a book benefit comprehension and provoke sustained effort, but providing a large quantity of interesting texts offers student choice among texts. Many researchers (e.g., Turner, 1995) report that allowing students some choice in the selection of interesting literature fosters both enjoyment of reading and engagement with literacy tasks. In a study that examined students' motivation for developing literacy, Gambrell, Palmer, and Codling (1993) interviewed fifth-graders about which books they found most interesting. Overall, students responded that "interesting books" were books they found personally relevant and that they self-selected.

Mrs. Bender's Perspective on Interesting Texts

"During the year, students want many different books to answer their personal questions. They use information books and field guides to help them investigate ideas. They read poetry to explore images and ideas. Their interest level is sparked through an exposure to a variety of books. Plus, different genres of books help the students put all of the ingredients together. It makes a more complete picture of the concept."

Mrs. Bender reported not only that her classroom library had 250 books related to ecological systems and interactions, but that her students organized the classroom library themselves. *"I place all of the books relating to the theme out on the students' tables. My students are shocked at first, but then I explain that it is extremely important for them to think of a way to organize the books—for two reasons. First, they will be able to preview the books and get an idea of what's available, and second, they will know where to find what they need when they begin their search for information.*

"Since I have students with various reading capabilities and interests, I make sure that I find interesting books from many different grade levels and genres. When I have a wide range of books available, the students use all of the books. At the beginning of their search, they may start with the books that have a lot of illustrations, and as they observe and figure out the vocabulary words related to the theme, they start to move on to the more difficult books to answer their questions."

Interesting Texts in the Classroom

Multiple texts from different genres offer students different perspectives on the same topic. All of these perspectives help build a more elaborate and complete concept. For a 16-week unit on ecological systems and interactions, Mrs. Bender provided the following: 2 class sets of information books; 3 group sets of information books, copies of one title per team of 4-5 students; two novels; a collection of folk tales, poetry, or short stories; and approximately 50 individual titles in a classroom collection. See the Appendix at the end of this chapter for an abridged list of these books.

When choosing which books to buy for a conceptual theme, Mrs. Bender explained, "I spend a lot of time in bookstores and I ask a lot of people for advice. You have to just get out there and see what is available. Once you start to realize the possibilities, you will be thrilled."

In Mrs. Bender's class, students were exposed to many different genres of text. Mrs. Bender explained that often students are not given opportunities to explore texts and then to think about why they like or dislike a particular book or passage and how they feel in general about reading. She makes sure her students do get ample opportunities for such reflection. For example, when she asked the students to share their thoughts on poetry, Denisha wrote,

> My favorite kinds of poetry are the kinds that make you think. I think poetry is something that makes you laugh, cry, think, and wonder. You know I think people write poetry to show their personality. If I were to write a poem, it would be about how I feel. I would make it humorous and put myself into an animal's or plant's shoes. I don't have a favorite poem but I will later in life. That's how I feel about poetry.

How did students use interesting texts in Mrs. Bender's class? In different parts of the unit, the students in Mrs. Bender's participated in the following:

- classified and organized books
- compared and contrasted different types of information books
- reflected on personal purposes for reading a particular book (e.g., enjoyment, information, practice)
- wrote reviews of books they read, describing the books' strengths and weaknesses
- wrote about interesting points that a book made
- wrote story summaries for peers
- participated in book discussions

Steps in Teaching with Interesting Texts

1. Provide an ample supply of books on the conceptual theme.
2. Spend enough time within a genre to allow students to learn strategies to understand that genre (at least 10 days per genre).
3. Have directed lessons for teaching strategies about each genre.
4. Link writing activities to reading within the genre type.
5. Select books with an abundance of illustrations, diagrams, and charts, and provide instruction for making meaning with them.
6. Provide time for self-selected reading for students to explore genres about the theme.
7. Choose a wide variety of reading levels (from 2 levels below to 2 levels above the current grade level).
8. Provide books that are culturally responsive to the students in your classroom.
9. For each conceptual theme, provide at least 2 class sets of information books, 4 group sets of information books, 2 novels or folk tale collections, 1 poetry collection, and 10 individual titles.
10. Get the media specialist involved in your program.

SELF-DIRECTED LEARNING

Helping Students Assume Responsibility with Self-Directed Learning

In general, the principle for self direction is that *teachers enable students to assume responsibility for learning by helping them to select the topics, texts, tasks, and media related to the conceptual theme.* CORI helps students customize their learning environments to accomplish their own personal goals for learning. Once they set their goals through the questions that they ask, students assume responsibility for attaining those goals. Researchers agree that recognizing the primacy of the learner's role as the agent in charge of his or her own literacy accomplishments is essential in helping students take ownership over their academic decisions (McCombs & Whisler, 1989).

Deci and Ryan (1987) suggested that perceived control or "self-determination" is satisfied when students maintain focus and effort toward a self-initiated goal and achieve despite potential distractions. Furthermore, supporting self-determination involves giving learners freedom to guide their own personal learning goals (Skinner & Belmont, 1993). According to this theory, self-determination increases as people accept their strengths and limitations, make meaningful choices, and determine ways to satisfy their personal needs (Deci, 1995).

Studies of the CORI program show that students participate in decisions; make academic rather than trivial choices; assume leadership roles; and form, execute, and monitor their own self-conceived goals. These conditions increase long-term motivation for reading and writing (Guthrie et al., 1996).

Mrs. Bender's Advice on Self-Direction

"Students investigate their own personal questions through reading and research. One thing that they do on their own is to go grab a field guide and whether it's a wall flower, or an insect, or a butterfly, they read about it. Having a private goal for reading opens doors for students and creates

literacy events ... an intimate relationship between the child and the book begins to develop.

"In my classroom, students must solve problems on their own and generate their own learning questions. Even though it is difficult, I watch them struggle and don't jump in when they have a disagreement or make an error. I think the self-direction aspect of CORI helps students legitimize their questions and different ways of learning."

Self-Directed Learning in the Classroom

There are four features of the CORI atmosphere that make self direction successful. First, since the CORI students are studying a topic of choice in depth, they become experts in their area. In the midst of learning about a concept, they realize that they can make a relevant and worthwhile contribution to the class. The teacher then retreats from being the sole authority, and the students stride into the role of expert. Consider the following example, in which Armando delights in his knowledge about the gender of the butterfly. Remember, this was one of his personal questions! Mrs. Bender asked students to observe a monarch that had just emerged from the chrysalis.

ARMANDO: They are practicing rolling their wings.

STUDENT 1: Opened its wings a little bit...

STUDENT 2: You sort of see..

STUDENT 1: It has four legs, wow, we couldn't see that on the other butterflies!

Mrs. B.: Can you see if it's a male?

ARMANDO: Nope. It's a female because look here when it opens her wings!

Many researchers concur that "distributing students' expertise" (Brown et al., 1993) or "honoring students' voices" (Oldfather & Dahl, 1994) encourages them to become masters over their own learning. In CORI, students lead discussions, explain their ideas, initiate topics, and share their expertise.

A second feature of CORI's self-direction principle that allows students to exercise freedom over their learning environment is that students organize the structural features of the classroom. Although at first this may sound trivial, Mrs. Bender explained that students feel good when they do not have to ask about locations of materials. Since the students organized and labeled the classroom library themselves, they knew exactly where to locate what they needed.

A third component that makes self-direction feasible is that the climate of the class is one of sharing rather than evaluating (Ames, 1992). Students in the CORI classroom are not continually concerned about evaluation; therefore, mistakes are not only allowed—they are expected. Mrs. Bender remarked that when students first arrive in her class, they are very dependent. "They need to be weaned from their reliance on me, and that was not always easy. This is the fourth week of school and I still have three students who are surprised when I do not just *tell* them the answer." In CORI, the teacher presents students with activities that require complex problem-solving and forces them to struggle through the difficult parts together, reminding them that mistakes are part of the process.

Turner and Meyer (1995) coined the term "constructive floundering" to describe an atmosphere where students learn to tolerate the inevitable mistakes and uncertainties of learning. Mrs. Bender described an activity that required first charting data and then graphing it to present to classmates: "After making an elaborate chart, one group of students realized that they could not transform their data chart into a graph. Together, they identified the mistake. Instead of worrying about not having a graph to present, they simply displayed their data chart on the overhead projector. The group explained to their classmates where they made the mistake and how they would do it differently next time."

A final characteristic of self-direction in the CORI classroom is that students learn to self-evaluate and monitor their own progress. They complete self-monitoring checklists (like the one in Table 3-2, p. 100) for most activities; these external reminders help advance students to begin developing internal standards for judging their own literacy. The students keep journals, portfolios and personal reflections to see physical evidence of their academic advancements.

Steps in Supporting Self-Direction

1. Give options for instructional activities.
2. Give choices for how your students will record their real-world intervention.
3. Help all students compose questions that will guide their learning of the concepts.
4. Help students find informational resources to fulfill their personal learning goals.

Table 3-2.

Self-Monitoring Checklist
Assignment: Written Summary of Data Analysis

Name_____

Date: _____

Topic: _____

	YES	NO
• I stated the topic of the graph	_____	_____
• I wrote at least 3 sentences describing what the graph displays	_____	_____
• I presented a clear explanation of any graph outliers	_____	_____
• My summary is only about information presented in the graph	_____	_____
• I used clear and complete sentences when writing my summary	_____	_____

Scoring Tool

5 out of 5 are checked — Summary is excellent

4 out of 5 are checked — Summary is satisfactory

Less than 4 are checked — Summary needs improvement

---

5. Provide a limited set of options for how students will communicate their knowledge gain from information books (i.e., composing letters, publishing books, writing essays).
6. Have students share their strategies for learning.
7. Ask for student input about the decisions you make about instruction.
8. Let your instruction follow your students' interests.
9. Ask students to keep a log of their own interests and curiosity.
10. Give students ample time to complete self-selected projects.
11. Support students in using text resources to extend their background knowledge.
12. Emphasize asking questions rather than giving answers when students struggle.
13. Have students construct their own knowledge (rather than giving them knowledge) and evaluate it themselves.

STRATEGIC LITERACY

Supporting Learning with Strategy Instruction

Cognitive research consistently demonstrates that strategy instruction is effective in promoting learning (Lipson et al., 1993). Moreover, for students with disabilities or other severe learning difficulties, strategy instruction is crucial (Graham & Harris, 1993). How do students become good strategy users? Pressley and his colleagues (1992) stressed that simply teaching a student how to use a strategy in no way guarantees that the student understands how that strategy benefits performance. Mrs. Bender's students quickly realized that without strategies, they simply could not perform as well.

The CORI program is unique because strategies are taught not only in the context of the conceptual theme, but *because of* conceptual understanding. Literary strategies such as attending to relevant features of a problem or text (Bransford, Franks, Vye, & Sherwood, 1989), engaging in reflective practice (Weinstein & Mayer, 1986), monitoring comprehension (Baker & Brown, 1984), using conscious approaches to regulating effort (Paris, Wasik, & Turner, 1991), and making inferences, finding the main idea, and summarizing (Stevens & Slavin, 1995) are the "tools" for gaining conceptual understanding.

There are a few powerful strategies that support learning in each of the phases of CORI. First, in the real-world interaction phase, students are taught how to observe in a full and detailed way, and to record their observations comprehensively through drawing, charting, or keeping a journal. Second, in the searching phase, students are taught how to form a good question, find relevant information, and integrate what they have found with their background knowledge (Guthrie, Weber, & Kimmerly, 1993). Third, students are taught to comprehend the informational texts by emphasizing main ideas and supporting details. Narrative comprehension is taught by emphasizing the basic structures of plot, character development, and theme in novels and stories. Fourth, students are taught strategies for composing that include planning, outlining, drafting, revising, and finally publishing their work (Danoff, Harris, & Graham, 1993). These strategies are supported by a variety of teaching techniques. The principle for strategic literacy is that *teachers provide a variety of supports for strategy learning—including modeling, explaining, coaching, peer discussions, practice, and student reflection.*

Mrs. Bender's Goals for Strategy Instruction

"I'll use our class book—Monarchs, by Katherine Lasky—to help students make links from experience to further explanation. The book will explain the things that they cannot observe directly and help answer the questions they develop as they observe. For example, links are made to the monarch's dependency on certain nectar in the Oyamel forests during crucial times of the year. I spot-check students' comprehension and understanding of what they are reading. We review scientific vocabulary and conceptual ideas in each chapter. This helps students to make connections between the words and ideas in the books and what they have already observed.

"In my classroom, students want to know strategies in order to obtain

their personal goals. For example, after establishing a special question about her butterfly, Denisha wants to know how to locate that butterfly profile in her field guide, and knowing how to use a table of contents will help her in her search. The strategic awareness that is taught within the conceptual goal of understanding often helps students realize when, how, and why to use their strategies."

Strategies in the Classroom

Mrs. Bender prompted students to be strategic in a number of different ways. First, she defined a strategy and explained how it is used, while simultaneously referring to strategy cues that were posted in the classroom. One example was her explanation of summarizing. "Students, let's get some of our ideas down on paper. Gather with your teammates and decide what the main topic of this chapter is." She pointed to a poster about summarizing. "Remember, the main topic is not simply the title of the chapter. Think about the details in the chapter that support your main idea and write them down in the order that they occur in the story." Additionally, she cued students to use comprehension strategies with comments such as, "Yes, you made an inference, and it is an especially good supporting detail—just as long as you can back it up with evidence from the book." Or, she sometimes asked students to think aloud, verify information with text, and revise their ideas.

At other times, she acknowledged a student's use of a strategy, saying, "OK, I like the way you checked your information with the book," or "Oh, that information came from your reading!" Or she prompted reflection, self-monitoring, and students' joint construction of meaning through waiting and modeling. In the following example, the students finished reading the chapter of the trade book, *Monarchs*.

> MRS. B.: *(holding the book and pointing at the map)* If butterflies do not actually make it back to Mexico all the way from, let's say here, Maryland—that's 2000 miles! What happens to them instead?

> *(The students do not respond. Mrs. Bender sits down at her desk and starts flipping through her own trade book. She looks at her book for almost three minutes, giving students time to reread and think about the question.)*

MRS. B.: What do you think about this?

STUDENT 1: They make babies.

MRS. B.: What is the science word instead of babies?

STUDENT 2: Eggs, and then they hatch and then they keep on going, you know, traveling down.

MRS. B.: OK, what is another word for eggs and hatching that the book uses?

STUDENT 3: Generations.

MRS. B.: Yes, the book describes generations of monarchs. [Student 2] described it very well when he said that one butterfly lays an egg and it hatches and it will feed and the others will die. Excellent thinking and reading! What other information did you get from your reading?

How did students use strategies? Students in Mrs. Bender's class:

- chose vocabulary words from a book chapter for the class "word wall"
- defined the words on the "word wall" before reading the text
- organized thoughts and ideas by summarizing chapters of readings in trade books
- discussed the author's purpose for writing
- charted vivid language used by the authors
- used concept maps to express ideas about monarchs
- wrote sentences using the ideas and vocabulary words from the concept map
- constructed KWL maps (what I *know*, what I *want* to know, what I have *learned*)
- used Venn diagrams, webbing, outlining
- wrote their own books that included tables of contents and bibliographies

- drafted when writing
- engaged in peer conferencing
- self-evaluated their work
- studied story elements
- learned note-taking skills
- interpreted figurative language and applied it in creative writing

Mrs. Bender also used visual aids to help prompt strategy use. Her students can't help noticing the:

- poster explaining Scientific Processes
- KWL posters
- book posters describing features of different genres of literature
- Word Webs
- Swelling Concept maps
- vocabulary "word wall"
- "How to Write a Summary" poster
- Venn diagrams
- "What to Do If I Come Across a Word that I Do Not Know" poster
- prompt words for observation techniques

Steps in Teaching Strategic Literacy

1. Make a list of the basic strategies you want students to learn.
2. Relate the strategies in your list to the phases of the theme (e.g., observing, searching, reading, collaborating, composing, communicating).
3. Identify specific strategies for *observing and interacting in the real world* (e.g., noticing the features of a bug).
4. Identify specific strategies for *searching* (e.g., using the library, locating references, identifying information in books, using the table of contents).

5. Identify specific strategies for *comprehension* (e.g., noting main idea and details, self-monitoring)

6. Identify specific strategies for *effective collaboration* (e.g., generating rules for group work, taking turns, listening, sharing roles, taking responsibility).

7. Identify specific strategies for *writing* (e.g., note taking, outlining, planning, drafting, revising, composing, publishing, writing to persuade vs. writing a narrative).

8. Identify specific strategies for *using scientific processes* (e.g., predicting, recording, inferring, drawing conclusions).

9. Teach strategies with multiple approaches (e.g., teacher modeling, student modeling, group discussion).

10. Encourage students to be reflective about the strategies they use.

11. Ask students to discuss and share strategies they find beneficial to their learning.

12. Link the use of strategies to learning the conceptual theme.

13. Talk about how you use strategies.

14. Put strategy instruction in the context of learning about personally relevant questions.

15. Help students to see how strategies empower them to learn independently.

COLLABORATION

Supporting Engagement and Learning with Collaboration

Over the past decade, research on learner collaboration has flourished (see, for example, Butler, 1995). One of the most significant findings in this research is that compared to competitive and individualistic classroom structures, collaboration facilitates learning (Stevens & Slavin, 1995), motivation (Ames, 1992), perceived social support (Wentzel, 1994), and effective help seeking (Butler, 1995). The principle guiding CORI in this area is that *students work together in a variety of social structures including individual work, partnerships, small teams, and whole-class activities as they learn the content and strategies relevant to the conceptual theme.*

As with the other principles, collaboration in CORI is intimately bound to conceptual understanding. Students collaborate when it is beneficial to the process of advancing conceptual knowledge. Some features of CORI that make collaboration beneficial both motivationally and cognitively are (1) the interdependence that the students share, (2) the convergence of meaning that evolves from bringing their expertise to the table, and (3) the positive feedback and social support they provide for each other.

Motivational research shows that students can pursue social and academic goals at the same time (Urdan & Maehr, 1995). Student needs for peer approval are fulfilled in the academic climate of CORI because in addition to sharing their expertise, students also maintain and refine their own individuality by owning their unique and special knowledge. Group collaboration in which students help each other builds conceptual learning for all (Stevens & Slavin, 1995).

Mrs. Bender's Goals for Collaboration

"I try to make sure that I have a cohesive group of students in each team. I choose the teams based on each student's strengths and weaknesses. I mix reading abilities and, if possible, genders. However, it is more important for me to make the decisions based on the students' individual differences. For example, I do have a group of all boys for this unit. It just worked out that way when I started thinking about what each person could add to the group.

"I put a lot of thought into the groupings. I do not just 'throw' students together. When the group has a problem, I try very hard to have them solve the conflict on their own. It is extremely rare that I allow a student to change from one team to another. Instead, I give them 'problem-solving time' to work out problems, and then when we come back together as a group, I ask the students to talk to each other about what worked and what didn't and why.

"Whenever the students work together, we always have a time when

we come back as a group and talk about the collaborative processes they used, like how they decided together to make one group chart or how they divided up the roles. When they talk about these issues together, the teams that had difficulty can pick up strategies from the other teams for next time."

Collaboration in the Classroom

In CORI, students collaborate in "idea circles" to build conceptual understanding (Guthrie & McCann, 1996). During idea-circle time, teams gather and integrate their information from multiple sources. For example, in a team, one student may have read all about the mating cycle of a monarch, while another student may have located facts about the destruction of the monarch's microclimate, and still another read about the importance of the monarch's flight to Mexico. When the team congregates, students begin forming links among all of their facts. The merging facts then construct a bridge of conceptual understanding. Each student's level of expertise converges to shape a team interpretation about the monarch's imperiled survival.

This explaining and elaborating enables students to refine their schemata and process information at deeper conceptual levels (Brown & Palincsar, 1989). Together, the team builds a cohesive explanation integrating all of their specialized knowledge. Furthermore, students delight in their ability to share what they know. One day, Mrs. Bender told the students to get together for idea-circle time, but was momentarily interrupted before she could give further directions. In one team, a student said, "How about everybody read what they have for notes." Immediately the team started reading in turn.

A CORI team typically remains a cohesive unit throughout the 16 weeks of study. Because of the team members' similarities in both search and observation experiences, they have an advantage in terms of hooking into their partners' background knowledge. Team members filter information for each other and guide one another in bridging what they know with what they still need to verify and explain (Palincsar, Anderson, & David, 1993). This external scaffold can serve as a metacognitive model and help ensure that students evaluate their thought processes. Mrs. Bender explained that she tried to encourage her students to view their peers as potential learning resources rather than rivals. Consider the following example, in which students are having an "instructional conversation" (Tharp & Gallimore, 1993):

STUDENT 1: Those little dots, they look like gold.

STUDENT 2: We don't see any behavior yet.

STUDENT 1: But there is color change.

STUDENT 3: Well, what is not happening could be important too.

STUDENT 2: We should write that.

STUDENT 1: It's mostly changing physical stuff, going through metamorphosis.

STUDENT 2: I see, it is mostly still so that it could complete its metamorphosis!

STUDENT 3: I'm writing that the color is changing and becoming more transparent.

STUDENT 1: It's the metamorphosis into a butterfly.

Mrs. Bender provides needed support for collaboration. In a study of fifth-graders, Turner and Meyer (1995) found that without scaffolding, students did not automatically push each other to think about concepts. Effective collaboration necessitates a shifting of roles in the classroom. As students take on more responsibility in the learning process, teachers need to move to a role of mediator, facilitator, scaffolder, and coach (Brown et al., 1993). Consider the following example, in which Mrs. Bender was working with a group engaged in measuring their butterfly for the tagging program.

STUDENT 1: Look, it's a male! You can see it spreading its wings, yeah!

MRS. B.: What does it have to have if it's a male?

STUDENT 1: Two black dots.

MRS. B.: Yes, well, they are not really dots. *(The student gets a book to look up what the dots are called.)*

STUDENT 2: OK, I have it here *(the ruler is in a good spot for measurement)*. What's the measurement?

STUDENT 3: Around...

MRS. B.: Not *around!* Science means *exact.*

STUDENT 3: 4½ centimeters.

STUDENT 2: Write that down.

Steps in Creating a Collaborative Community

1. Form teams of 4–6 students differing in achievement and ability levels.
2. Arrange classroom to permit students to sit with their desks clustered together.
3. Discuss and have students formulate rules for teamwork.
4. Plan for students to work in their teams for short periods several times a day.
5. Give students group objectives such as discussing a concept in a text.
6. Form literature circles in which teams discuss diverse perspectives on the same novel.
7. Organize idea circles to help students learn concepts from multiple texts.
8. Assign group projects in which students create exhibits to share with other groups.
9. Discuss and monitor the effectiveness of teamwork and cooperation.
10. Teach students to view each other as resources rather than rivals.
11. Discourage competition within and between groups.
12. Have students form interest groups about topics for limited amounts of time.
13. Balance time given to individual work, partnerships, teamwork, and class discussion.
14. Actively monitor and troubleshoot communication during group activities.

15. Help groups monitor their own goals and progress toward their goals.

SELF-EXPRESSION

Expressing Knowledge and Imagination

Encouraging self-expression in the classroom involves creating an atmosphere in which students communicate their science knowledge and their reading and writing competencies in ways that are meaningful to them and tailored to their interests. In a classroom that supports self-expression, teachers provide ample time for students to think about, write about, and revise their ideas on a topic they have selected (Oldfather & McLaughlin, 1993). If students feel that they are able to choose how they will show their knowledge and viewpoint, they believe in themselves as the creators of knowledge, and they feel empowered as learners (Belenky, Clinchy, Goldberger, & Tarule, 1986). Oldfather and Dahl (1994) found that students were motivated to write extensively when they trusted that the teacher and their peers would appreciate their work. When students make a diorama of their own choice, they feel inventive (Blumenfeld, et.al., 1991). When students can compose stories with themes that reflect their personal joys, sorrows, and conflicts, they grow as persons and as writers.

As in real-world communication, the CORI students make personal decisions based on their own perceptions about which avenue best expresses their conceptual understanding. Students shape their products to reflect their interests, which enables them to use their interest, background knowledge, and favorite strategies (Schiefele, 1991). The principle that summarizes this aspect of CORI is that *students are supported in articulating their understanding of the conceptual theme in ways that are personally and culturally relevant to them and their audiences.*

Mrs. Bender's Views on Self-Expression

"For self-expression, I try to make sure that the problems are open-ended enough so that the students can share understanding of their personal questions. They write in journals, debate ideas, and make posters. We publish books and write poetry. The big word I try to keep in mind is sharing.

"The 'Invent an Animal' project synthesizes all of their knowledge about adaptation, biomes, survival, protection from energy, body features, food, predators, and shelter. The students use their teammates when they need to, and they monitor their own progress. They help to make the criteria rubric for evaluation. In this way, they write, justify, and have opinions about everything ... the whole process."

Guiding Self-Expression in the Classroom

For one type of self-expression, Armando decided to construct a diorama describing a desert biome. Armando's diorama expressed his understanding of a desert terrain. For example, his diorama featured bland colors of Play-doh pieces that created desert images, a genuine cactus plant, sand woven with dried roots, and some insects that would survive in the desert. On index cards, Armando described the function of desert plants, outlined desert weather conditions, and explained animal survival in the desert. Finally, he cited six references—one of which was a Native American folktale!

A diversity of thought and language permeates our principle of self-expression. Because tasks can be approached in a variety of different ways, students of very different ability levels are able to participate fully in the process. In fact, they can come up with ingenious and creative solutions. Consider the following story written by a student named Tanner who struggled with his literacy skills. When introducing his narrative he explained, "This book contains a nonfiction story but factual about a green chameleon and his mate for life. I really hope you find the story interesting."

It was a hot day in Africa when a green Chameleon came out of a log. Chameleons are one of the many lizards that are hard to find because they are camouflaged. Its skin changes colors. Its skin becomes the color of the place it is sitting. It starts to look for food early in the morning. The Chameleon spots a spider which is easy prey to catch. Its tongue gets the spider and the Chameleon swallows the spider in one gulp.

The story continued, describing the chameleon's mating cycle and its fear of predators like the gila monster. Tanner's narrative ended when the chameleon met his mate for life: "Later, when it gets hot, the female lays 2-12 eggs that should hatch in a month. The green Chameleon calls the female and they watch their beloved eggs together." This is just one of many examples showing how personal expression highlighted both students' strengths and their conceptual understanding.

Since the specific purpose is to communicate knowledge, students discover quickly not to focus on the surface features of a task that may prevent them from effectively demonstrating what they know. Therefore in CORI, the "pretty" poster is not a valued piece of work; rather, the treasured commodity is the factual, comprehensive poster reflecting conceptual understanding of the theme. The level of difficulty is one that communicates high expectations embedded in realistic and intriguing scenarios.

Self-expression may take shape in written compositions, publications, performances, dioramas, posters, videos, narrative stories, or the creation of personal artifacts. Students talk to each other about the strengths and weaknesses of their different expressive strategies and brainstorm methods of improving their styles of communication. Mrs. Bender explained that her students understood that *she* was not the ultimate audience. Therefore, they sought multiple opinions about their work. As with success in the work force, what is more appropriate than to consult resources, ask questions, and document progress?

Self-expression activities in Mrs. Bender's class were varied.

Students:

- maintained portfolios
- maintained personal journals
- shared journal responses
- compiled an anthology of original poetry
- debated issues
- compared and contrasted observations, interpretations and conclusions
- published results of monarch activity
- wrote original poetry and folktales
- created dioramas illustrating a biome
- invented an animal to suit a biome
- shared expertise with their peers
- constructed a class quilt of the life cycle
- published informational fiction stories
- maintained book logs with personal thoughts and critiques of each book

Steps in Developing Student Self-Expression

1. Encourage students to choose their own topics within the conceptual theme.
2. Give students options for how to display and express their knowledge about a topic.
3. Allow students to discuss their ideas about self-expression with other students.
4. Help students develop explanations for their ideas.
5. Allow students to choose different literary genres as bases for their reflective writing.
6. Give students choices about different audiences they will select for their expression.
7. Review strategy instruction for effective communication.
8. Help students pursue a group writing activity with the members of their team.

9. Provide ample time for individual reflections in their journals.

10. Make available a generous supply of materials for communicating.

11. Encourage student expression through fine arts activities within the conceptual theme.

12. Create occasions for students to present their work to community members, local scientists, or politicians.

13. Use student self-expressive work for developing report cards and other evaluations.

14. Avoid high-stakes assessment that is tangential to the conceptual theme.

15. Admire variations in expression.

COHERENCE OF CURRICULUM

Linking Instruction to Support Learning

The coherence of instruction varies dramatically. Some teachers tie everything together. Their instruction is interconnected and coherent, flowing naturally from phase to phase. Other teachers have a large number of separate activities. In these classrooms, subject matters, skills, and activities do not necessarily overlap. In a coherent curriculum, the different disciplines are integrated (Beane, 1995). At a basic level, reading and writing are integrated into a language arts unit which is present in a majority of elementary classrooms (Mullis, Campbell, & Farstrup, 1993). At higher levels, language arts are being integrated with social studies. For example, the literature and history of Colonial times complement each other well (Lipson et al., 1993). Many teachers are combining science and language arts through conceptual themes such as environmental science, or physical structures of the earth (e.g., formation of rivers, mountains, and continents). Environmental science is especially fruitful for teaching life science concepts (Brown et al. 1993), and reading, writing, and thinking skills (Guthrie, 1996).

In addition to connecting two or more disciplines, a coherent classroom links the contexts of learning to each other. Any comprehensive classroom must create contexts to teach reading skills, support the social life of students, enable students to become independent, help students connect the classroom to the real world, and meet many other objectives. A coherent classroom fuses these objectives together. For example, teachers enable students to develop self-direction as they improve their writing skills. They set up group work that fosters social learning while it fosters strategy learning. They teach reading skills in the midst of student learning about the literature and mythology of a social group, such as native North Americans. They support motivation for school—not with a separate incentive program, but with a set of curriculum-relevant choices, opportunities for social exchange, and empowering strategy instruction. The principle that captures this perspective is that *classroom instruction integrates the contents, cognitive strategies and social interactions for learning by linking the expectations, activities, materials and displays of understanding around multi-disciplinary, conceptual themes.*

Mrs. Bender's Vision of Coherence

"I want my students to see the broader picture of habitat, adaptation, man's effect on our environment, and global concerns. During my ecological system unit there are cognitive skills that are taught within the conceptual theme so that the students will remember why these skills are important. The students in my class do not have difficulty trying to figure out how note taking or poetry fits with science, or how literacy skills and strategies are necessary in math, because here it is a daily event for them. The skills they learn are meaningful and valuable because without them they simply would not have been able to do the work."

Coherence in the Classroom

The fusion of these learning activities is perhaps best illustrated by one of Denisha's activities. This activity exemplified how each dimension was woven in to offer a unified plan. First, Denisha's team was given a terrarium with a monarch larva in it. Each morning, Denisha watched the larva very carefully. She wrote in her "Larva Log" (see Figure 3-2, p. 118) about the physical and behavioral changes undergone by the monarch.

Further, as an observational activity, Denisha sketched each phase of metamorphosis (see Figure 3-3, p. 119). She was careful to include all of the notes from her "Larva Log," and she used her trade books as resources to be sure that she was providing an accurate and detailed portrait of the metamorphosis process.

Next, Denisha used her chart of observations to construct data tables (see Table 3-3, p. 120). These tables helped her gain conceptual understanding of her own monarch's processes compared to those of the others in the classroom. Using her observational data, Denisha drew a line graph depicting the daily growth of her caterpillar (Table 3-4, p. 121). Next, she wanted to explain what her graph meant. Denisha knew that she wanted to be clear and accurate when she wrote her graph summary (Table 3-4, p. 122). She used the writing strategies that she learned and asked two of her teammates to complete a "Peer Response Form" to help her to better communicate with her intended audience. Last, Denisha wrote a final draft of her summary so that when her classmates looked at her graph hanging on the wall, they would understand what they were seeing. This one activity exemplified the principles of observation, use of interesting texts, self-direction, strategies, peer collaboration, and self expression.

Steps to Building Coherence

1. Relate literacy activities to science activities and discuss how learning in English and Science are connected.
2. Have students read about the real-world objects they observe.
3. Encourage students to link their self-directed learning and their collaboration.
4. Teach writing skills in the context of their science work.
5. Teach writing mechanics in connection with students com-

Figure 3-2. Denisha's Larva Log

Date	Physical Characteristics	Behavioral Characteristics
9/18 caterpillar	Length: 1.5 cm / Width: 2 mm –has yellow, black, white stripes –looks like it has 2 head, 2 antennae	–crawling on milkweed –looking around –nibbling on food
9/20	Length: 1.5 cm / Width: 3 mm –has a little black spot on second yellow stripe near head –little white stuff underneath yellow stripe	–staying on leaf –crawling on leaf –looking around
9/22	Length: 2 cm / Width: 4 mm –larger and fatter –black little spot at the very end	–not moving at all –alert –sticking to the wall –molted –wiggled antennae
9/25	Length: 2.3 cm / Width: 5 mm –fatter and longer	–crawling –looking around –touching leaf
9/26	Length: 3 cm / Width: 6 mm –8 pairs of legs –getting larger and fatter –added more stripes and colors	–sticking head up –turning around –exploring –moving the filaments around
9/27 chrysalis	Length: 3.5 cm / Width: 6 mm –jade green with gold spots on the chrysalis –lines on it –oval shape on the wings	–hanging on a cremaster? –staying very still in the chrysalis
9/29	Length: 2.5 cm / Width: 9 mm –jade green with gold dots –veins on the butterfly wing are black –stem hanging	–very still –forming into a butterfly
10/2	Length: 3 cm / Width: 1 cm –black vein on wing –little transparent –gold dots are bigger –darker jade green	–very still
10/6 butterfly	Length of body: 3 cm / Wing: 4 cm –black veins	–just emerged –flapping wings very calmly

Figure 3-3. Denisha's Phases of Metamorphosis Sketches.

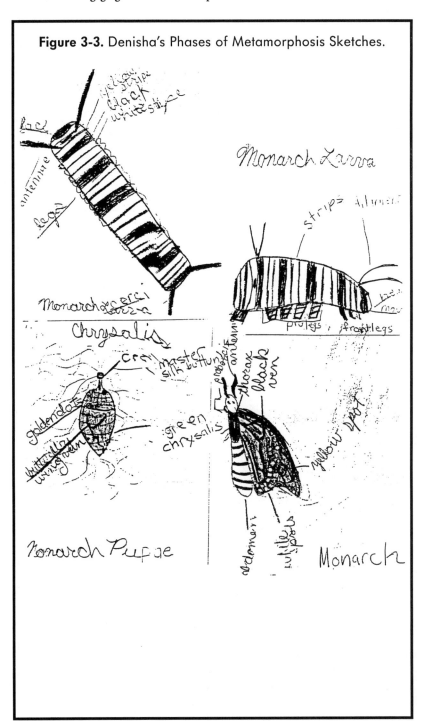

Table 3-3. Denisha's Data Tables

Using her chart of observations, Denisha made two data tables; one charted the dates of her specimen's phases of metamorphosis and the second charted the team and class growth rate of each of the caterpillars.

Denisha's Phases of Metamorphosis Data Table

Date	Caterpillar Length	Width	Chrysalis Formation	Butterfly Emerged	Gender	Tagged/ Released
9/29	35mm	6mm	10/2	10/13	M	10/16

Class Growth Rate Data Table

Team	Caterpillar length		Number of days		Gender
	Beginning	End	Caterpillar	Chrysalis	
1	10 mm	34 mm	11	10	F
2	10 mm	36 mm	10	11	F
3	10 mm	35 mm	12	12	M
4	10 mm	35 mm	14	11	F
5	10 mm	48 mm	13	12	M
6	5 mm	40 mm	11	11	M
7	10 mm	30 mm	13	16	M
8	10 mm	34 mm	11	15	M

Daily growth rate of the caterpillar	Length = 2.1 mm per day
Estimate of average daily growth rate of the caterpillar	Length = 2.9 mm per day
Class Average of the daily growth rate of the caterpillar	Length = 2.5 mm per day

Fraction Male	5/8	*% Male*	63%
Fraction Female	3/8	*% Female*	37%

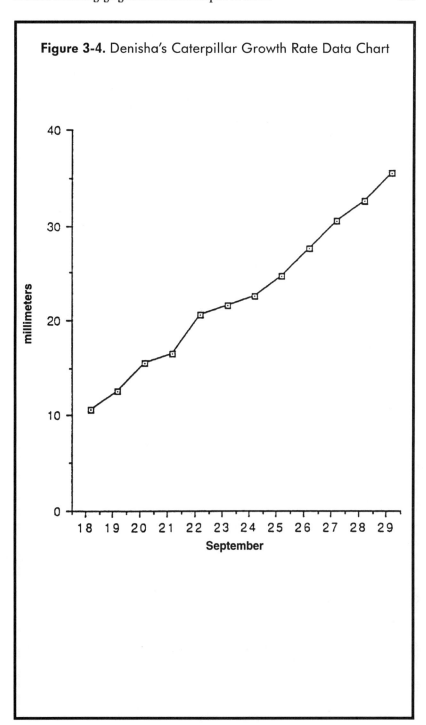

Figure 3-4. Denisha's Caterpillar Growth Rate Data Chart

Table 3-4. Denisha's Summary

Denisha wrote a summary about her caterpillar's growth rate that she illustrated in a line graph. She wrote two drafts and asked her peers to complete a response form. Finally, she edited her graph interpretation. Listed below is an example of the peer response form that her teammates completed and her final version of the summary.

Peer Response Form

1. Ask your partners to listen carefully as you read your rough draft out loud.

2. Ask your partners to help you improve your writing by telling you the answers to the questions below.

3. In the space provided, jot down notes about what your partners say.

What did you like best about my rough draft? _____

What did you have the hardest time understanding about my rough draft? _____

What else can you suggest that I do to improve my rough draft?

_____

Some of the responses that Denisha received included comments that she explained what the graph meant very well and that they liked how she was very specific about the big increase between the 27th and 29th of September. They had the hardest time understanding some of the sentence structure, and one peer noted that it was not specific enough to say that the caterpillar grows rapidly. Finally, some peers suggested that she should try to write in daily growth and that she should not number the sentences, but instead put the information in paragraph form.

Caterpillar Growth in Length

What my graph is about is the growth in the length of a caterpillar until it turned into a chrysalis. You can tell from my graph that the caterpillar grew a little each day. Between the 27th and 29th of September, it increased from 30 mm to 35 mm. Our caterpillar was a caterpillar for 12 days until it became a chrysalis. Really what the graph shows is that a caterpillar grows rapidly daily!

munication with audiences outside the classroom.

6. Teach comprehension skills in connection with learning about the conceptual theme.
7. Relate literary texts such as poems to science concepts.
8. Make cooperative learning relevant to the conceptual theme.
9. Connect strategy learning and social interaction to each other.
10. Have students link in-school and out-of-school learning through community-based connections to the conceptual theme.

TEACHING DIVERSE STUDENTS IN CORI

The principles of Concept-Oriented Reading Instruction are intended to accommodate diverse students. There are several aspects of CORI that are particularly helpful for students who speak English as a second language, who have learning disabilities, or who face other serious academic or social challenges.

First, as a centerpiece of instruction, the conceptual theme is accessible to all students. A topic such as adaptation can embrace multilevel subtopics. For example, animal homes may be understood at many levels. We advise careful determination of language and background knowledge needs for all students. If some topics will be too hard to adapt, use more adaptable ones.

CORI begins with real-world interactions for students. Observing and interacting with the physical environment or people in the community are activities that are available to all students. On some occasions, for example, students with reading problems may be excellent at observing and drawing birds. More importantly, all students are equally excited by these interactions. Regardless of their academic histories and achievements, all students are motivated by seeing and interacting with something concrete. The capability to get interested and motivated is distributed equitably across students of diverse academic accomplishments.

CORI uses interesting texts to accommodate diverse learners. Using texts with a wide range of difficulty provides access to the conceptual theme for all students. For example, in grade 3, texts from grade levels 1-5 may be included. In grade 5, texts from grade 3 through grade 7 (and lower or higher if needed) may be incorporated into the unit. As students gain knowledge, they become increasingly able to use higher-level books, as expertise in a particular topic enables students to understand texts that would otherwise be above their reading level. Informational books can be especially valuable if they are lavishly illustrated. The pictures, diagrams, and captions can be sources of connection to real-world observing that benefit diverse learners. Students with learning or language problems can construct links between their observations and the texts through pictures, captions, and headings in informational books. Enabling students to choose their own books as sources of learning about the conceptual theme provides multiple avenues into content learning for all students and gives learners a sense of equal participation.

When the conceptual theme is the center of the learning environment, all students can participate equally in writing. By keeping logs, maintaining a journal, and writing reports, all students can address the same goals in their writing, and they will feel a sense of efficacy. The level of stylistic polish and conceptual coherence will vary. However, including all students in the same writing tasks will provide a base for improvement for each individual.

Collaboration in CORI occurs in heterogeneous groups. Students are not placed in homogeneous ability groups but, rather, are widely distributed. Emphasizing full participation by each team member increases the opportunities for reading, writing, and discussing for diverse students. The conceptual theme invites contributions from all types of learners and allows individual strengths to be recognized. Although each student is expected to read, write, and gain knowledge, each student can also contribute special expertise. For example, a student who is good at drawing can provide illustrations, while a student who is comfortable on the computer can provide information retrieval or word processing for group reports. However, it is important that all students be expected to read and write extensively at their instructional level.

We believe that all students benefit particularly from coherence. The supportive milieu of interdisciplinary learning is valuable for students who are struggling with skills. When reading is related to real-world observing, and writing is connected to reading activities, academically challenged students are better able to find meaning. Ironically, though, students with academic challenges such as learning or social difficulties or language differences usually experience the most fragmented instruction—they are pulled out for special reading instruction, provided out-of-class language help, and given a variety of learning experiences disconnected from each other. We believe that academically challenged students need an *increase* in integration rather than a decrease in the coherence of their school experience. CORI teachers have noted that it is their lowest-achieving students who make the most dramatic progress. Research studies, too, point in this direction. CORI provides an environment where diverse students can capitalize on their strengths to address their learning needs in a long-term endeavor that produces substantial cumulative effects.

AFTERWORD

Concept-Oriented Reading Instruction (CORI) can be thought of as a web. The web is woven from the threads we have described as principles. Each teacher has her own distinctive weave. She creates a pattern that is adapted to her students and suits her personality. In all the engaging classrooms we have observed, teachers include self-direction, real-world connections, strategy teaching, and the other principles in this chapter. One teacher may strongly emphasize one principle, such as direct strategy teaching. But if her web includes all of the threads, the classroom will be engaging.

A potential hazard is the neglect of some of the threads. A secure web cannot be woven with too few threads. Teachers of CORI find that as their students participate in the classroom context, they become weavers, too. Students contribute to the context by becoming engaged in literacy and their own development. CORI is a collaboration between teacher and students to weave a web that supports and delights them.

APPENDIX: ABBREVIATED BOOK LIST
(THEME: INTERACTION OF LIVING THINGS)

CLASS SETS

Lasky, K. (1993). *Monarch*. Orlando, FL: Harcourt Brace & Co.

Babbitt, N. (1975). *Tuck Everlasting*. Canada: Harper Collins.

Bruchac, J. (1991). *Native American Stories*. Golden, CO: Fulcrum.

George, J.C. (1995) *The Missing 'Gator of Gumbo Limbo*. Canada: HarperCollins.

Penny, M. (1989). *Animal adaptations*. New York: Bookwright Press.

Taylor, M. (1979). *Song of the trees*. New York: Bantam Books.

GROUP SETS (8 each)

Science

British Museum of Natural History (1982). *Nature at work*. New York: Cambridge University Press.

Feltwell, J. (1992). *Animals and where they live*. New York: Dorling Kindersley, Inc.

Lye, K. (1991). *The earth*. Brookfield, CT: Millbrook Press.

Folktales

Bruchac, J. (1995). *Gluskabe and the four wishes*. New York: Dutton.

Goble, P. (1983). *Star boy*. Scarsdale, NY: Bradbury Press.

Goble, P. (1984). *Buffalo Woman*. New York: Macmillan.

Poetry

Booth, D. (1989). *'Til all the stars have fallen: a collection of poems*. New York: Puffin Books.

Livingston, N.C. (1994). *Flights of fancy and other poems*. New York: Macmillan.

Yolen, J. (1990). *Birdwatch*. New York: Putnam & Grosset.

INDIVIDUAL TITLES IN CLASS LIBRARY (1 copy of each)

Poetry

Bennett, J. (1987). *Noisy Poems.* Oxford: Oxford University Press.

Fleischman, P. (1988). *Joyful noise.* New York: Harper Collins.

Ryder, J. (1992). *Dancers in the garden.* San Francisco: Sierra Club Books for Children.

Viorst, J. (1981). *If I were in charge of the world and other worries.* New York: Macmillan.

Stories/Novels

Bailey, J. (1992). *Operation elephant—Earth's endangered creatures.* Austin, TX: Steck-Vaughn.

Folktales

* Anderson, D. (1991). *The origin of life on earth.* Mt. Airy, MD: Sights Productions.

Science

Amsel, S. (1993). *Grasslands* (Habitats of the World series). Austin, TX: Steck-Vaughn.

* Bailey, D. (1990). *Butterflies* (Animal World series). Austin, TX: Steck-Vaughn.

George, J. C. (1993). *Moon of the Monarch.* New York: Harper Collins.

* Norden, C. R. (1991). *Deserts* (Read About series). Austin, TX: Steck-Vaughn.

Pope, J. (1994). *Animal Homes.* NJ: Troll Associates

Field Guides

The Audubon Society Field Guide to North American Insects and Spiders

Peterson First Guides

REFERENCES

Alexander, P.A., Kulikowich, J.M., & Jetton, T.L. (1994). The role of subject matter knowledge and interest in the processing of linear and nonlinear texts. *Review of Educational Research, 64*(2), 201-252.

Ames, C. (1992). Classroom: Goals, structures, and student motivation. *Journal of Educational Psychology, 84,* 261-271.

Anderson, R., Shirey, L., Wilson, P., & Fielding, L. (1987). Interestingness of children's reading material. In R. Snow and M. Farr (Eds.) *Aptitude, learning,*

---

*Lower reading level book.

and instruction III: Conative and affective process analysis (pp. 287-299). Hillsdale, NJ: Erlbaum.

Baker, L., & Brown, A.L. (1984). Metacognitive skills and reading. In P.D. Pearson, M. Kamil, R. Barr, P. Mosenthal (Eds.), *Handbook of reading research* (Vol. 1, pp. 353-394). White Plains, NY: Longman.

Beane, J.A. (1995). What is coherent curriculum? In J.A. Beane (Ed.), *Toward a coherent curriculum* (pp. 1-5). Alexandria, VA: 1995 Yearbook of the Association for Supervision and Curriculum Development.

Belenky, M.F., Clinchy, B.M., Goldberger, N.R., & Tarule, J.M. (1986). *Women's ways of knowing: The development of self, voice, and mind.* New York: Basic Books.

Blumenfeld, P.C. (1992). Classroom learning and motivation: Clarifying and expanding goal theory. *Journal of Educational Psychology, 84,* 272-281.

Blumenfeld, P.C., Soloway, E., Marx, R.W., Krajcik, J.S., Guzdial, M., & Palincsar, A.S. (1991). Motivating project-based learning: Sustaining the doing, supporting the learning. *Educational Psychologist, 26,* 369-398.

Bransford, J.D., Franks, J.J., Vye, N.J., & Sherwood, R.D. (1989). New approaches to instruction: Because wisdom can't be told. In S. Vosniadou & A. Ortony (Eds.), *Similarity and analogical reasoning.* Cambridge: Cambridge University Press.

Brown, A.L., & Palincsar, A.S. (1989). Guided, cooperative and individual knowledge acquisition. In L.B. Resnick (Ed.), *Knowing, learning, and instruction: Essays in honor of Robert Glaser.* Hillsdale, NJ: Erlbaum.

Brown, A.L., Ash, D., Rutherford, M., Nakagawa, K., Gordon, A., & Campione, J.C. (1993). Distributed expertise in the classroom. In G. Salomon (Ed.), *Distributed Cognitions: Psychological and educational considerations* (pp. 188-228). New York: Cambridge University Press.

Butler, R. (1995). Motivational and informational functions and consequences of children's attention to peers' work. *The Journal of Educational Psychology, 87*(3), 347-359.

Danoff, B., Harris, K.R., & Graham, S. (1993). Incorporating strategy instruction into the school curriculum: Effects on children's writing. *Journal of reading behavior, 25,* 295-322.

Deci, E.L. (1995). *Why we do what we do: The dynamics of personal autonomy.* New York: G.P. Putnam's Sons.

Deci, E., & Ryan, R. (1987). The support of autonomy and the control of behavior. *Journal of personality and social psychology, 53*(6), 1024-1037.

Dewey, J. (1913). *Interest and effort in education.* Boston: Riverside Press.

Dewey, J. (1938). *Education and experience.* Boston: Riverside Press.

Gambrell, L.B., Palmer, B.M., & Codling, R.M. (1993). *Motivation to read.* Washington, DC: Office of Educational Research and Improvement.

Graham, S., & Harris, K. (1993). Self-regulated strategy development: Helping students with learning problems develop as writers. *Elementary School Journal, 94*, 169-181.

Guthrie, J.T. (1996). Educational contexts for engagement in literacy. *The Reading Teacher, 49*(6), 432-445.

Guthrie, J.T., & McCann, A.D. (1996). Idea circles: Peer collaborations for conceptual learning. In L. Gambrell & J. Almasi (Eds.), *Lively discussions!* (pp. 87-105). Newark, DE: International Reading Association.

Guthrie, J.T., Van Meter, P., McCann, A.D., Wigfield, A., Bender, L., Poundstone, C.C., Rice, M.E., Faibisch, F.M., Hunt, B., & Mitchell, A.M. (1996). Growth of literacy engagement: Changes in motivations and strategies during concept-oriented reading instruction. *Reading Research Quarterly, 31*, 306-325.

Guthrie, J.T., Weber, G., & Kimmerly, N. (1993). Searching documents: Cognitive processes and deficits in understanding graphs, tables, and illustrations. *Contemporary Educational Psychology, 18*(2), 186-221.

Hartman, D.K., & Allison, J. (1996). Promoting inquiry-oriented discussions using multiple texts. In L. Gambrell & J. Almasi (Eds.), *Lively discussions!* (pp. 87-105). Newark, DE: International Reading Association.

Linn, M.C., & Muilenburg, L. (1996). Creating lifelong science learners: What models form a firm foundation? *Educational Researcher, 25*, 18-24.

Lipson, M.Y., Valencia, S.W., Wixson, K.K., & Peters, C.W. (1993). Integration and thematic teaching: Integration to improve teaching and learning. *Language Arts, 70*, 252-271.

McCombs, B.L., & Whisler, J.S. (1989). The role of affective variables in autonomous learning. *Educational Psychologist, 24*(3), 277-306.

Mullis, I., Campbell, J.R., & Farstrup, A.E. (1993). *Executive summary of the NAEP 1992 Reading Report Card for the nation and the states* (Report No. 23-ST08). Washington D.C: U.S. Government Printing Office.

Oldfather, P., & Dahl, K. (1994). Toward a social constructivist reconceptualization of intrinsic motivation for literacy learning. *Journal of Reading Behavior, 26*, 139-158.

Oldfather, P., & McLaughlin, J. (1993). Gaining and losing voice: A longitudinal study of students' continuing impulse to learn across elementary and middle school contexts. *Research in middle level education, 11*, 1-25.

Palincsar, A.S., Anderson, C., & David, Y.M. (1993). Pursuing scientific literacy in the middle grades through collaborative problem solving. *Elementary School Journal, 93*, 643-658.

Paris, S.G., Wasik, B.A., & Turner, J.C. (1991). The development of strategic readers. In R. Barr, M.L. Kamil, P.B. Mosenthal, & P.D. Pearson (Eds.), *Handbook of Reading Research* (Vol. 2, pp. 609-640). New York: Longman.

Pressley, M., El-Dinary, P.B., Gaskins, I., Schuder, T., Bergman, J.L., Almasi, J, & Brown, R. (1992). Beyond direct explanation: Transactional instruction of reading comprehension strategies. *Elementary School Journal, 92,* 513-555.

Renninger, A., Hidi, S., & Krapp, A. (1992). *The role of interest in learning and development.* Hillsdale, NJ: Erlbaum.

Schiefele, U. (1991). Interest, learning, and motivation, *Educational Psychologist, 26,* 299-323.

Schraw, G., Bruning, R., & Svoboda, C. (1995). Sources of situational interest. *Journal of Reading Behavior, 27*(1), 1-17.

Skinner, E.A., & Belmont, M. (1993). Motivation in the classroom: Reciprocal effects of teacher behavior and student engagement across the school year. *Journal of Educational Psychology, 85*(4), p. 571-581.

Stephenson, C., & Carr, J.F. (1993). *Integrated studies in the middle grades: Dancing through walls.* New York: Teachers College Press.

Stevens, R.J., & Slavin, R.E. (1995). The cooperative elementary school: Effects on students' achievement, attitudes, and social relations. *American Educational Research Journal, 32,* 321-351.

Tharp, R.G., & Gallimore, R (1993). Teaching mind in society: Teaching, schooling, and literate discourse. In L. Moll (Ed.), *Vygotsky and education* (pp. 175-205). Cambridge: Press Syndicate of the University of Cambridge.

Turner, J.C. (1995). The influence of classroom contexts on young children's motivation for literacy. *Reading Research Quarterly, 30,* 410-441.

Turner, J.C., & Meyer, D.A. (1995). Motivating students to learn: Lessons from a fifth grade math class. *Middle School Journal, 27,* 18-25.

Urdan, T.C., & Maehr, M.L. (1995). Beyond a two-goal theory of motivation and achievement: A case for social goals. *Review of Educational Research, 65*(3), 213-243.

Weinstein, C.E., & Mayer, R.E. (1986). The teaching of learning strategies. In M.C. Wittrock (Ed.). *Handbook of research on teaching* (3rd ed., pp. 315-327). New York: Macmillan.

Wentzel, K. (1994). Relations of social goal pursuit to social acceptance, classroom behavior, and perceived social support. *The Journal of Educational Psychology, 86*(2), 173-182.

CHAPTER FOUR

Every Child Can Write: Strategies for Composition and Self-Regulation in the Writing Process

KAREN R. HARRIS, TANYA SCHMIDT, & STEVE GRAHAM,
University of Maryland

Few people—either children or adults—would describe writing as a very easy process that they complete without much effort. Writing is a highly complex and demanding process. While negotiating the rules and mechanics of writing, the writer must maintain a focus on factors such as organization, form and features, purposes and goals, audience needs and perspectives, and evaluation of the communication between author and reader. Self-regulation of the writing process is critical; the writer must be goal-oriented, resourceful, and reflective.

Even highly skilled professional writers speak to the demanding and complex mix of composition and self-regulatory abilities involved in writing. For example, Susan Sontag has said that when writing *On Photography*, she often drafted each page 30 to 40 times (Burnham, 1994). Joseph Heller, author of *Catch-22*, carried index cards in his wallet so that he could write down ideas whenever they came to him (Plimpton, 1989).

Research on expert writers has further clarified the importance of self-regulation in writing. For skilled authors, writing is a flexible, goal-directed activity, scaffolded by a rich source of cognitive processes and strategies for planning, text production, and revision. Skilled authors also engage in purposeful and active self-direction of these processes and strategies. As Flower and Hayes (1980) note, "a great part of skill in writing is the ability to monitor and direct one's own composing processes" (p. 39). Research on and descriptions of expert writers—both children and adults—has been an important factor in understanding and improving children's writing abilities (Harris & Graham, 1992).

CHILDREN'S WRITING

While we know what is required for effective writing, we also know that many children, and especially those who experience significant difficulties with writing, do not exhibit critical self-regulation and composition strategies, skills, and beliefs. Often, children act more like Snoopy does in one Peanuts cartoon. Sitting on top of his dog house, paws at the typewriter, he types the sentence, "The light mist turned to rain." He types the next sentence, "The rain turned to snow." At this, he rips his paper out of the typewriter and throws it away, muttering, "The story turned boring..." Much like Snoopy, many children fail to plan ahead when they write. Instead, they view writing as a task of telling what one knows—as remembering or *knowledge telling* (Scardamalia & Bereiter, 1986). Any somewhat-appropriate information is retrieved from memory and written down, with little attention directed at choice of topic, the needs of the audience, the constraints imposed by the topic and the audience, the organization of the text, or the development and evaluation of goals. Writing remains a problematic area for many children in our country (Applebee, Langer, Jenkins, Mullis, & Foertsch, 1990).

Research also indicates that affect (including attitudes, beliefs, and emotions) needs to be considered when students experience difficulty in writing or other academic areas (Harris & Graham, 1996a). It is important to understand the reciprocal relationships among academic difficulties or failure, self-doubts, learned helplessness, attributions, pre-task expectancies, self-efficacy and motivation (Alexander, in press; Garner & Alexander, 1989; Licht, 1983; Sawyer, Graham, & Harris, 1992). In addition, other characteristics such as impulsivity, difficulty with memory or other aspects of information processing, low task engagement and persistence, devaluation of learning, and low productivity create further challenges for some children (for a detailed discussion, see Harris & Graham, 1996a). Children who consider themselves poor writers, who have negative attitudes and emotions about writing, or who have learning difficulties that make writing even more challenging need an approach to instruction that directly addresses these issues.

SELF-REGULATED STRATEGY DEVELOPMENT: EVERY CHILD CAN WRITE

More than 15 years ago, Karen Harris and Steve Graham began developing the instructional approach now known as self-regulated strategy development (SRSD). They started with the premise that all children—and especially those who face significant difficulties—would benefit from an integrated instructional approach that directly addressed their affective, behavioral, and cognitive characteristics, strengths, and needs (Harris, 1982; Harris & Graham, 1996a). The SRSD approach integrates findings from researchers and educators who have focused on cognitive development and learning, those who have focused on behavior, and those who have emphasized the role of affect in learning and development (cf. Harris, 1982). Harris and Graham believed that such an approach must integrate competing viewpoints about effective learning environments and approaches to teaching, while remaining dynamic and open to change as knowledge of teaching and learning expands and new approaches are validated. They have also emphasized that approaches to teaching and learning need to be flexible and modifiable to meet the styles and needs of both teachers and students (Harris & Graham, 1992).

Self-regulated strategy development has been used to support students in a variety of academic areas—including reading, spelling, math, and writing (see Case, Mamlin, Harris & Graham, 1995; Harris & Graham, 1992). However, the heart of SRSD has been establishing that every child can write, and validating powerful strategies for planning, writing, revising, editing, and managing the writing process. In tandem with composition strategies, children develop self-regulation strategies and abilities crucial to orchestrating the writing process—including *goal setting, self-instructions, self-monitoring and self-assessment,* and *self-reinforcement* (a detailed discussion of these skills and how they can be developed in the classroom is included in Harris & Graham, 1996a).

In writing, the major goals of SRSD are threefold:

1. Assist students in developing knowledge about writing and powerful skills and strategies involved in the writing process, including planning, writing, revising, and editing.
2. Support students in the ongoing development of the abilities needed to monitor and manage their own writing.
3. Promote children's development of positive attitudes about writing and themselves as writers.

To reach these goals, teachers using the SRSD model provide whatever level of support and scaffolding necessary—from explicit instruction to guided discovery—in the development of (a) skillful use of strategies that make a difference, (b) self-regulation of strategic performance and knowledge of one's own cognitive processes and other learning characteristics, and (c) understanding of the purpose, significance, and limitations of the strategies used.

INTEGRATING SRSD AND THE WRITING PROCESS APPROACH

A product-oriented model of writing instruction prevailed in American schools until relatively recently (Applebee et al., 1990; Harris &

Graham, 1992; Graham & Harris, in press). In this model, mechanics and grammar were emphasized over content and process. Further, writing was given limited time and attention, and few activities pursued in classrooms required sustained writing. Students were taught little about the processes and strategies involved in writing, and little was done to promote their development. Students were expected to learn to write in isolation, typically by reading the work of others and creating similar compositions. First drafts were often final drafts, read only by the teacher—who primarily marked errors in mechanics and assigned grades. The roles of writing in learning and communicating were neglected.

Instructional practices in writing today evidence significant change from that model. A process-oriented approach to writing has emerged, as seen in Writers' Workshop and whole-language approaches (Applebee et al., 1990; Atwell, 1987; Graves, 1985). The process approach to writing places the learner and the learner's needs at the center of interactive learning among teachers and students. Learning is seen as a socially situated activity enhanced in functional and meaningful literacy contexts. Emphasis is placed on creating a community of learners who:

- share and help each other,
- make personal choices about what they read and write,
- take ownership of and responsibility for their learning,
- see writing as a process—and a first draft as just that,
- take risks in their reading and writing, and
- collaborate in evaluating their efforts and progress.

Students write for real audiences and for real purposes, and are given opportunities for extended writing. Writing conferences, peer collaboration, mini-lessons, modeling, sharing, and classroom dialogue are all essential components of this approach. Students should come to see writing as a process that is difficult and frustrating at times, yet is also a challenging and enjoyable vehicle for learning and self-expression.

Good strategy instruction embraces every one of these principles and teacher actions (cf. Harris & Pressley, 1991; Pressley, Harris, & Marks, 1992; Pressley & Rankin, 1994). We have strongly supported the shift toward the writing process approach, and toward authentic learning approaches in general, for all children (Harris & Graham, 1992, 1996b). However, the integration of strategy instruction with process writing or whole-language approaches has generated considerable debate. There are those who view strategy instruction as similar to the teacher-centered, "drill and kill" approach, and those who argue that such integration is impossible and dangerously misguided (cf. Edelsky, Altwerger, & Flores, 1991; Goodman, 1986; Harris & Graham, 1994, 1996b; McIntyre & Pressley, 1996). Some whole-language advocates encourage teachers to inoculate themselves against criticisms or concerns regarding the approach (see Edelsky et al., 1991; Manning & Manning, 1995). These advocates believe that rich social interaction and immersion in meaningful literacy activities will teach children all they need to know, and develop all the skills and abilities they need to have, in due developmental time. In their view, it is not necessary, and may even be harmful, to teach explicitly.

Researchers and practitioners, however, are increasingly demonstrating that neither whole language nor process approaches to writing are uniformly effective for all children (Graham & Harris, 1994, 1997). Immersion in reading and writing, informal methods of instruction, and "teachable moments" do not provide all children with the level of explicit instruction, practice, and feedback they need to master critical skills and strategies. For students who struggle with reading and writing, and those with pronounced learning difficulties or disabilities, the limitations of process writing and whole-language approaches may be even more pronounced. These students often require more extensive, structured, and explicit instruction in the skills and strategies critical to literacy (Brown & Campione, 1990; Englert et al., 1991; Graham & Harris, 1994; Harris & Graham, 1996b; Wong et al., 1994).

Teachers and researchers have argued that explicitness and structure should not be equated with decontextualized learning of meaningless skills, passive learning, or the teaching of gradually accruing basic skills before allowing higher-order thinking, problem-solving, and conceptual learning. In fact, Harris and Graham (1994, 1996a) have argued that SRSD depends upon teachers engaging students as active collaborators in their own learning and development; modeling, dialogue, sharing, and scaffolding are critical. It is also important to note that SRSD was not designed to replace any particular writing curriculum, but rather to complement existing, effective practices in writing instruction. Further, SRSD emphasizes providing instruction that is only as explicit and supportive as is required by individual students' self-regulation and writing needs—needs that are realized in authentic literacy contexts, such as that provided by the process writing approach. Thus, the full SRSD model is not needed with all students, nor do all students need the same self-regulation or writing strategies. The SRSD approach also stresses that teachers are active learners; as they engage in collaborative strategy instruction, they and their students construct knowledge of

- writing and self-regulation strategies;
- difficulties that students encounter in attempting to regulate strategic performance;
- ways to facilitate development of strategies; and
- ways to promote sustained and generalizable self-regulated, strategic performance.

Many teachers have "adapted, rather than adopted" whole language and other authentic learning approaches (Pearson, quoted in Willis, 1993, p. 8). In a national study of outstanding teachers of reading and writing, Pressley, Rankin, and Yokoi (in press) found that these teachers typically blend together whole language and explicit instruction. Commenting on how she integrated SRSD with Writers' Workshop, one teacher noted,

It's perfect. I think it fits Writers' Workshop really well because there were plenty of opportunities for student choice ... I think it really clarifies for kids what the planning stage of Writers' Workshop is all about, and the writing process (MacArthur, Schwartz, Graham, Molloy, & Harris, 1996, p. 174).

RESEARCH BASE SUPPORTING SRSD

To date, over 20 studies using SRSD to teach writing strategies have been conducted (cf. Case et al., 1995; Harris, Graham, & Schmidt, 1997). These studies have taken place in classrooms or tutoring settings, with instruction typically given by preservice or inservice teachers. Many of the studies involve teachers who have integrated SRSD with Writers' Workshop or whole-language approaches (e.g., Danoff, Harris, & Graham, 1993; MacArthur et al., 1996; Sexton, Harris, & Graham, in press). Studies have been conducted by Harris, Graham, and their colleagues, as well as others (Albertson & Billingsley, 1997; Collins, 1992; De La Paz, in press; Tanhouser, 1994). While Harris and Graham have worked primarily in the elementary and middle grades, SRSD has also been used with high-school students.

SRSD has made significant differences in children's development of a variety of planning and revising strategies, including brainstorming (see Harris & Graham, 1985); self-monitoring (Harris, Graham, Reid, McElroy, & Hamby, 1994); reading for information and semantic webbing (MacArthur et al., 1996); generating and organizing writing content using text structure (Graham & Harris, 1989; Sawyer, Graham, & Harris, 1992); advanced planning and dictation (De La Paz & Graham, 1997); goal setting (Graham, MacArthur, & Schwartz, 1995; Graham, MacArthur, Schwartz, & Voth, 1992); revising using peer feedback (MacArthur, Schwartz, & Graham, 1991); and revising for both mechanics and substance (Graham & MacArthur, 1988; Graham et al., 1995). Writing strategies have been developed, typically with the assistance of teachers and students, for a variety of genres—such as story writing, opinion essays, persuasive essays, report writing, and so on (see Harris & Graham, 1996a, for detailed descriptions of the strategies and how to help students develop them).

SRSD leads to changes and improvements in four main aspects of students' performance: quality of writing, knowledge of writing, approach to writing, and self-efficacy (cf. Graham, Harris, MacArthur, & Schwartz, 1991; Harris & Graham, 1992). Specifically, across a variety of strategies, the quality, length, and structure of students' compositions have improved. Depending on the strategy taught, improvements have also been documented in planning, revising, substantive content, and mechanical concerns. Further, these improvements have been consistently maintained over time (with some students needing booster sessions for long-term maintenance), and students have shown generalization across settings, persons, and writing medium—i.e., from word processor to paper and pencil (Harris & Graham, 1996a; Graham, Harris, & Troia, in press). These improvements occurred among normally achieving students as well as students with learning problems (Graham et al., 1991). In several studies, in fact, improvements for students with learning disabilities have been so pronounced that following SRSD instruction, these students did as well as their normally achieving peers (cf. Danoff et al., 1993; Graham & Harris, 1989).

FROM CHILDREN'S PORTFOLIOS

The stories below, from three elementary school students' portfolios, illustrate how SRSD helps children develop as writers. The first two children, Mike and Christie, were described to us by their teachers as "non-writers." Both were also identified as learning disabled. Mike, our first author, was said to "very much dislike writing." Christie did not particularly dislike writing (her teacher attributed her more positive attitude to the Writers' Workshop used at the school), but felt she was simply not much good at it.

Mike

Mike wrote the following story before SRSD instruction:

> The boy is running through the meadow where there is a lot of water
> and trees and high hills. He is running up and down to get to another
> side and he must be happy or he would stop running.

Together with other students who were having difficulty with writing, Mike was offered SRSD instruction in a basic three-step planning
strategy adapted for story writing (Harris & Graham, 1996a):

1. Think   —Who will read this?
                —Why am I writing this?
2. Plan what to say—Use S-P-A-C-E
3. Write and say more

SPACE is an acronym used to help students remember the parts if a
good story; it stands for Setting, Purpose, Action, Conclusion, and
Emotions. Mike and his peers were able to use this strategy effectively
in six to eight class sessions. The following story is one Mike wrote
after SRSD instruction.

> Once upon a time long ago an animal was shipped to a small country
> in Brazil. The men that lived there did not know what it was and they
> went to their master and told their master what had happened. He
> came out, took the box to a top of a hill because whatever was in the
> box he did not want it to kill his men. The man got a net and went
> to open the box. He opened the box. The animal got out and bit him
> and was running towards his men. The men did not want to get hurt,
> so they ran into their tent with fear and the animal ran away. The
> leader got a bandage for his leg and got the net and started after him.
> He finally caught the animal and found out it was only a scared lion
> and carried him back. He told his men to come out and look. They
> walked out slow. The leader said, "Look, it is only a baby lion." They

all pet it and played with it, fed it and they all became good friends with the lion. They were all happy, but pretty soon after that, the tiger got bigger and wasn't friendly any more. So they let it go free. They were all upset, but then they remembered all the good time they had with the lion.

Christie

Christie's teacher, Barbara Danoff, decided to offer instruction in a different story writing approach at her school—the "W-W-W" or Story Grammar strategy. While she felt that all of the students would profit from learning about the strategy, she was surprised (but pleased) to find that the entire class wanted to receive this instruction. The students who were struggling with writing needed seven to nine class sessions and considerable support (the full SRSD model) to make the strategy theirs; others caught "the trick of it" in the first few mini-lessons. (For a complete description of how Barbara and her students worked together during Writers' Workshop to develop each student's abilities with this strategy and with other aspects of story writing, see Harris & Graham, 1996a.) This planning strategy has five steps:

1. Think of a story that you would like to share with others.
2. Let your mind be free.
3. Write down the story part reminder:
   W-W-W
   What=2
   How=2
4. Make notes of your ideas for each part.
5. Write your story—use good parts, add, elaborate, revise as you write or afterwards, and make sense.

The mnemonic in Step 3 of this strategy stands for the following questions: Who is the main character, and who else is in the story? When does the story take place? Where does the story take place?

What does the main character do or want to do, and what do other characters do? What happens when the main character does or tries to do it, and what happens with other characters? How does the story end? How does the main character feel, and how do other characters feel?

Barbara taught students the W-W-W strategy in the context of the Writers' Workshop approach at her school. Before SRSD instruction, Christie's stories looked much like Mike's pre-instruction story, but after working with Barbara and her peers, she wrote the following story.

Baseball and Tommy

One hot, humid day in April (April 22, 1990) there was Tommy, who lived in Maryland-Virginia. Tommy is a short boy, he is 9 years old with brown hair. And he loved to wear his red hat, blue jeans, and his gray sweatshirt. One afternoon Tommy saw his friends (Jim, Scott, Fred, Tod) were playing ball. But when he went home he tried to play but he was not good. He practiced and practiced, finally he was getting good. So when he told his friends they said, "Lets see how good you are." So they went to Tod's house and played in his backyard. It was a hot, humid day so they had to stop. They went in and got drinks. Then Scott said, "Hey, you're pretty good." "Thank you," Tommy said. When Tommy tried out for the team (neighborhood) he made it. When he got home he was so proud of himself. He told his father and his father said if you're so good then try out for the school team. The next day he watched the team and tried to learn the plays. When he went home he played with his friends, like the team. The next day he went in to talk with the coach and ask if he could try out. The coach said sure, we're looking for another player. So Tommy went for it and made the team. When he got home he told his father. His father was so proud he took him out for ice cream. Tommy's father said, "I am sorry for acting so rude before and being so forceful." Tommy said, "It's OK."

The End

Vanessa

Vanessa, also in Barbara Danoff's class, was one of the more capable writers. However, review of her portfolio indicated that she typically did not use all of the story components in her writing. In addition to including all the story components, Vanessa also wanted to include more elaboration, detail, and actions in her stories. After discussion and modeling of the strategy (just a few class sessions or mini-lessons), she wrote the following story—and clearly met her goals.

The St. Patrick's Day Leprechaun

One day in Doggy Land, Valerie (a poodle) was walking through the forest. It was March 31, 1990. Valerie was a white poodle with a green bow in her hair. Since it was St. Patrick's Day, Valerie was going to find a leprechaun.

She was skipping along when all of a sudden she heard a moan. Then she heard a whimper. Now, Valerie was a very curious dog. She started to walk east. That was where the sound was coming from. In surprise she found out that it was a dog too. He was tan and white with big, brown, sad eyes. He also had on a green top hat and a bow-tie with clovers on it. It was a leprechaun! Valerie said, "Why are you crying Mr. Leprechaun?"

"Because I have scratched my paw on a thorn bush! Could you please help me!" begged the leprechaun. Well, Valerie wanted a little something out of this too. So she said, "Only if you give me three wishes!"

"Oh, all right!" said Mr. Leprechaun. Valerie got a band-aid out of her purse and put it on the leprechaun. He felt much better. "Now what do you wish for?"

"I want a bike, a new dress, and a pot of gold!" said Valerie. Out of mid-air came a bike, and a new dress. "But where's my pot of gold?" asked Valerie.

"Well for that we'll have to go over the rainbow. Hop on!" shouted Mr. Leprechaun. Together they rode up onto the rainbow on the magic carpet. When they got on top they slid down. They landed on a cloud. Under a rock was the pot of gold.

After that Valerie went home. She laid her things down on the table. She was thirsty from the long ride. She went into the kitchen. When she came back her bike, dress, and pot of gold were gone. "Oh no!" thought Valerie. She ran back to the woods. But he wasn't there. She looked up at the sky. The rainbow was gone! For it was only her imagination.

The End

SRSD STAGES OF INSTRUCTION

How do students achieve such developments in their writing? Children like Vanessa, who enjoy writing and do not struggle with it, may merely need opportunities to share, discuss, and try out strategies for different genres or forms of writing. For other students, much more is needed—more explicit instruction, more support, and more attention to their attitudes, beliefs, and feelings about writing.

Six instructional stages provide the framework for self-regulated strategy development (Harris & Graham, 1992, 1996a). These stages represent a "metascript," providing a general guideline; they can be reordered, combined, revisited, modified or deleted to meet student and teacher needs. Furthermore, the stages are designed to be recursive—so that if a concept is not mastered at a certain stage, students and teachers can revisit or continue that stage as they move on to others. In fact, a typical lesson (as we illustrate shortly) involves two or three stages.

The six stages in the SRSD model are listed below. ("It" refers to the writing process using both self-regulation and specific writing strategies).

1. Develop Background Knowledge
2. Discuss It
3. Model It
4. Memorize It

5. Support It
6. Independent Performance

Some stages may not be needed by all students. For example, some students may have already mastered the background knowledge needed to use the writing strategy and self-regulation processes targeted for instruction. These students may skip this stage or act as a resource for other students who need this stage.

Procedures for promoting maintenance and generalization are integrated throughout the SRSD model. These include: identifying opportunities to use the strategies in other classes or settings, discussing attempts to use the strategies at other times, reminding students to use the strategies at appropriate times, analyzing how these processes might need to be modified with other tasks and in new settings, and evaluating the success of these processes during and after instruction. Other teachers can be asked to prompt students to use the writing and self-regulation strategies when appropriate in their classrooms. Booster sessions, in which the strategy is reviewed and discussed, are very important in maintaining strategy use for some students.

Rather than simply describing each stage, we will illustrate the SRSD process with two case studies of its use in actual classrooms.

SRSD INSTRUCTION: TWO TEACHERS AND THEIR STUDENTS

SRSD can be conducted with individual students, small groups, or entire classes. While Barbara Danoff (whose students Christie and Vanessa were described above) involved her whole class in at least the first stages of SRSD (Danoff, Harris, & Graham, 1993), the teachers in the following two examples are working with small groups of students. In both groups, the students have serious difficulties with writing, and are identified as having a learning disability in this area. In the second example, the teacher has modified SRSD instruction in some interesting ways.

Melissa Sexton's SRSD Group

The first group included six fifth- and sixth-grade students with learning disabilities, who were taught a strategy for writing opinion essays (Sexton et al., in press). These students were involved in SRSD instruction because they experienced difficulties with writing, displayed a low level of motivation, and had maladaptive beliefs about the causes of success and failure in their writing. The school was implementing an inclusion model; these six students were part of a multi-grade team with their general education peers. Their writing class was team taught by general and special education teachers, using the Writers' Workshop approach. The students continued to participate in Writers' Workshop, receiving instruction in the composition strategy in a small group. Since mini-lessons and conferences are a common part of Writers' Workshop, Melissa Sexton, the teacher, did not have a problem integrating SRSD within this approach.

Develop Background Knowledge. Melissa began instruction by leading a discussion on what the students already knew about opinion essays, including the elements that are commonly found in such an essay. This knowledge was considered an essential prerequisite to using the target writing strategy, as these elements of opinion essays served as prompts for generating information to include in the outlines. Melissa and her students read and discussed several good essays. They identified three elements commonly included in opinion essays: a premise, supporting reasons, and a conclusion. Next, they identified examples of these elements in essays they were reading in class and essays written by other children. They then spent some time generating ideas for essay parts, using various topics.

Discuss It. Following this initial lesson, an individual conference was held with each student. Each student examined previous opinion essays he or she had written to determine which elements were included and to assess the quality of each element. Melissa and the student also talked about any strategies or self-statements that he or she currently used when writing. At this point, Melissa indicated that she would like to teach the student a strategy for writing essays. She talked with the student about the goals for learning the strategy (to write better essays), and about how including and expanding essay parts could improve the student's writing, and thus improve communication with the reader. Melissa also introduced self-monitoring, explaining that self-assessment and self-recording would allow the student to monitor the components in his or her essays and the effects of learning the writing strategy. Together, she and the student counted and graphed the number of elements included in the student's earlier essays. Melissa explained how the graph would continue to be used for self-monitoring as the writing strategy was learned. Before completing the conference, she emphasized the student's role as collaborator, and together they developed a written goal to learn the strategy.

After each child had participated in an individual conference, Melissa and the students resumed their group discussion of the writing strategy during a second lesson. Each student was given a chart listing the steps of the strategy:

1. Think, who will read this, and why am I writing it?
2. Plan what to say using TREE (note *Topic* sentence, note *Reasons*, *Examine* reasons, note *Ending*).
3. Write and say more.

(Mike's class used the same basic three-step strategy, but with a story-writing component—SPACE—as explained previously.)

The first step in the strategy involves identifying the intended audience and reasons for writing the paper. During the second step, each student develops an outline for his or her essay. This includes establishing the premise for the paper, generating ideas to support the premise, evaluating readers' reaction to each idea (and eliminating unsound ideas), noting a conclusion for the paper, and determining how the argument will be structured or sequenced. The third step is a reminder to continue revising and improving the outline while writing.

Melissa asked the students what they thought the reason for each step might be, and the group discussed how and when to use the strategy (e.g., whenever you are asked, or want, to give your opinion or tell what you believe). Melissa then described the procedures for learning the strategy. She stressed the importance of effort, since a strategy can't work if it hasn't been mastered.

To help them remember the steps in developing an outline (TREE), students were given various verbal prompts to visualize a tree: "The trunk is like your *Topic* sentence or premise. How are the trunk of a tree and your topic sentence similar? [Everything is connected to each of them.] The roots are like your *Reasons*. How are the roots of a tree like the reasons that support your topic sentence? [They support the trunk—just like reasons support the topic sentence.] It is also important to *Examine* the roots—just like you examine reasons. If they are strong, the trunk and the whole tree will be strong."

Model It. During the third lesson, Melissa modeled how to use the writing strategy, thinking out loud as she worked. The students participated during modeling by helping her as she planned, made notes, and wrote the first draft of her essay. Together they accepted and rejected possible ideas to support her premise, and they continued to modify the plan while writing the paper. Once a first draft was written, they reread the paper and made revisions.

While planning and writing, Melissa used a variety of self-instructions to help her manage the strategy, the writing process, and her behavior. These included self-statements involving problem definition (e.g., "What do I need to do?"), planning, (e.g., "OK, first I need to ..."), self-evaluation (e.g., "Did I say what I really believe?"), and self-reinforcement (e.g., "Great, this is a good reason!"). In addition, she emphasized that her success in writing the essay was due to effort in the use of the writing strategy. (As noted earlier, these children had maladaptive beliefs about the causes of success and failure in their writing). The attributional self-statements Melissa used included: "If I work hard and follow the steps of the strategy, I'll write a good essay" and "I want to write a good essay, so I will try hard to use the strategy and include good essay parts."

Discuss It (revisited). After Melissa modeled how to use the writing strategy, she and her students discussed the importance of what we say to ourselves while we work; students volunteered examples of positive and negative self-statements they used when writing. They also identified the types of things Melissa said that helped her work better, stressing statements that emphasized the role of effort and use of the strategy in success. After discussing how these self-statements were helpful, each student generated and recorded on a small chart self-statements he or she would use to (1) manage the strategy and the writing process (e.g., "Slow down and take my time") and (2) attribute success to effort and use of the strategy (e.g., "Work hard—Write better.").

Memorize It. During a fourth lesson, students worked on memorizing the strategy, the mnemonic (TREE), and several self-statements they planned to use. Melissa felt this stage was important to include, because several of her students experienced memory problems (as do many children with learning disabilities). Students practiced memorizing this information in pairs—typically by quizzing each other. Most students memorized the items easily, but some needed more practice, and continued to work on memorization as they began writing essays.

Support It. In subsequent lessons, students received assistance from Melissa and from each other as they applied the writing strategy and accompanying self-regulation procedures while writing opinion essays. The goal during this stage of instruction was to support the students' efforts as they learned to use these procedures successfully and independently. Melissa gradually adjusted the level of support provided, reducing assistance as each child became increasingly adept at using the procedures.

At first, students received considerable support in developing a writing outline. Based on her previous experience with the students, Melissa thought this part of the strategy would be particularly challenging for them (an excellent example of anticipating and planning for difficulties). Support initially involved her acting as the lead collaborator in the planning process. As she and the students planned together, she intentionally committed a few errors, such as forgetting a step of the strategy. This led to discussions about the impacts of and reasons for such errors. Melissa then modeled correcting the mistake, combining the correction with a positive attributional self-statement (e.g., "I need to try to follow all of the strategy steps, so I can write a good essay"). If students subsequently made mistakes in using the strategy, the possible consequences of the errors were examined again, and students were encouraged to redo the step while using a positive attributional statement.

Melissa's role as a planning collaborator was quickly (as students became ready) replaced with less intrusive forms of assistance and scaffolding, including reminders to carry out a step or use self-statements, prompting to devote more attention to a specific aspect of the process (e.g., generate more possible supporting reasons), and feedback on the use of the strategy and accompanying self-regulation procedures. In some instances, it was necessary for her to revisit the rationale underlying an individual step in the process (e.g., the need to evaluate the readers' reactions to each idea). Assistance also included helping students determine which self-statements were especially useful to them. References to the strategy chart and self-statement lists as prompts or reminders were faded, and students were encouraged to use their self-statements covertly (in their heads).

As students worked on their essays, Melissa encouraged them to use goal setting and self-assessment (continuing the use of the graphs) in conjunction with the writing strategy and self-statements. Prior to planning an essay, each student set a goal to include all of the essay parts in his or her paper. Once an essay was completed, the student reviewed the paper, determining if any parts were missing and counting and graphing the number of essay elements that were included. Students then shared their essays with each other, providing feedback on both strengths and areas where improvements could be made in each other's arguments.

Independent Performance. After writing three or four essays, all of the students were able to use the writing strategy and accompanying self-regulation procedures without teacher support. At this point, students planned and wrote essays independently. Melissa provided positive and constructive feedback as needed, and the students continued to share their essays with each other. While some students still relied on their strategy charts and lists of self-statements as a prompt or reminder, they were encouraged to work without them. Students were asked to continue using the goal setting and self-assessment (graphing) procedures on at least two more essays. After that, they were told that use of these procedures was up to them.

In a group conference, students discussed how what they were learning could be used in other classes. Several students indicated that they now told themselves "to try harder" when writing or asked themselves if their paper was "good enough." The students identified opportunities they might have to use the writing strategy and self-regulation procedures in the future. Each student also evaluated the strategy and the instructional process. They all indicated that they enjoyed learning the writing strategy and that other students would benefit from learning it as well; as one student put it, "All schools in the country should learn this!" When asked if they would change anything about instruction, the only recommendation was to give homework assignments to use the strategy.

Formal evaluation indicated that instruction changed both how and what students wrote (Sexton, Harris, & Graham, in press). Before SRSD instruction, when students were asked to write an essay, they began to write immediately; these essays were of poor quality, containing only two or three ideas. They typically started their essays by stating their position, then gave a single supporting reason, and ended abruptly, without a concluding statement. Following instruction, the students typically planned papers in advance, and the quality of the resulting essays improved. Papers became longer, the number of reasons supporting the premise increased, text was coherently ordered, and all of the basic elements of a good essay were present. The students were more confident about their ability to write a good essay, and more positive about the role of effort and strategy use in writing.

Gary Troia's SRSD Group

The second group included three fifth-graders in a tutoring setting, who were taught a planning strategy for story writing (Troia, Graham, & Harris, 1997). The strategy involved using three important writing processes: *goal setting, brainstorming,* and *organizing.* As in the previous example, these students had learning disabilities and experienced severe difficulties with writing. Gary modified the SRSD approach by leading students to derive the nature and importance of these three processes across both writing and reading tasks, and by using "homework" (practice at home or school) to promote generalization and maintenance.

Develop Background Knowledge. Instruction began with reviewing and expanding what each child knew about good stories and story writing. In an approach similar to Melissa's, Gary incorporated discussion and examination of stories students were reading to help establish the common components of a good story: setting, problem, action, consequence, and reaction. At this point, however, rather than first describing the writing strategy he planned to offer and then asking students to reflect on the rationale and value of each step, Gary decided to model several literacy tasks involving reading and writing.

Model It and Discuss It. As he modeled each writing task, he used goal setting, brainstorming, and organizing, and let the students derive the essential features, rationale, and value of these three processes. To help students see the importance and generalizability of these processes, Gary led three lessons where he modeled different tasks, including reading tasks and both essay and story writing. The students identified, discussed and evaluated these three processes, and

Gary introduced outlining as a reminder for employing these processes with writing and other tasks. During each of the three lessons, students were encouraged to assist him in goal setting, brainstorming, and organizing.

In the first lesson, Gary modeled—while "thinking out loud"— the use of these processes to read a chapter and write a story. In reading the chapter, he set a goal ("find out how plants fit into the food chain"), brainstormed and listed what he already knew, and organized his ideas by topic. As he read, he modified his outline by adding, deleting, changing, and rearranging both ideas and categories. Similarly, when writing a story, Gary set a goal ("to write a good story to share with my creative writing class"), brainstormed ideas to include in the story, and sequenced the ideas he planned to use. While writing, he modified his outline by adding, changing, deleting, and rearranging ideas. Throughout the modeling, Gary provided a rationale for each of his actions and verbally reinforced himself for a job well done.

After the two tasks were modeled, the students were encouraged to take some time to think about what they had just seen and heard. Guided discussion helped them identify the rationales for and essential features of the three processes used to accomplish the tasks. First, Gary asked a series of questions focused on what was similar and different in the reading and writing activities. All of the students identified goal setting, brainstorming, and organizing as similar. Gary then posed more focused questions, asking the students to think about why he had used each of these processes and how they had helped him. Discussion then shifted to how this approach to writing a story was similar to or different from the students' approaches on a story written a few days earlier. Each student was asked to evaluate the possible use of the processes in her or his own writing.

In the next two lessons, Gary modeled (thinking aloud, and involving students in the process) preparing for a speech, planning a trip, and, once again, writing a story. Discussion resumed about what was similar and different in the conduct of these three tasks. This series of lessons ended with the introduction of a mnemonic that would act as a prompt to set goals, brainstorm, and sequence when writing or doing other tasks involving planning. A small chart was used to introduce the mnemonic, STOP & LIST: Stop Think Of Purpose & List Ideas Sequence Them.

Discussion of STOP & LIST resumed during the following lesson. With Gary's guidance, each student self-evaluated a recent story. Students determined if each common story element (i.e., setting, problem, action, consequence, and reaction) was included and rated the quality of the elements present on a five-point Likert-type scale. They also assessed the overall quality of the story using the same rating system, and identified strategies used in writing the story. Students were then asked to specify how goal setting, brainstorming, and sequencing had helped or would help them with story writing. Together with Gary, they created a list of when, where, and why students used the three processes. At this point, Gary described how they would work together to learn to use STOP & LIST to write stories. He indicated that the purpose of learning the strategy was to "write better stories and use it with other tasks." Each student noted what he or she would do to facilitate the learning process, such as "not give up" or "work hard."

Memorize It. During this lesson, the students also briefly practiced the STOP & LIST mnemonic and the sentence it represented. This continued in succeeding lessons until students could repeat the information easily and quickly. Gary believed such practice to be particularly important for this group of students, as all of them had difficulties with long-term memory, and a strategy cannot be used if it cannot be recalled!

Support It. In the next lesson, students began writing stories using STOP & LIST. Gary collaboratively planned a story with each student, and made sure the strategy and mnemonic were used appropriately. The mnemonic chart was set out to remind students to set goals, brainstorm, and sequence. Gary modified the amount of input and support provided to meet each child's needs. Assistance included prompting, guidance and feedback, and re-explanations.

This scaffolding, including use of the mnemonic chart, was faded as each student grew ready to use the strategy independently.

After completing a story, each student was asked to determine which story elements were present in the story, evaluate their quality (using the rating scale described earlier), and determine if the goal(s) for the story had been met. The student discussed with Gary where and why he or she was successful, unsuccessful, or both; the role of goal setting, brainstorming, and sequencing in writing the story; and what could have been done to write an even better story.

At the end of each lesson, each student identified an opportunity to apply STOP & LIST at home or school, and this became a "homework" assignment. Students explained how the strategy would be helpful and what modifications were needed to enable it to work. Examples of homework assignments included planning a report, a trip, or supplies needed for school. At the start of the next lesson, each student turned in his or her outline or planning sheet, reported on the success of the assignment, and assessed the role and value of the strategy in carrying out the task. Each child also described any other times goal setting, brainstorming, or sequencing had been used since the prior lesson. Most of the students' examples centered on the completion of writing assignments.

Independent Performance. After writing two stories with assistance, each student was able to use STOP & LIST without Gary's support. At this point, students planned and wrote stories independently; Gary provided positive and constructive feedback as needed. Homework continued, and students evaluated their stories and reflected on the outcomes and relevance of using the strategy.

At the end of instruction on this strategy, each student was asked to further consider how goal setting, brainstorming, and sequencing were helpful when writing stories and completing homework assignments. They discussed how STOP & LIST had to be modified for these tasks, and they identified opportunities for applying the strategy in the future (e.g., in writing assignments, homework, shopping, and organizing their rooms).

Formal evaluation of the students' stories revealed that prior to SRSD instruction, none of the participating students had done any planning in advance of writing, following instruction they consistently used STOP & LIST to plan and organize. The students' papers became longer and included more story elements. These improvements also generalized to a second genre, the writing of opinion essays, and were maintained on writing probes administered almost a month after instruction was terminated. Students had positive comments about the strategy and the way they had learned it; they said it would help them "get better grades in school," "think of ideas I might not have," and "write good stories."

"It's Not Just What You Do, But How You Do It"

Our work with teachers and children learning self-regulation and writing strategies has convinced us that *how* is every bit as important as *what* in strategy instruction. Teachers and children have helped us to identify several characteristics of the SRSD approach that are critical to effective implementation in schools and classrooms (Harris & Graham, 1996a).

First, the self-regulated strategy development model *emphasizes collaborative learning* among teachers and students. While the teacher initially provides the necessary degree of scaffolding or support, the responsibility for recruiting, executing, monitoring, evaluating, and modifying strategies is gradually transferred to the student. For example, students can act as collaborators in determining the goals of instruction; completing the task; implementing, evaluating, and modifying the strategy and self-regulation procedures; and planning for maintenance and generalization. Students also collaborate with and provide support for each other.

Individualization of instruction based on students' characteristics and skills is a second important feature. Instruction does not need to be one-to-one, but teachers should strive to understand each child's current approach to writing and then work with students to select and modify strategies and instructional components that fit their needs and promote development. As mentioned earlier, SRSD has been successfully used with individual students, small groups, and entire classes. Regardless of the number of students and teachers working together, the preskills, skills, strategies, and self-regulatory procedures used should be chosen and developed in accordance with a thorough understanding of each student and of the writing task, and should be tailored to individual students' capabilities. Even when the composition and self-regulatory strategies are appropriate for a group or entire class, the teacher can individualize certain aspects of instruction (the nature and content of self-instructions, goals for writing and self-regulation, affective goals, feedback and reinforcement, etc.). Ongoing self-evaluation, using techniques such as self-monitoring or portfolio assessment, can also promote individualization (Harris & Graham, 1996a).

The third characteristic of SRSD is that *instruction is criterion based*, rather than time based. Each student should be given adequate time to meet affective, cognitive, and composing goals. Students progress through the stages at their own pace, moving on as they become ready to do so. Thus, teachers do not plan to teach a strategy in a set period of time, and when they are working with groups, they may frequently shift between entire-group, smaller-group, and individual lessons. Teachers have found that it typically takes only six to nine class sessions or lessons, using the full SRSD model, for students to reach independent performance. As we have noted, many students will not need the full SRSD model, and thus will come to understand and work with a strategy in less time.

The fourth aspect of SRSD is true of teaching in general; teachers in all areas have found it important to *anticipate and plan for glitches— areas of instruction that may be difficult*. Before introducing a new strategy, teachers have found it beneficial to brainstorm things that could go wrong or prove especially problematic, given what is known about the learners and the composition task. Students can collaborate in anticipating glitches as well. For example, maintaining and generalizing strategy use can be challenging for some students. Together with their teacher, students can set a plan for booster sessions (reviewing and revisiting strategies) after they have learned the strategies.

Because teachers play such a pivotal role in helping students understand the meaning and efficacy of self-regulation and writing strategies, the fifth characteristic involves having *enthusiastic teachers working within a support network*. Enthusiastic, responsive teaching is an integral part of SRSD, as it is with all effective teaching. Given the complexity and demands of strategy instruction, a supportive network of teachers and administrators who can problem-solve and share both their successes and their failures makes implementation considerably easier. Moreover, the impact of instruction on students is much greater, and generalization of strategic performance across the curriculum and grades is more likely, when strategy instruction is embraced across a school or district.

The final characteristic teachers need to consider is *developmental enhancement*. With SRSD, teachers consider how a strategy fits into the larger scheme of things in relation to each student's development both as a writer and as a self-directed learner (Harris & Graham, 1992). The teacher needs to understand the many ways strategies can empower students in order to help students take full advantage of them. Students need to learn the meaning and significance of strategy usage, as well as the strengths and weaknesses of particular strategies. For example, strategy instruction might begin with a traditional story grammar strategy (such as the SPACE and W-W-W strategies described here). Once students develop ownership of this strategy, the class may move on to other types of story grammars—such as those used by African tribal story tellers, or structures focused more on character development than action—or they might expand the story grammar strategy by working on writing biographical stories. The strengths and weaknesses of various strategies can then be compared, and new strategies may be discovered or created.

EVALUATING SRSD

Students who are taught a strategy that does not improve their performance will certainly not be enthusiastic about learning a second strategy. Conducting ongoing assessment, rather than assessing the methods only at the end of instruction, allows teachers and students to determine what is working and what changes need to be made. SRSD facilitates meaningful, ongoing assessment. The interactive, collaborative nature of the SRSD learning process allows teachers to assess changes in affect, behavior, and cognition. The following is an explanation of some basic principles for assessing SRSD methods and procedures. The list is certainly not exhaustive, but it provides a good stating point for effective evaluation.

Involve Students as Co-Evaluators

Students should be included as partners in the strategy evaluation process. Not only does co-evaluation increase students' sense of ownership and reinforce the progress they are making, but it also provides teachers with much greater insight into the effectiveness of the strategies and SRSD instruction. Students can participate in many ways, such as learning to evaluate their writing based on their goals (self-assessment), or discussing with the teacher which components of instruction are most helpful to them and where they would recommend changes. Helping students ask appropriate self-questions (e.g., "Am I ready to move on to the next step?" "Is this working for me?" "Do I need to do anything differently?") is another effective way to help students evaluate their own progress. By asking students to share their reflections, teachers gain valuable insight into their progress and readiness for moving on. Collaborative peer evaluation, using strategies such as peer revising (see Harris & Graham, 1996), is also a valuable component of the assessment process.

Consider the Level of Evaluation Needed

Strategies, methods, and procedures such as TREE or STOP & LIST that have been previously validated (both by research and by teachers in the classroom) typically need less scrutiny than a strategy being used for the first time. The amount of time and effort expended on assessing the usefulness of a strategy should depend on the established validity of the strategy and a teacher's experience with it. However, it is important to remember that even well-validated strategies need evaluation. At a minimum, teachers should know whether (a) students are actually using the strategy, (b) use of the strategy has a positive impact on performance and affective characteristics, and (c) students see the strategy as being valuable and manageable.

Assess Changes in Performance, Attitudes, and Cognition

Because the benefits of SRSD go beyond improving a student's performance, teachers should also look for changes in students' attitudes and cognitive processes. While teaching writing and self-regulation strategies, teachers might observe students for improvements in attitudes toward writing or confidence in their abilities. They might also gather information about the amount and quality of writing a student does before and after SRSD instruction, or listen for spontaneous statements made about writing assignments. Open-ended questions—such as "What is good writing?" or "What do you most like to say to yourself while you write?"—can help provide insight. When evaluating performance, attitudes, and cognition, it is important to remember that some changes (such as reducing writing anxiety or improving attitudes) take more time than others to obtain.

Assess How Students Actually Use the Strategy

Over time, students will often modify a strategy or the ways in which they use it. As a result, it cannot be assumed that students are using the strategy as intended. Some modifications allow a strategy to meet a student's unique needs, but others (such as eliminating a necessary step) may not be useful or desirable. Teachers can monitor strategy usage through direct means (such as observing what students do as they write, asking questions, discussing how things are working), or indirectly (by looking for evidence of strategy usage in students' papers).

Assess Students' Use of the Strategy Over Time and In New Situations

We cannot assume that students will continue to use a particular strategy or successfully adapt a strategy to new situations. Therefore, it is beneficial to actively enhance maintenance and generalization of strategy usage from the very beginning of SRSD instruction. This might be done by periodically inviting students to explain the purpose of a strategy, or by having students (and teachers) share ways they've used the strategy. A teacher might also ask students to keep a record of each time they use a strategy or the ways they modify it for other tasks. Ultimately, the goal is to determine whether students need additional support to consistently apply the strategy in appropriate situations.

Collaborate with Colleagues During the Evaluation Process

If students are being taught a strategy that can be applied in different content areas or classrooms, it is important for teachers to involve colleagues in promoting this generalization and assessing whether the transition across subjects and settings is being made. It is also important to discuss with other teachers the strategy's effectiveness and whether it is appropriate in their classes—and, if not, how it could best be modified, or what other strategies would be more useful. Working together in this way, teachers in different classes can provide reminders for students to use the strategy, help students with a particular aspect of the strategy, or suggest modifications to make the strategy more effective for a certain task.

Use Portfolio Assessment Procedures

Portfolio assessment is an ideal way to bring together many of the recommendations we have presented for SRSD evaluation. When students maintain portfolios, both teachers and students benefit. Students learn to engage in reflective self-evaluation, come to understand that development is as important as achievement (a major tenet of many process approaches to writing), and begin to take greater responsibility for their own learning. Teachers gain new insights about both assessment and teaching, and a greater understanding of their students' development and learning. Portfolio assessment does require that teachers establish the credibility of this approach with students and then become intimately involved in the maintenance and evaluation of student portfolios. However, once teachers and students become comfortable with this form of assessment, positive results occur for both.

A FEW FINAL TIPS FOR SRSD

Take It Slow

For teachers just starting out with strategy instruction, we recommend starting slowly. It is tempting to try SRSD in the areas of instruction that present the greatest challenges or with students who are experiencing the most difficultly. However, despite good intentions, it is not fair to either party to take on too much too fast. Instead, begin with relatively simple strategies in an area with which you are comfortable and anticipate success, and with students who are willing to learn the strategies. Initial failure can make it difficult for both teachers and students to persist, and conversely, nothing succeeds like success. Teachers can move on to greater challenges as they gain experience. We also recommend that strategies be *offered* to students, not forced on them.

Take Advantage of Strategies Already Developed

It is often easier to begin strategy instruction with an existing, already proven strategy, such as the three-step strategy with TREE or SPACE, the W-W-W strategy, or the STOP & LIST strategy. Rather than attempting to simultaneously create an effective strategy and become comfortable with the process of helping students master the strategy, teachers can take advantage of a strategy that has already been developed and validated (cf. Harris & Graham, 1996a). Once the teacher and students are familiar with SRSD, then they can work together to create and evaluate new strategies, as they will often need to do to address their unique needs and situations.

Learn Together

If at all possible, teachers should collaborate with other teachers, as well as their students, while they learn to implement SRSD in the classroom. Professional collaboration allows teachers to share their personal triumphs and challenges with strategy instruction and serves to facilitate supportive feedback and problem solving.

CONCLUSION

Harris and Graham have emphasized from the beginning that SRSD should not be thought of as a panacea; promoting students' academic competence and literacy requires a complex integration of skills, strategies, processes, and attributes. However, by establishing affective, behavioral, and cognitive goals for instruction, SRSD represents an important contribution to teachers' instructional repertoires.

Evaluations of SRSD by teachers and students have been positive, indicating sound social validity. One teacher, for example, commented that she could "see light bulbs going on" as her students learned to use writing strategies (Danoff et al., 1993, p. 315). One student proclaimed that SRSD should be "taught to all schools in the country" (Graham, Harris, & Troia, 1997, p. 16), and another noted that "the W-W-W strategy really builds up your resources." Perhaps the best description of our goals for SRSD was one student's comment that "*Now* this writing stuff makes sense!" When writing makes sense and children develop ownership of powerful self-regulation and writing strategies, every child can indeed write.

REFERENCES

Albertson, L., & Billingsley, F. (1997, March). *Improving young writers' planning and reviewing skills while story-writing.* Paper presented at the American Educational Research Association Conference, Chicago.

Alexander, P. (in press). Mapping the multidimensional nature of domain learning: The interplay of cognitive, motivational, and strategic forces. In P. Pintrich & M. Maehr (Eds.), *Advances in motivation and achievement: Vol. 10.* Greenwich, CT: JAI Press.

Applebee, A., Langer, J., Jenkins, L., Mullis, I., & Foertsch, M. (1990). *Learning to write in our nation's schools.* Princeton, NJ: Educational Testing Service.

Atwell, N. (1987). *In the middle: Reading, writing, and learning from adolescents.* Portsmouth, NH: Heinemann.

Brown, A., & Campione, J. (1990). Interactive learning environments and the teaching of science and mathematics. In M. Gardner, J. Green, F. Reif, A. Schoenfield, A. di Sessa, & E. Stage (Eds.), *Toward a scientific practice of science education* (pp. 112-139). Hillsdale, NJ: Erlbaum.

Burnham, S. (1994). *For writer only.* New York: Ballantine Books.

Case, L., Mamlin, N., Harris, K., & Graham, S. (1995). Self-regulated strategy development: A theoretical and practical perspective. In T. Scruggs & M. Mastropieri (Eds), *Research in Learning and Behavioral Disabilities* (pp. 21-46). Greenwich, CT: JAI Press.

Collins, R. (1992). *Narrative writing of option II students: The effects of combining the whole-language techniques, writing process approach and strategy training.* Unpublished master's thesis, State University of New York, Buffalo.

Danoff, B., Harris, K.R., & Graham, S. (1993). Incorporating strategy instruction within the writing process in the regular classroom. *Journal of Reading Behavior, 25,* 295-322.

De La Paz, S. (in press). Strategy instruction in planning: Teaching students with learning and writing disabilities to compose narrative and expository essays. *Learning Disability Quarterly.*

De La Paz, S., & Graham, S. (1997). The effects of dictation and advanced planning instruction on the composing of students with writing and learning problems. *Journal of Educational Psychology, 89,* 203-222.

Edelsky, C., Altwerger, B., & Flores, B. (1991). *Whole language: What's the difference?* Portsmouth, NH: Heinemann.

Englert, C., Raphael, T., Anderson, L., Anthony, H., Stevens, D., & Fear, K. (1991). Making writing strategies and self-talk visible: Cognitive strategy instruction in writing in regular and special education classrooms. *American Educational Research Journal, 28,* 337-373.

Flower, L., & Hayes, J. (1980). The dynamics of composing: Making plans and juggling constraints. In L. Gregg & R. Steinberg (Eds.), *Cognitive processes in writing* (pp. 31-50). Hillsdale, NJ: Erlbaum.

Garner, R., & Alexander, P.A. (1989). Metacognition: Answered and unanswered questions. *Educational Psychologist, 24,* 143-158.

Goodman, K. (1986). *What's whole in whole language.* Portsmouth, NH: Heinemann.

Graham, S., & Harris, K.R. (1989). Improving learning disabled students' skills at composing essays: Self-instructional strategy training. *Exceptional Children, 56,* 201-214.

Graham, S., & Harris, K.R. (1994). The effects of whole language on children's writing: A review of literature. *Educational Psychologist, 29,* 187-192.

Graham, S., & Harris, K.R. (1997). It can be taught, but it does not develop naturally: Myths and realities in writing instruction. *School Psychology Review, 26,* 414-424.

Graham, S., & Harris, K.R. (in press). Whole language and process writing: Does one approach fit all? In J. Lloyd, E. Kameenui, & D. Chard (Eds.), *Issues in educating students with disabilities.* Hillsdale, NJ: Erlbaum.

Graham, S., Harris, K.R., MacArthur, C., & Schwartz, S. (1991). Writing and writing instruction with students with learning disabilities: A review of a program of research. *Learning Disabilities Quarterly, 14,* 89-114.

Graham, S., Harris, K.R., & Troia, G. (in press). Writing and self-regulation: cases from the self-regulated strategy development model. In D. Schunk & B. Zimmerman (Eds.), *Developing self-regulated learners: From teaching to self-reflective practices.* New York: Guilford.

Graham, S., & MacArthur, C. (1988). Improving learning disabled students' skills at revising essays produced on a word processor: Self-instructional strategy training. *Journal of Special Education, 22,* 133-152.

Graham, S., MacArthur, C., & Schwartz, S. (1995). The effects of goal setting and procedural facilitation on the revising behavior and writing performance of students with writing and learning problems. *Journal of Educational Psychology, 87,* 230-240.

Graham, S., MacArthur, C., Schwartz, S., & Voth, T. (1992). Improving the compositions of students with learning disabilities using a strategy involving product and process goal setting. *Exceptional Children, 58,* 322-335.

Graves, D. (1985). All children can write. *Learning Disability Focus, 1,* 36-43.

Harris, K.R. (1982). Cognitive-behavior modification: Application with exceptional students. *Focus on Exceptional Children, 15,* 1-16.

Harris, K.R., & Graham, S. (1985). Improving learning disabled students' composition skills: Self-control strategy training. *Learning Disability Quarterly, 8,* 27-36.

Harris, K.R., & Graham, S. (1992). Self-regulated strategy development: A part of the writing process. In M. Pressley, K. Harris, & J. Guthrie (Eds.), *Promoting Academic Competence and Literacy in Schools.* San Diego: Academic Press.

Harris, K.R., & Graham, S. (1994). Constructivism: Principles, paradigms, and integration. *Journal of Special Education, 28,* 275-289.

Harris, K.R., & Graham, S. (1996a). *Making the writing process work: Strategies for composition and self-regulation.* Cambridge, MA: Brookline Books.

Harris, K.R., & Graham, S. (1996b). Memo to constructivists: Skills count, too. *Educational Leadership, 53,* 26-29.

Harris, K.R., Graham, S., Reid, R., McElroy, K., & Hamby, R. (1994). Self-monitoring of attention versus self-monitoring of performance: Replication and cross-task comparison studies. *Learning Disability Quarterly, 17,* 121-139.

Harris, K.R., Graham, S., & Schmidt, T. (1997). *Self-regulated strategy development: Two decades of classroom-based research.* Manuscript submitted for publication.

Harris, K.R., & Pressley, M. (1991). The nature of cognitive strategy instruction: Interactive strategy instruction. *Exceptional Children, 57,* 392-404.

Licht, B. (1983). Cognitive-motivational factors that contribute to the achievement of learning-disabled children. *Journal of Learning Disabilities, 16,* 483-490.

MacArthur, C., Schwartz, S., & Graham, S. (1991). Effects of a reciprocal peer revision strategy in special education classrooms. *Learning Disabilities Research and Practice, 6,* 201-210.

MacArthur, C., Schwartz, S., Graham, S., Molloy, D., & Harris, K.R. (1996). Integration of strategy instruction into a whole language classroom: A case study. *Learning Disabilities Research & Practice, 11,* 168-176.

Manning, M., & Manning, G. (1995). Whole language: They say, you say. *Teaching preK-8, 25,* 50-55.

McIntyre, E., & Pressley, M. (1996). *Balanced instruction: Strategies and skills in whole language.* Norwood, MA: Christopher-Gordon.

Plimpton, G. (Ed.) (1989). *Writers at work: The Paris Review Interviews* (3rd series). New York: Viking Press.

Pressley, M., Harris, K.R., & Marks, M. (1992). But good strategy instructors are constructivists!! *Educational Psychology Review, 4,* 3-31.

Pressley, M., & Rankin, J. (1994). More about whole language methods of reading instruction for students at risk for early reading failure. *Learning Disabilities Research and Practice, 9,* 157-168.

Pressley, M., Rankin, J., & Yokoi, L. (in press). A survey of instructional practices of primary teachers nominated as effective in promoting literacy. *Elementary School Journal.*

Sawyer, R., Graham, S., & Harris, K.R. (1992). Direct teaching, strategy instruction, and strategy instruction with explicit self-regulation: Effects on learning disabled students' compositions and self-efficacy. *Journal of Education Psychology, 84,* 340-352.

Scardamalia, M., & Bereiter, C. (1986). Written composition. In M. Wittrock (Ed.), *Handbook of research on teaching* (3rd ed., pp. 778-803). New York: Macmillan.

Sexton, M., Harris, K.R., & Graham, S. (in press). The effects of self-regulated strategy development on essay writing and attributions of students with LD in a process writing setting. *Exceptional Children.*

Tanhouser, S. (1994). *Function over form: The relative efficacy of self-instructional strategy training alone and with procedural facilitation for adolescents with learning disabilities.* Unpublished doctoral dissertation, Johns Hopkins University.

Troia, G., Graham, S., & Harris, K.R. (1997). Teaching planning strategies to students with writing and learning problems. Manuscript submitted for publication.

Willis, S. (1993). Whole language in the '90s. *ASCD Update, 35*(9), 1-8.

Wong, B., Butler, D., Ficzere, S., Corden, M., & Zelmer, J. (1994). Teaching problem learners revision skills and sensitivity to audience through two instructional modes: Student-teacher versus student-student interactive dialogues. *Learning Disabilities Research and Practice, 9,* 78-90.

CHAPTER FIVE

Mathematics Instruction in Diverse Classrooms

MARJORIE MONTAGUE, University of Miami

Nearly 10 years have passed since the publication of the *Curriculum and Evaluation Standards for School Mathematics* (National Council of Teachers of Mathematics [NCTM], 1989). This document, along with *Everybody Counts,* a report from the National Research Council (Mathematical Sciences Education Board [MSEB], 1989) and NCTM's *Professional Standards for Teaching Mathematics* (NCTM, 1991) set the stage for the curriculum reform movement in mathematics education that is currently underway. At the same time, other curricular areas were also responding to the call for educational reform (American Association for the Advancement of Science, 1989; Bradley Commission on History in the Schools, 1988; National Center for History in the Schools, 1992; National Commission on Social Studies in the Schools, 1989). Reform efforts such as these are frequently responses to trends and changes in society (Pugach & Warger, 1996a).

The current curricular reform movement is part of the response to the diversity that is becoming more evident in our nation's schools. In 1992, 50 of the 99 largest school districts in the United States enrolled about 23% of all students in our nation's schools, and over 50% of these were minority students (Nieto, 1996). The Sixteenth Annual Report to Congress on the Implementation of the Individuals with Disabilities Act (U.S. Department of Education, 1994) indicated that approximately 95% of students in special education received their education in regular school buildings during the 1991-92 school year. Of this number, 35% were served in regular classes and 36% were served in resource rooms. The increasing diversity of students in general education programs—due largely to changing demographics and the inclusion of students with disabilities—places a great responsibility on teachers to understand student variations in ability, achievement, motivation, and behavior, and to make curricular and instructional adaptations to increase learning opportunities for all students.

Another trend influencing curricular reform in the schools involves the changing expectations of the nation's work force. Technology has rapidly altered manufacturing and is now the primary basis for economic advancement. As a result, education has been charged with developing curricula that prepare students for a fast-paced technological and knowledge-driven society. In this age of information, workers must be able to think analytically and creatively, communicate effectively in diverse communities, and work cooperatively with others to solve problems and complete tasks (Allington, 1995; Darling-Hammond, 1993; Pugach & Warger, 1996b). The NCTM and MSEP recommendations highlight the need to develop mathematics competencies that clearly lead to improved problem-solving ability and technological literacy.

Researchers and practitioners have begun to address the NCTM and MSEB recommendations by making changes in mathematics content, pedagogy, learning experiences, time allocation, and testing or evaluation (e.g., Owens, 1993). The content of the mathematics curriculum is shifting to include a greater emphasis on conceptual understanding, mathematical reasoning, and problem solving. Pedagogy, as underscored by the move toward constructivism, encourages teacher facilitation and scaffolded instruction, thus replacing antiquated, didactic instructional models. Learning experiences focus on communicating about mathematics, solving problems cooperatively, using manipulatives to enhance conceptual learning, and incorporating calculators and other technology into daily routines. Less time is being allocated to paper-and-pencil drill and practice exercises, allowing more time for interactive problem solving and mathematical reasoning activities. Finally, assessment and evaluation of mathematical learning is embracing more authentic measures of student progress related to both academic and real-life experiences.

The purpose of this chapter is to describe effective instruction in mathematics that addresses the diversity of learners in inclusive, general education classrooms. First, several issues concerning students, teachers, the mathematics curriculum, and instructional models and procedures are discussed. Then, research findings associated with mathematics educational reform are presented as they relate to outcome expectations. These expectations provide the rationale for using a variety of techniques and strategies to enhance mathematical learning by developing conceptual, declarative, algorithmic, and strategic knowledge.

Finally, several principles are identified to help mathematics teachers improve their ability and skills in meeting the needs of diverse learners in general education classrooms. Illustrations of effective mathematics instruction that reflect each principle are provided. Classroom management and motivational strategies are presented and discussed as they complement procedures and techniques that enhance the mathematical development of all students. The focus is on developing mathematical skills and concepts while teaching students to become proficient mathematical problem solvers.

STUDENT, TEACHER, CURRICULUM, AND INSTRUCTIONAL ISSUES

The following questions pertaining to students and teachers of mathematics, the mathematics curriculum, and instructional models and procedures are posed to provoke dialogue about reform in mathematics education.

- What does diversity in the classroom mean?
- What types of students can teachers expect to meet in their

general mathematics classes?

- How do teachers perceive the diversity in their classes?
- Should additional preparation at the preservice or in-service level be required of teachers?
- Should teachers be required to implement new and innovative programs without additional support and resources?
- Are the curriculum and the instructional procedures appropriate for all students, or must adaptations be made? Who makes the adaptations if needed?
- How can teachers overcome their biases with respect to student differences, curricular shifts, and style of teaching?
- Can teachers meet the diverse needs of their students on their own, or is collaboration with other teachers or support personnel necessary?
- Who has ultimate responsibility for the students in a diverse classroom? Should teachers be held accountable for the performance of all students in the diverse classroom?
- What are the expectations as diverse classrooms and mathematics reform become more common in today's schools?
- How does effective change occur?

Nearly all of these questions are addressed in this chapter. None are fully answered, however, because we are only beginning to understand and evaluate diversity and reform in our schools.

The Students

The students in a diverse mathematics classroom have a range of characteristics that either enhance or hinder their mathematics learning. They represent a multitude of backgrounds and bring to the classroom a variety of experiences. The majority of students will be average-achieving and will generally need little in the way of curricular adaptations or specialized instructional techniques. Some students will be high-achieving or even gifted in mathematics and may require more challenging tasks and activities. Other students, however, may generally perform poorly in mathematics due to cultural and linguistic differences, impoverished backgrounds, or cognitive disorders. Historically, females, African-Americans, Latinos, and economically disadvantaged students have performed poorly in mathematics. As a result, they are under-represented in mathematics programs in colleges and in positions that require mathematical ability (Maple & Strange, 1991). In addition to these low-performing students are students with mild to moderate mathematical disabilities who are underachieving in mathematics. These students typically require curricular and instructional modifications to succeed in mathematics classes.

Enright (1989) identified several categories of students that teachers will find in diverse classrooms. For example, educationally disadvantaged students often display limited mathematics vocabulary, experience difficulty shifting from one computation to another, comprehend only surface meanings in word problems, have low motivation, and do not achieve to their ability level. In contrast, students with learning disabilities frequently perform unevenly and inconsistently, demonstrate gaps in mathematics skills, are easily distracted and often off-task, have difficulty remembering words and their meanings as well as math facts, and experience considerable difficulty solving mathematical problems. There is a wide range of student characteristics in a typical diverse classroom. Thus, the first task for teachers of mathematics is to identify the characteristics of students in their classes and, as they implement the curriculum, make adjustments as needed to achieve a maximum match between learner characteristics and the curriculum.

To illustrate, let us take a look at Mr. Hunt's sixth-grade mathematics class, which has 32 students enrolled. Among these students are four students who have been identified as having learning disabilities and/or emotional and behavioral problems. English was not the first language for approximately one third of the students in the class; in fact, two students are recent immigrants and are just learning English. The students vary considerably in their ability, achievement, motivation, English proficiency, social skills, and mathematical knowledge levels (conceptual, declarative, procedural, and strategic). The primary challenge that Mr. Hunt faces is how to provide the opportunity for all students to benefit.

Mr. Hunt's school had adopted a specific problem-solving model as a means for meeting the challenges of diversity in the classrooms. The school team members had agreed on using an approach termed *curriculum-centered collaborative consultation*—a model in which the curriculum, rather than the student, becomes the source of the identified problem (Warger & Pugach, 1996; Pugach & Warger, 1996b). The school team members had also decided that the collaboration team would consist of general, special, and bilingual education teachers. Professionals representing other areas of expertise would be enlisted on an as-needed basis.

Mr. Hunt met with Ms. Garcia, the learning disabilities specialist, and Mr. Hernandez, the bilingual education specialist, for an hour every week to make decisions about how to tailor the curriculum so that all students in the general mathematics class could benefit from instruction. The collaborative consultation process, as proposed by Pugach and Warger (1993), consists of four phases: (a) orientation, (b) problem identification, (c) intervention, and (d) closure.

During the orientation phase, the team became familiar with the curriculum, the expected outcomes for the students, and Mr. Hunt's teaching style. Mr. Hunt provided the team with data he had collected on his class. He had devoted the first few weeks of school to ascertaining the strengths and weaknesses of the students in his class and noting the problems that students seemed to have given the standard curriculum. He decided that one student, Sara, typified the types of problems that many students were experiencing. Sara was in the learning-disabilities program and was mainstreamed for mathematics. Her reading level and mathematical computation scores both tested out at about the fourth-grade level. In the cooperative problem-solving groups, Sara seemed distracted and uninterested. She rarely contributed to the group even when prompted by Mr. Hunt, who noticed that most students were having difficulty interacting with one another. His evaluation was that they needed the direction of the teacher to engage in the problem-solving process. They did not seem to know how to talk about mathematical problems, and usually used a trial-and-error approach to solve them. Often, they complained that the problems were too hard and simply gave up. Many did not seem to have the social skills or the mathematical skills to be successful with the mathematics program.

During the problem identification phase, the team reviewed the curriculum, specifically focusing on Mr. Hunt's goals for the following week. The primary goal was to have students work in groups of four to solve multi-step word problems having to do with the perimeter and area of rectangles. The team identified three potential problems that could prevent the students from meeting the goal:

- Students might lack the mathematical problem-solving strategies necessary to solve the problems.
- Students might lack the social skills needed to work in cooperative groups.
- Students might lack the persistence and motivation needed to complete the problem-solving activities.

Mr. Hunt, Ms. Garcia, and Mr. Hernandez decided that they needed a strategy to remedy the problems they anticipated. As teachers, they accepted their responsibility to deal effectively with the diversity in Mr. Hunt's general mathematics classes. They also knew that teaching in diverse classrooms was not an easy task, and that this challenge was not unique to their school. They decided to do some reading to discover how other teachers felt about this challenge and how they were coping with diversity.

The Teachers

In a synthesis of 28 studies of teacher perceptions of mainstreaming (including students with disabilities in general education classes), Scruggs and Mastropieri (1996) found that about two thirds of general education teachers were in favor of inclusion. Yet although at least half of the teachers felt that inclusion could be beneficial for students, only about one third of the teachers felt they had enough time, skills, training, or resources needed for inclusion to be effective for their classes. This finding is consistent with recent studies in which teachers identified several barriers to successful inclusion, such as large class size and inadequate preparation and resources (Houck & Rogers, 1994; Vaughn, Schumm, Jallad, Slusher, & Saumell, 1996).

Teachers whose classes include children with disabilities have repeatedly reported needs associated with time, training, support personnel, materials, class size, and type of disability (Scruggs & Mastropieri, 1996). Across studies there is general agreement that at least one hour per day is needed for planning, that intensive training in classroom management and curricular modifications is required, that class size should not exceed 20 students, that more materials and equipment are necessary, and that students with severe disabilities are particularly challenging in the general education setting.

Additional resources and support could have a positive impact on teacher attitudes and perceptions of inclusion. The collaborative model of providing educational programs for students seems to be effective in meeting the challenge of diversity in the classroom (Aldinger, Warger, & Eavy, 1991). A study of 628 general and special education teachers and administrators from 32 school sites that provided heterogeneous educational opportunities indicated that, overall, the educators believed the inclusion model could be successful through collaborative relationships among all educators (Villa, Thousand, Meyers, & Nevin, 1996). For mathematics reform to be successful in diverse classrooms, general and special educators and bilingual education specialists must work together in planning and delivering instruction. Resources must be used efficiently and effectively as teachers collaborate and cooperate in planning and implementing curricular adaptations, instructional modifications, and classroom accommodations. Assessment should be a cooperative endeavor to identify and address the strengths and weaknesses of students. A team approach helps teachers develop the knowledge and skills needed to implement and evaluate mathematics instruction for their students.

After reviewing the literature, Mr. Hunt's team was gratified to know that other teachers were feeling as frustrated as they did at times. They also knew that administrative support was crucial to effective instruction for diverse learners. Because they had a cooperative team in place, Mr. Hunt knew the mathematics curriculum, Ms. Garcia and Mr. Hernandez were specialists in teaching diverse learners, and they were using curriculum-centered collaboration as their model, they felt that they could make mathematics a positive learning experience for all of the students in Mr. Hunt's class.

The Curriculum

The NCTM *Standards* (1989) set goals for mathematics education that require fundamental changes in curriculum. The goals focus on developing students' conceptual understanding of mathematics, improving their ability to communicate about mathematics, and increasing their understanding of mathematical problems and strategies for solving them. A curriculum that reflects these goals would emphasize deep conceptual understanding rather than rote computational skills, innovative problem solving rather than simple computational exercises disguised as word problems, flexibility in doing mathematics, and novel uses of mathematical tools.

Conceptual understanding is the foundation for the acquisition of declarative and procedural knowledge in mathematics. For example, an understanding of the concepts underlying addition and subtraction facilitates learning computational facts and algorithms for those operations. As children engage in mathematical activities using manipulatives and symbols, they develop the ability to think conceptually, mentally represent problem situations, and construct new knowledge that extends their mathematical knowledge base (Davis & Maher, 1996; Montague, 1996b). Real-world problem solving becomes the basis for developing strategic knowledge, a critical cornerstone of effective problem solving.

Curriculum reform in mathematics is based on the premise that the type of thinking involved in mathematics relies on several skills—the ability to understand and represent problem situations; to organize and classify relevant information; to draw upon relevant mathematical knowledge and know where, when, how, and why to apply that knowledge; to explain the concepts underlying problem solutions, and to explain why certain procedures are used. The traditional mathematics curriculum is based on rote acquisition of declarative and procedural knowledge without much regard for conceptual and strategic knowledge. The new curriculum is much more relevant to real-world experiences. With this new curriculum, the emphasis is on teaching students to use the mathematics they are learning in their everyday lives.

According to Pugach and Warger (1996b), numerous developments have been observed as teachers move toward the new curriculum. Teachers are covering less material in more depth; teaching concepts rather than facts or skills; facilitating learning; linking ideas across subject areas; building on students' prior knowledge; creating authentic learning activities; teaching basic skills in the context of meaningful activities; using cooperative learning techniques; focusing on problem solving; and seeing the relationships among assessment, curriculum, and instruction.

The Instruction

As the curriculum changes to meet the needs of a changing society, so must methods of instruction. The traditional model—in which a teacher first shows students how to do the problem and then provides time for drill and practice—does not meet the educational needs of most learners. In addition, this approach limits creative thinking, a skill which is heavily emphasized in new curriculum standards (Woodward & Baxter, 1997). Thus, there is a need for instructional models and approaches that accommodate the new standards as well as diversity in the mathematics classroom.

Pressley and McCormick (1995) contend that explicit teaching in the context of multi-component instruction is necessary for many students to become proficient problem solvers. The multi-component approach includes varying types of instruction, including constructivism, group investigation, scientific inquiry methods, mnemonic instruction, and explicit instruction. Mercer, Jordan, and Miller (1996) provided a continuum of explicit to implicit instruction in mathematics by describing the degree and intensity of teacher assistance, the level of student independence, and the typical content that characterizes each type of instruction. In their view, by selecting elements of each type, instruction will incorporate sound techniques such as (a) scaffolded instruction that could hasten students' acquisition of basic skills and mathematical concepts and relationships, (b) teacher and student interaction during instruction, (c) dialogues about mathematics and problem solving, and (d) guided discovery in which the teacher facilitates rather than directs learning.

Traditional approaches to mathematics instruction have not been very effective for low-achieving students and students with learning disabilities. Two studies of traditional approaches conducted in third- and fourth-grade and middle-school classes compared a typical basal series and a commercially available direct instruction program for teaching subtraction. Of the 143 students, 15 elementary and all 10 middle-school students were enrolled in learning disabilities programs. All students were categorized as low-, average-, or high-achieving based on the results of a group achievement test.

Results of a computerized error analysis program indicated that these students—and particularly the low achievers—performed inconsistently on computational problems following instruction, seemed to plateau at about 70% correct, and committed various types of errors as the task demands changed (Woodward, Baxter, & Scheel, 1997). As the low-achieving elementary students progressed through the curriculum, their error patterns shifted from simple inversions of numbers when regrouping to errors with zeros and multiple borrows. The middle-school students (all of whom had learning disabilities) had more computational subtraction skills at the outset of the study and did well with simple subtraction. By the end of the school year, however, they evidenced the same types of errors with zeros and borrowing as the low-achieving elementary students. Additionally, student interviews showed that the middle school students had little conceptual knowledge about subtraction (e.g., place value, the role of zero) and showed poor word-problem-solving skills (e.g., extracting numbers without reading the problem, reacting impulsively, and failing to correct their responses even when evidence clearly indicated that they were wrong). The basal series and the direct instruction program produced similar results, suggesting that both traditional methods focus on functional rather than conceptual explanations.

In their study of an innovative mathematics curriculum, *Everyday Mathematics* (Bell, Bell, & Hartfield, 1993), Woodward and Baxter (1997) found that the program generally benefited students, but that average and high achievers made relatively greater progress than low-achieving students. The program used a curriculum and pedagogical techniques that reflected the NCTM standards. Woodward and Baxter suggested that although the new curriculum and pedagogy may be necessary, and seemed sufficient to have a positive impact on typical learners, they may be insufficient to make the same kinds of differences for students who have difficulty in mathematics.

To address the needs of the diverse population of students in mathematics classrooms, Woodward, Baxter, and Scheel (1997) recommend using an instructional assistance model that fits with the new curriculum and pedagogy. According to these researchers, classrooms should be organized so that grouping of students is flexible and there is ample opportunity for students to interact and discuss problems; also, instruction should focus on central concepts and exercises that reinforce the concepts rather than on fragmented series of skills. Further, they maintained (as do the NCTM standards) that students should learn calculator skills. They suggest that calculators be used daily in class to solve real-world problems that may be approached in multiple ways and require considerably more time to solve than typical textbook problems. In this model, teachers would provide ongoing scaffolded instruction in communication skills and plenty of practice, feedback, and success on selected mathematical exercises and activities.

As teachers become more comfortable with this new approach to the mathematics curriculum, we should expect that (a) teachers will feel more capable of meeting the needs of all the students in their classroom and be more successful in doing so and (b) students will be more motivated and successful mathematical problem solvers. To achieve these goals, teachers must be willing to change the way they teach mathematics. A bottom-up approach to change—in which teachers volunteer to participate as collaborators or change agents— seems to be more appealing to teachers and, thus, more effective than the top-down approach, in which the school administration requires teachers to participate (Englert, 1996). With this approach to change, teachers become empowered and initiate new programs, techniques, and instructional strategies in their classrooms. Teachers collaborate and consult with one another or with university researchers using action research principles to investigate the effectiveness of these programs and techniques. The primary benefit of teachers serving as researchers is that the research findings can be immediately translated into practice (Clouthier & Shandola, 1993).

Even with this new approach to mathematics instruction, students who perform poorly will need explicit instruction in mathematical skills and strategies. Harris and Graham (1996) have advocated integrating explicit instruction for students who need it into a constructivist framework—one in which learning occurs in communities of active learners who are both self-regulating and self-directed. The beginning point in a constructivist learning community is the learner's prior knowledge and experience in a given domain. Presented with relevant activities and authentic experiences in mathematics, the learners construct new knowledge and acquire new expertise.

This model seems to be consistent with the NCTM standards and provides the basis for realizing many of the goals set by NCTM. However, many students, by virtue of their limited backgrounds (often exacerbated by cognitive, language, behavioral, social, and emotional difficulties) will not be able to function independently in such environments without additional supports. By using a variety of approaches, techniques, and strategies—including explicit instruction for students who need it—teachers should be able to accommodate all students in a diverse classroom and assist students in developing their conceptual understanding of mathematics.

KEY PRINCIPLES FOR EFFECTIVE MATHEMATICS INSTRUCTION

This section presents several principles that help to guide practitioners as they instruct students in diverse mathematics classrooms. These principles are important because they focus on understanding how students learn and how to engage them in learning. Even the best curriculum will be ineffective if instruction is poor. Teachers who know and understand the curriculum, and who use sound instructional principles to teach students, have a greater chance to benefit all students. Thus, it is important that teachers

1. understand and accommodate diversity in general education classrooms;
2. use a positive approach in the classroom;
3. use functional assessment to identify student strengths and weaknesses;
4. adapt the curriculum to meet the needs of students;
5. select the most appropriate and effective instructional strategies;
6. decide between individual, small-group, or whole-class instruction; and
7. monitor student progress, making modifications when necessary.

Following a brief discussion of each principle, scenarios are described that illustrate common problems teachers face in diverse mathematics classes and some possible solutions to the problems.

Principle 1: Understand and Accommodate Diversity in General Education Classrooms

Research suggests that teachers currently have limited understanding of diversity in their classrooms and, as a result, do little to accommodate the range of physical, psychological, and social-emotional attributes of their students (Hocutt, 1996). Students differ widely in cognitive ability, learning style, knowledge base, achievement, motivation, social behavior, and interests. It is important for teachers to become aware of the diversity of their students, to accept their students' differences, and to use techniques and strategies that have proven effective in improving outcomes for students. Dealing with diversity is often frustrating for teachers. The following scenario describes what Mr. Sanders, an experienced fourth-grade teacher, does to understand and accommodate the range of learners in his class.

Mr. Sanders takes the first week or two of each new school year to become acquainted with his students. This year, his class includes a diverse group of 28 students. Mr. Sanders first assesses the students to determine their mathematical levels. Early on in this assessment process, Mr. Sanders realizes that there is considerable diversity— even beyond the three students who are in the ESL program, the two students with learning disabilities, the gifted student who has an attention deficit disorder, and the student in the developmental disabilities program. Several of the other students appear to be low achievers, and some seem to be functioning well above the beginning fourth-grade level in some areas. Two students seem to be inordinately hostile, and many students have difficulty staying on task. Two students are noticeably isolated by their classmates, but there are also a couple of emerging class leaders. Tailoring the curriculum, instructional procedures, and learning environment to meet the needs of all these students will indeed be a challenge.

Mr. Sanders selects several informal assessment tools and techniques. These include paper-and-pencil tasks as well as interactive and application tasks and exercises. He then assesses the students' computational skills, conceptual understanding, mathematical vocabulary and expression, problem-solving strategies, measurement and estimation abilities, and competence in using manipulatives, calculators, and computers. During these activities, he also keeps track of students' affective behaviors, compliance with classroom standards or rules, and social interactions with other students and himself.

Mr. Sanders values goal-oriented teaching and learning and the development of self-regulated learners. He realizes that management systems must support instructional systems, and he understands the importance of socializing students to function successfully within the diverse classroom (cf. Brophy, 1996). A well-managed classroom in which students know the expectations and limits is the foundation for an effective and flexible learning community. Research-based classroom management principles and procedures set the stage for mathematics instruction that stresses conceptual understanding and applications.

A teacher must establish procedural guidelines that reflect academic and social goals, while fostering a cooperative classroom spirit and individual student pride. Keeping in mind the strengths and needs of his students, Mr. Sanders selects from several instructional formats that reflect the new approach to teaching mathematics. These formats include interactive lectures to introduce new concepts, mathematical discussion groups to increase use of mathematical vocabulary and improve communication about mathematics, cooperative problem-solving groups to explore alternative solutions to challenging mathematical problems, computer dyads for reinforcing skills and concepts, and investigative triads to do research in mathematics and to engage in authentic mathematical applications. As needed, Mr. Sanders provides small-group instruction in skills and concepts that some students have not mastered. He also provides mathematics enrichment activities for students who have shown mastery.

Mr. Sanders promotes a climate of trust and cooperation. He discusses the benefits associated with each instructional format before trying it out with his students. Using Brophy's (1996, p. 17) "informational style of presenting guidelines," he explains the reasons for the guidelines he uses. ("Use low voices during your problem-solving groups. There will be at least three groups meeting at the same time. All group members need to be able to hear what the other members are saying.") Second, he establishes a cueing system for reminding students to remind themselves to follow the guidelines, and he phrases the reminders in a friendly, positive manner. The cues are both auditory and visual, and are posted in the classroom. ("It's math concept time. Clear your desk, put away your pencil, close your eyes, and think about the concepts you have learned. Be ready to tell the class.") Third, for students who repeatedly transgress, he uses a procedure that redirects students and is productive. ("Juan, you are talking too loudly. Go to the Remember the Guidelines area, write Guideline 3 two times, and then try using the Guideline with your group.")

Mr. Sanders' goal is to teach students how to function successfully within a community that is supportive and cooperative and that sets expectations for all its participants. Teaching students how to regulate their behavior and accept responsibility for behaving in a way that will enhance their learning is fundamental to instruction.

Principle 2: Use a Positive Approach in the Classroom

Children who display behaviors that deviate from the norm receive a higher proportion of negative to positive teacher feedback than other students do (Lago-Delello, 1996). This places many children with learning, behavior, and emotional problems in jeopardy in general education classrooms. Positive programming for students who are low-performing, disruptive, or low in motivation can be very powerful if it is implemented correctly and consistently. On the other side, negative feedback can be deleterious to students' classroom performance as well as self-esteem. A supportive classroom that provides many opportunities for children to receive positive reinforcement is critical for learning.

Verbal praise and positive feedback have been shown to enhance students' intrinsic interest in tasks and activities (Cameron & Pierce, 1994). When interest had been established, it seemed to be maintained by most students even after the reinforcers were withdrawn. A curious finding in this research is that rewards can impact *negatively* on intrinsic motivation and performance when they are offered simply for task completion, rather than for meeting preset standards of performance. Thus, reinforcement programs must be carefully planned to ensure successful performance rather than simple task completion.

A classroom climate that focuses on cooperation rather than competition, and that teaches students how to set learning goals and evaluate their own achievement, can help students develop flexibility in learning and recognize their effort and progress (Schunk, 1996). Students should be taught to set *learning goals* rather than *performance goals* (e.g., to learn how to solve problems rather than simply to get an answer to a specific problem). They should also be taught to evaluate their performance and reward themselves when they do well. Teaching students to aim for a "personal best" rather than compete with other students can improve self-efficacy and personal achievement (Montague, 1992). Ms. Walker, a sixth-grade teacher, uses three basic steps to teach her students to set learning goals and monitor their own performance. In the following example, Ms. Walker assisted one student, Janice, who was having difficulty with mathematics.

- The first step involves assessment, goal setting, and explicit instruction. Ms. Walker reviewed Janice's baseline performance with her. Then, based on their review of Janice's mathematical problem solving, they set realistic goals. It appeared that Janice simply extracted numbers from word problems and then added or subtracted haphazardly. Ms. Walker's first goal was to teach Janice how to paraphrase mathematical word problems by "saying the problem in a different way." She explicitly taught Janice how to paraphrase problems, and then reviewed the strategy with the entire class.

She provided activities to practice paraphrasing—including tape-recording the paraphrases, using paper and pencil, using a word processor, and working with a partner to rephrase the problems orally or in writing. Janice's first personal goal was to learn how to paraphrase two one-step problems successfully each day for a week.

- The second step involves monitoring progress toward the goal. Janice's progress was monitored daily using a graph. (If Janice did not make *any* progress, the goal would have been adjusted.) Grades can be awarded for meeting personal goals.

- When the criterion for the goal is met, another goal should be selected that extends current learning. Janice was praised for meeting her goal and given a star to put on her "ladder of effort and success." She then moved on to a more challenging goal. She kept her graphs and "ladder" in her "Personal Best" folder.

Several general "rules of thumb" should be followed in the mathematics classroom. These "rules" should be used consistently to reinforce effort, productivity, and learning (Montague, 1997). To illustrate these principles, let us return to Mr. Hunt's sixth-grade mathematics class. This class is quite diverse in ability and achievement, and the students do not seem to have the knowledge and skills needed to engage in cooperative problem solving activities.

- Teach students how to try hard and use new strategies to improve performance and goal attainment. After students solve a problem, discuss how the strategy was useful in reaching that solution. Periodically, have the students tell how strategies are useful in solving mathematical problems.

    For example, Mr. Hunt taught his students to draw pictures to represent the perimeter and area problems they were working on. Students within each problem-solving group drew pictures independently for each of the practice problems and then took turns explaining one another's illustrations, giving positive feedback and suggestions for improvement. They were given grades for completing and discussing the drawings. Then the students independently solved a problem. The students voted on the best solution and explained why they thought it was the best.

- Teach students how to articulate the effort they expend as they solve problems; relate progress to effort and convey a positive tone (e.g., "You worked a long time on that problem, and you solved it well. Tell me what you did to solve it.").

Mr. Hunt taught his students how to monitor and evaluate their performance—by self-recording their progress on graphs in their portfolios and, for each recording, making a brief note explaining why they performed as they did.

- Teach students to self-instruct and self-regulate by slowing down, telling themselves what to do, backing up, and correcting themselves when they are unsure or "something feels wrong." ("I do not know if I should add or subtract. Let me see. I will go back and read the first sentence and draw a picture to show the meaning. Then I will read the next sentence," and so forth.)

Mr. Hunt realized that his students did not use self-regulation strategies well, so he taught students to "talk through" the problems as they solved them. He taught them to give themselves instructions, ask themselves questions, and then check that they had done everything correctly. Students were also taught to ask for help if they needed it.

- Teach students to reinforce themselves for all activities associated with good problem solving, such as setting goals, using strategies, asking questions, communicating with other students about the problems, using manipulatives when appropriate, and attributing success to effort and failure to lack of effort.

After the students in Mr. Hunt's class recorded their progress notes, they explained them to the other members of their groups. The group then helped each student decide on a realistic progress grade and rewards for using strategies and expending effort.

- Teach students to demonstrate effective problem solving for other students and to ask good questions about problem solving.

   When the students in Mr. Hunt's class learned the problem-solving strategies, they took turns demonstrating good problem solving for the class. The students were taught to think aloud (*cognitive modeling*) as they demonstrated solving the problem. They used an overhead projector to show their work as they talked through the problem. The other students in the class used the "TAG" strategy to facilitate interaction: *Tell* what you liked about the problem solution. *Ask* good questions about the problem and the way it was solved. *Give* suggestions about other ways to solve the problem.

- Teach students to compliment one another for asking good questions, trying hard, and being successful.

   The students in Mr. Hunt's class helped and supported one another as they became good problem solvers. They developed a cooperative rather than competitive spirit and became good at describing the problem-solving strategies they learned and why they were useful.

Principle 3: Use Functional Assessment to Identify Student Strengths and Weaknesses

Functional assessment is a systematic method for identifying academic and personal-social behaviors that may interfere with students' success in the classroom. This assessment method is based on the following assumptions: (a) Understanding the context or setting in which a behavior occurs is important, because the behavior is functionally related to the setting. (b) Each behavior serves a particular function for the student and is gratifying to the extent that the student is reinforced in some way (e.g., negative or positive attention, avoidance of an unpleasant task or situation). (c) Changing the antecedents or consequences in the behavioral sequence changes the behavior. (d) Positive reinforcement is a powerful procedure for teaching new behaviors and extending or maintaining learned behaviors. Foster-Johnson and Dunlap (1993, p. 46) defined functional assessment as a process in which "informed hypothesis statements are developed about relationships between events in the environment and the occurrence of a student's challenging behavior." Functional assessment can be as simple or as complex as time and resources permit; the assessment procedure can be a simple observation followed by a 5-minute interview with the student, or a series of lengthy systematic observations conducted by a trained behavioral analyst. It can focus on classroom behavior, learning strategies and processes, attitudes toward learning, or other student characteristics and behaviors that affect school performance.

For example, Ms. Sosa noticed that several students in her eighth-grade general mathematics class were performing well below other students in solving mathematical word problems. She wanted additional data in order to address their problem-solving strengths and weaknesses, so she decided to functionally assess the students' mathematical problem-solving strategies. Ms. Sosa knew that the information from the assessment would help her select appropriate instructional strategies to improve the performance of these students.

Because it is easy to administer and requires only about 25 minutes to give and score, Ms. Sosa selected the Mathematical Problem Solving Assessment–Short Form (MPSA-SF; Montague, 1996a). The MPSA-SF includes three word problems of increasing complexity in terms of number of operations needed. There are also 10 interview items related to attitude and perception of mathematics and 30 items designed to reveal students' levels of mathematical knowledge (conceptual, declarative, procedural, and strategic). The assessment yields an affective and cognitive profile for each student, providing a graphic display of the student's strengths and weaknesses in mathematical problem solving.

Ms. Sosa used the results of the assessment to guide her instructional decisions for the students. For instance, Elliott's results indicated that he had a relatively poor attitude toward mathematics and used only a few rudimentary problem-solving strategies. He could do computations but often made mistakes. He seemed to have no plan for determining which operations to use to solve problems. Ms. Sosa decided that Elliott needed positive learning experiences in math and a program that builds on his computational strengths. She decided to have another student teach Elliott how to use a fairly sophisticated calculator. Additionally, to address his weaknesses, he received explicit instruction in mathematical problem-solving strategies. In just a few weeks, Ms. Sosa noticed a marked improvement in Elliott's problem solving and general attitude toward mathematics.

Principle 4: Adapt the Curriculum to Meet the Needs of Students

The NCTM's set of recommendations was the impetus for the real changes we are currently witnessing in the mathematics curriculum. The emphasis on developing conceptual understanding, improving communication about mathematics, and creating proficient problem solvers has revolutionized thinking about mathematics instruction. Curricular changes reflect this new conceptualization of mathematics education; basic skills instruction, rote learning, and show-and-do approaches to teaching have been distinctly de-emphasized in the curriculum. NCTM's *Professional Standards for Teaching Mathematics* (1991) presented various instructional suggestions for teachers to use so that all students would "benefit from an opportunity to study the core curriculum specified in the Standards" (NCTM, 1989, p. 253).

After reading about other teachers' experiences in modifying curricula for diverse learners, Mr. Hunt and his team entered the intervention phase of collaborative consultation. In this phase, they discussed alternatives to the standard curriculum that would make material more accessible to students. They identified strategies for modifying the curriculum, made suggestions about support practices and instructional procedures, and developed an implementation plan. As a framework, they decided to use principles suggested by Kameenui, Chard, and Carnine (1996) for designing and enriching the mathematics curriculum for students with diverse needs. These included (a) teaching strategies based on big ideas, (b) using time efficiently, (c) providing clear and explicit instruction, and (d) providing appropriate and sufficient practice and review.

To help students solve multi-step perimeter and area problems, the team's objectives were to teach students (a) problem-solving strategies, (b) appropriate skills for working together in groups, and (c) the concepts associated with perimeter and area. The team decided to follow the suggestions of Kameenui, Chard, and Carnine (1996) and teach fewer objectives more thoroughly, ease into complex strategies and problems, and use a strand organization for lessons (i.e., break the time period into segments that address each objective).

The team of instructors set up a general plan for instruction, allowing for some flexibility. They decided that the first part of each class would focus on teaching cognitive and metacognitive strategies for mathematical problem solving (Montague, 1992; Montague, Applegate, & Marquard, 1993). The students learned how to read, paraphrase, and visualize problems, and how to make hypotheses based on the information provided. Then, they learned how to estimate and compute answers. Finally, they learned a number of techniques for verifying or checking their answers. The metacognitive strategies they learned to use included self-instruction, self-questioning, and self-checking.

The team decided that some time should also be directed at improving students' communication skills. To accomplish this, the problem-solving groups practiced the problem-solving strategies, reviewed the mathematics skills and concepts they learned, and discussed why the strategies, skills, and concepts were important. The last part of each class was devoted to introducing new mathematical skills, concepts, and tools. The team agreed that Ms. Garcia, the special education teacher, should co-teach the class with Mr. Hunt for two days each week, and that once a week, Mr. Hernandez should work with the students who had limited English proficiency to reinforce new mathematics vocabulary.

During the closure phase of collaborative consultation, the team developed an evaluation plan that determined what and how well the students learned, and what other curricular modifications might be necessary to meet the diverse needs of the students. Evaluation techniques included "Personal Best" folders, student interviews, and teacher logs. All of the students in Mr. Hunt's class improved in mathematics. Several became quite proficient in solving mathematical word problems. Mr. Hunt was gratified to see the improvement in interactions among the students; he noticed that they helped one another, worked compatibly and cooperatively, and seemed to enjoy the class environment.

Principle 5: Select the Most Appropriate and Effective Learning and Instructional Strategies

Learning strategies or *cognitive strategies* are defined by Pressley, Forrest-Pressley, Elliott-Faust, and Miller (1995, p. 4) as being "composed of cognitive operations over and above the processes that are a natural consequence of carrying out a task, ranging from one such operation to a sequence of interdependent operations. Strategies achieve cognitive purposes (e.g., memorizing) and are potentially conscious and controllable activities." The cognitive or metacognitive strategies used for mathematical problem solving (e.g., problem representation strategies such as visualization and graphic displays) are controllable. Good problem solvers often access them without thinking about them, especially if the problems are perceived as easy or routine; however, when problems are perceived as difficult or challenging, even good problem solvers will consciously select and apply strategies. Students can be taught to use strategies to facilitate learning. There are domain-specific strategies that are appropriate for academic domains such as reading, writing, science, and mathematics, or for non-academic domains such as running a long-distance race or interacting successfully with peers. In the domain of mathematics, a host of strategies can be taught to help students solve mathematical problems.

Strategic approaches to problem solving are evident even among preschoolers, especially when they are provided with concrete manipulatives such as bottlecaps or discs (e.g., Levine, Jordan, & Huttenlocher, 1992). As children mature, they develop a repertoire of general and domain-specific problem-solving strategies. Mathematical problem solving is a recursive process composed of problem representation and problem execution strategies (Montague & Applegate, 1993). Many students, like Juan, who is in Mr. Hunt's sixth-grade class, do not acquire these strategies naturally, and thus require explicit strategy instruction in mathematical problem solving. To become a proficient problem solver, Juan needs to learn how to represent problems, develop a plan to solve them, execute the plan, and then verify his solution.

When attempting to solve a problem, Juan must first read the problem and understand it. To do this, he may read and then reread the problem, read parts of the problem, underline the important information, circle the numbers and number words, and use other effective reading strategies. Then, Juan must represent the problem through paraphrasing or visualizing. Juan may put the problem into his own words, retell the "story," draw a picture, make a graph or a table, or "see" the problem in his head. Often students will imagine that they are engaged in the activities mentioned in the problem. Based on his representations, Juan must transform the linguistic and numerical information in the problem into algorithmic plans or equations. Throughout the process, he should reflect on his decisions and make "educated" hypotheses about the outcome—logical estimations of the answer that stem from the information provided. Finally, Juan must do computations and verify his solution by checking that the procedures he used were correct, the computations were accurate, and the answer makes sense. If he has any doubts, he can return to the problem at any point in the problem-solving process or ask for help.

In contrast to learning strategies, *instructional strategies* are used by the teacher to foster or enhance student learning. These can range from a particular model of instruction, such as direct instruction, to a specific strategy such as cognitive modeling (in which the teacher thinks aloud as she or he performs a task). To teach students problem-solving strategies, Mr. Hunt needs to select appropriate instructional strategies. Most students with learning, language, or behavioral problems do not learn independently; they need explicit instruction in mathematics vocabulary, skills, concepts, strategies, and communication skills. All students come to the classroom with some prior knowledge of mathematics. However, the observant teacher will recognize the gaps in their knowledge bases and their misconceptions about mathematics. Instructional strategies should be selected that are effective and efficient in helping students to develop new knowledge, concepts, skills, and strategies; to complete partial understandings and knowledge bases; and to replace misconceptions with accurate knowledge.

Strategies such as verbal rehearsal, visualization, and self-regulation techniques can be taught individually or as part of a routine or package (see Montague, 1992; Montague et al., 1993). To teach these strategies, activity-based and interactive instructional formats should be used. It is extremely useful to use cognitive modeling to demonstrate how to think through a problem, as well as various types of practice activities and role playing. The teacher can model strategy recitation and application using an overhead projector, exchange roles with students during demonstration exercises, and give corrective and positive feedback during guided practice. Instructional procedures for strategy application include independent practice, practice in pairs, teacher-student role exchanges, and student demonstration of problem solving using an overhead projector. Systematic reinforcement programs should be implemented for using appropriate social and communication skills in groups and for contributing to group discussions in a positive, team-player manner.

Pressley and McCormick (1995, p. 316) discussed several guidelines for promoting good instruction in mathematics:

- Provide authentic experiences in mathematics that allow students to construct their knowledge and regulate application of concepts and procedures.
- Encourage students to think about mathematics and reflect on their problem solving.
- Provide a variety of manipulatives to promote conceptual understanding and problem representation.
- Teach students how to use calculators and other technology for mathematics.
- Help students understand the symbolic system and the relationships and patterns inherent in mathematics.
- Emphasize mathematical problem solving using word problems from an early age.
- Provide a myriad of everyday examples, activities, and experiences to promote generalization of learning.
- Teach students to ask questions and communicate about mathematics.
- Use different groupings of students to engage them in mathematics.

Principle 6: Decide on Individual, Small-Group, or Whole-class Instruction

Grouping students in a diverse classroom for mathematics instruction that is aligned with the NCTM *Standards* can be difficult. Should whole-class instruction be used, or are small groups better for student learning? Furthermore, if some students need individual attention, how can that instruction be provided within a typical classroom?

Mason and Good (1993) discuss the difference between structural and situational adjustment, two strategies for grouping students for mathematics instruction in diverse elementary classrooms. *Structural adjustment* is predetermined by student achievement levels and occurs before instruction. The structural approach entails placing students in either a high- or a low-achievement group. Instruction varies in content and pace for the two groups, and high-ability students learn higher-level concepts than low-ability students. *Situational adjustment* involves frequent changes in grouping based on student performance following instruction. The situational approach uses a whole-class ad hoc process in which teachers adapt instruction to individual students or small groups following whole-class presentations or active learning activities. All students are provided an opportunity to learn the same content, and then the teacher assesses performance, forms ad hoc groups, and provides remediation and enrichment activities that reflect students' needs.

In a study with upper elementary students in 81 classrooms, Mason and Good (1993) trained teachers to use either the structural or the situational approach. The results indicated that whole-class ad hoc grouping (the situational approach) yielded significantly higher computational scores than within-class ability grouping (the structural approach). The implication is that ongoing assessment is vital to addressing individual student needs, and that groups based on class performance are more beneficial to student learning than fixed-ability groups.

In making grouping decisions, teachers should consider the purpose and goals of the lesson, the resources and constraints of the setting, and the context in which the outcomes are to be performed. The 32 students in Mr. Hunt's class vary considerably in their background knowledge and mathematical achievement, especially with respect to conceptual understanding. This was particularly evident after a lesson on equivalence of fractions. Mr. Hunt's classroom is relatively small, but he does have Ms. Garcia and Mr. Hernandez helping. Mr. Hunt decided to focus on improving students' conceptual understanding of fractional equivalents, first using common fractions and then moving on to decimal fractions. On the days when Ms. Garcia and Mr. Hernandez are unavailable, he decided to hold 35-minute whole-class sessions, then divide students into pairs to complete paper-and-pencil reinforcement exercises for 15 minutes. On the days when another teacher was present, Mr. Hunt decided to form small remedial or enrichment groups and also provide individual instruction. He used a concrete, process-oriented approach, and the outcome measures focused on having students explain and demonstrate equivalency. Real-world experiences such as cooking and science activities were incorporated into the lessons. Mr. Hunt gathered the following books to help him plan activities:

- Ashlock, R.B. (1982). *Error patterns in computation: A semi-programmed approach* (3rd ed.). Columbus, OH: Charles Merrill.
  Provides multiple examples of common computational errors. Using a diagnostic-prescriptive approach, clearly presents procedures for diagnosing and correcting errors.
- Bley, N.S., & Thornton, C.A. (1995). *Teaching mathematics to students with learning disabilities* (3rd ed.). Austin, TX: Pro-Ed.
  Emphasizes problem solving, decision making, and mathematical reasoning. Suggests a variety of adaptations that are appropriate for students with diverse needs in general education classes.
- Cawley, J.F., Fitzmaurice-Hayes, & Shaw, R.A. (1988). *Mathematics for the mildly handicapped: A guide to curriculum and instruction.* Boston: Allyn & Bacon.
  Stresses both concept and skill development with an emphasis on problem solving. Provides multiple suggestions for curriculum adaptations for specific problems in mathematics displayed by students who have learning and attentional difficulties.
- Meltzer, L.J., Roditi, B., Haynes, D., Biddle, K., Paster, M., & Taber, S. (1996). *Strategies for success: Classroom teaching techniques for students with learning problems.* Austin, TX: Pro-Ed.
  Highlights organizational strategies, planning strategies, and specific learning strategies in reading, writing, spelling, and math. Presents procedures for understanding and teaching students with learning and attentional problems, with an emphasis on the learning process.

Principle 7: Monitor Student Progress

Determining how well instruction works for individual students is crucial to meeting learning and instructional goals and achieving desired outcomes. Just as instructional accommodations must be made to meet the needs of all students in a diverse classroom, assessment accommodations must be made as well. Simple accommodations for traditional paper-and-pencil testing—such as using computers for responding, allowing more time to complete tests, providing break time during tests, and giving individual rather than group tests—may provide necessary support for students who have difficulty sustaining attention or need more time to process information.

Curriculum reform necessitates even greater reform in how students are assessed. This is particularly evident in mathematics with the publication of *Assessment Standards for School Mathematics* (NCTM, 1995). These new assessment standards are grounded in the conceptualization that learners construct knowledge by drawing on previous experiences. Although traditional assessment techniques—such as standardized tests or typical classroom paper-and-pencil tests—do provide some information about students' strengths and weaknesses in general areas of mathematics, they fall short in ascertaining students' knowledge bases, learning styles, cognitive processes and strategies, self-concepts, and motivation. Therefore, nontraditional assessment techniques such as performance assessment (Elliott, 1994) and assisted assessment (Campione & Brown, 1987) have begun to supplement or even replace traditional measures of student learning.

Performance assessment is an alternative to traditional techniques for monitoring student progress and evaluating the effects of mathematics instruction. This approach is similar to authentic assessment of performance, in which skills and behaviors are assessed during real-life applications, using real-life tasks, in the context of real-life situations—rather than using only approximations of the task and content (Elliott, 1994). Direct observation and permanent products are the cornerstones of this approach to assessment. Students develop individual portfolios in which they evaluate their performance in school and in other settings using skills and strategies they have learned. These portfolios are supplemented by teacher observations of students working independently or in cooperative groups. Other measures of performance—including questionnaires, informal dialogues, think-aloud activities, audiotapes or videotapes of problem-solving sessions, self-evaluations of performance, teacher and self-evaluations of group interaction skills, error analyses of completed work, error detection and correction exercises, and interviews with peers about the problem-solving process—can be used as well. Several aspects of a mathematics program should be evaluated, including (a) the mathematics that students know and can do, (b) students' dispositions toward mathematics, (c) *program equity,* the assurance that all students have the opportunity to reach their potential in mathematics, and (d) overall program effectiveness in reaching the preset mathematics program goals (Webb & Welsch, 1993).

Assisted assessment, another alternative to traditional assessment, is based on the dynamic assessment or test-teach-retest model (Feuerstein, Miller, & Jensen, 1981; Vygotsky, 1986). Using this approach, the teacher attempts to understand how the learner approaches problem solving and what cognitive processes the learner utilizes to solve the problem. The learner's potential for cognitive change is also assessed. First, students are given a traditional problem-solving pretest. Then, they receive problem-solving instruction and are tested again with maintenance and transfer problems. The goal of assisted assessment is to determine the quantity of instruction and the nature and form of prompts and cues needed for students to be successful and independent problem solvers.

Smaller-scale, individual assisted assessments can be done in 5 to 10 minutes. First, a problem is presented for the student to solve. If the student's solution is incorrect, the teacher and student then solve the problem together. The teacher provides appropriately timed cues and prompts, gathering information about the strengths, limitations, and learning style of the student. In this way, the student eventually solves the problem (a positive experience), and the teacher gains valuable information about the student's problem-solving processes and strategies.

Unlike traditional approaches to assessment, assisted assessment involves considerable and ongoing interaction between students and teachers. Following assessment, the teacher should have a fairly clear idea of each student's cognitive and strategic strengths and weaknesses. This approach has been shown to be as good as or better than standardized measures in predicting academic achievement longitudinally (Guthke & Wingenfeld, 1992; Spector, 1992).

Mr. Hunt wanted to assess whether his students met the preset learning and instructional goals relating to equivalency of common and decimal fractions. He also wanted to be innovative in his approach and use a variety of assessment techniques. Mr. Hunt decided that he would consider students to have mastered the basics of equivalency once they could perform the following tasks:

(a) explain and discuss the meaning of *equivalent* and cite several instances in mathematics when equivalence is used,

(b) explain and discuss how equivalent fractions are the same and how they are different,

(c) demonstrate generalization of the symbolic algorithms from their experiences with manipulatives, and

(d) demonstrate understanding of the ways in which fractions that appear to be very different are the same.

Performance measures gave Mr. Hunt information about how individual students were progressing toward the goals of the mathematics program and provided the information needed to make adjustments in the mathematics curriculum. Assisted assessment enabled Mr. Hunt to identify the type and amount of assistance students needed to solve certain problems.

CONCLUSION

To conclude this chapter, it seems appropriate to return to the questions posed at the beginning of the chapter. Brief responses are presented, in light of the relatively limited information we have about teaching and learning in diverse mathematics classrooms.

What does diversity in the mathematics classroom mean? What types of students can teachers expect to meet in their general mathematics classes?
Diversity in a mathematics classroom means not only that students will have different ethnic and cultural backgrounds, but also that they may have learning and behavioral problems that interfere with performance. Students will vary considerably in their mathematics backgrounds, abilities, and achievements. They will also differ in their interest in, attitude toward, and motivation for doing mathematics. Teachers need to adjust their curricula and instructional approaches to accommodate these individual differences in the classroom.

Should additional preparation at the preservice or in-service level be required of teachers? Should teachers be required to implement new and innovative programs without additional support and resources? Are the curriculum and instructional procedures appropriate for all students, or must adaptations be made? Who makes the adaptations if needed?
Research indicates that teachers generally have a positive attitude toward the concept of inclusion but feel unprepared to deal effectively with the range of student characteristics (Scruggs & Mastropieri, 1996). They feel particularly inexperienced in teaching students with identified disabilities. The solution to this problem is to provide better preservice and in-service education for teachers, as well as better classroom support and resources. Curricular and instructional adaptations should be made by the classroom teacher, often in collaboration with colleagues who have expertise in teaching students with diverse learning needs.

How can teachers overcome their biases with respect to student differences, curricular shifts, and styles of teaching?

Some teachers may be better than others at meeting the diverse needs of the students in their classes because they are better prepared, have a good attitude toward students and their individual differences, and enjoy the challenge of constructing a learning environment in which all students will achieve some level of success. These teachers will continue to strive to improve their teaching, will learn how to adapt their curriculum and instruction, and will seek new and improved methods to enhance learning for their students. Other teachers will need more in-service preparation and direct support to help them structure the classroom and adapt the curriculum and instruction to meet the needs of diverse learners in their classes. Gaining an understanding of the range of characteristics among students and various techniques, as well as instructional strategies that promote learning for students, should help teachers overcome their anxiety and lack of confidence in teaching students with special needs.

Can teachers meet the diverse needs of their students on their own, or is collaboration with other teachers or support personnel necessary?

Some teachers may be able to manage quite well on their own in meeting the individual needs of their students. Other teachers will do much better if they have cooperative and collaborative relationships with one another as they adapt curricula and instruction to enhance learning for students. A structured process, such as the problem-solving model that is the basis for curriculum-centered collaboration, facilitates collaboration and improves instruction in diverse class-rooms (Pugach & Warger, 1996b).

Who has ultimate responsibility for the students in a diverse classroom? Should teachers be held accountable for the performance of all students in the diverse classroom?

Teachers are held responsible for the performance of all students in their classes despite the variance among learners. The new curriculum reforms are responsible for the rethinking of current assessment practice. A greater emphasis is being placed on alternative types of assessment that are performance-based and measure real-life applications. In gauging what children have learned and what they can do, these alternative assessments are more realistic than standardized tests, which have been the traditional method of measuring progress.

What are the desired outcomes as diverse classrooms and mathematics reform become more common in today's schools? How does effective change occur?

Meeting the needs of all students in a diverse classroom requires the dedication and cooperation of administrators, general education teachers, special education teachers, and support personnel. With a focus on curriculum-centered collaborative consultation to address student learning and instructional issues, these key players can set common goals and work together to achieve them.

This discussion has addressed, to a degree at least, nearly all of the questions posed at the beginning of the chapter. No definitive answers were provided, but a direction toward clearer and more complete answers to these questions was established.

REFERENCES

Aldinger, L.E., Warger, C. L., & Eavy, P.W. (1991). *Strategies for teacher collaboration.* Ann Arbor, MI: Exceptional Innovations.

Allington, R.L. (1995). Literacy lessons in the elementary schools: Yesterday, today, and tomorrow. In R.L. Allington & S.A. Walmsley (Eds.), *No quick fix: Rethinking literacy programs in America's elementary schools* (pp. 1-15). New York: Teachers College Press.

American Association for the Advancement of Science (1989). *Science for all Americans: Project 2061.* Washington, DC: Author.

Bell, M., Bell, J., & Hartfield, R. (1993). *Everyday mathematics.* Evanston, IL: Everyday Learning Corporation.

Bradley Commission on History in the Schools (1988). *Building a history curriculum: Guidelines for teaching history in the schools.* Washington, DC: Educational Excellence Network.

Brophy, J. (1996). *Teaching problem students.* New York: Guilford.

Cameron, J., & Pierce, W.D. (1994). Reinforcement, reward, and intrinsic motivation: A meta-analysis. *Review of Educational Research, 64,* 363-423.

Campione, J.C., & Brown, A.L. (1987). Linking dynamic assessment with school achievement. In C.S. Lidz (Ed.), *Dynamic assessment: An interactional approach to evaluating learning potential* (pp. 82-115). New York: Guilford Press.

Clouthier, G., & Shandola, D. (1993). Teacher as researcher. In D.T. Owens (Ed.), *Research ideas for the classroom: Middle grades mathematics* (pp. 319-336). New York: Macmillan.

Darling-Hammond, L. (1993). Reframing the school reform agenda. *Phi Delta Kappan, 74,* 752-761.

Davis, R.B., & Maher, C.A. (1996). A new view of the goals and means for school mathematics. In M.C. Pugach & C.L. Warger (Eds.), *Curriculum trends, special education, and reform: Refocusing the conversation* (pp. 68-83). New York: Teachers College Press.

Elliott, S.N. (1994). *Creating meaningful performance assessments: Fundamental concepts.* Reston, VA: Council for Exceptional Children.

Englert, C.S. (1996, October). *Creating collaborative communities of teachers to support educational change.* Paper presented at the meeting of the International Academy for Research in Learning Disabilities, Detroit, MI.

Enright, B.E. (1989). *Basic mathematics: Detecting and correcting special needs.* Boston: Allyn & Bacon.

Feuerstein, R., Miller, R., & Jensen, M.R. (1981). Can evolving techniques better measure cognitive change? *The Journal of Special Education, 15,* 201-270.

Foster-Johnson, L., & Dunlap, G. (1993). Using functional assessment to develop effective, individualized interventions for challenging behaviors. *Teaching Exceptional Children, 25,* 44-50.

Guthke, J., & Wingenfeld, S. (1992). The learning test concept: Origins, state of the art, and trends. In H.C. Haywood & D. Tzuriel (Eds.), *Interactive assessment* (pp. 64-93). New York: Springer-Verlag.

Harris, K.R., & Graham, S. (1996). Constructivism and students with special needs: Issues in the classroom. *Learning Disabilities Research and Practice, 11,* pp. 134-137.

Hocutt, A. (1996). The effectiveness of special education: Is placement the critical factor? *Monographs of the Center for the Future of Children, 56.* Los Altos, CA: The Lucile Packard Foundation.

Houck, C.K., & Rogers, C.J. (1994). The special/general education integration initiative for students with specific learning disabilities: A "snapshot" of program change. *Journal of Learning Disabilities, 27,* 435-453.

Kameenui, E.J., Chard, D.J., & Carnine, D.W. (1996). The new school mathematics and the age-old dilemma of diversity: Cutting or untying the Gordian knot. In M.C. Pugach & C.L. Warger (Eds.), *Curriculum trends, special education, and reform: Refocusing the conversation* (pp. 94-105.). New York: Teachers College Press.

Lago-Delello, E. (1996). *Classroom dynamics and young children identified as at risk for the development of serious emotional disturbance.* Unpublished doctoral dissertation, University of Miami, Florida.

Levine, S.C., Jordan, N.C., & Huttenlocher, J. (1992). Development of calculation abilities in young children. *Journal of Experimental Child Psychology, 53,* 72-103.

Maple, S.A., & Strange, F.K. (1991). Influences on the choice of math/science major by gender and ethnicity. *American Educational Research Journal, 28,* 37-62.

Mason, D.A., & Good, T.L.(1993). Effects of two-group and whole-class teaching on regrouped elementary students' mathematics achievement. *American Educational Research Journal, 30,* 328-360.

Mathematical Sciences Education Board (MSEB). (1989). *Everybody counts: A report to the nation on the future of mathematics education.* Washington, DC: National Academy Press.

Mercer, C.D., Jordan, L., & Miller, S.P. (1996). Constructivistic math instruction for diverse learners. *Learning Disabilities Research and Practice, 11,* 147-156.

Montague, M. (1992). The effects of cognitive and metacognitive strategy instruction on mathematical problem solving of middle school students with learning disabilities. *Journal of Learning Disabilities, 25,* 230-248.

Montague, M. (1996a). Assessing mathematical problem solving. *Learning Disabilities Research and Practice, 11,* 238-248.

Montague, M. (1996b). Response: What does the "new view" of school mathematics mean for students with mild disabilities? In M.C. Pugach & C.L. Warger (Eds.), *Curriculum trends, special education, and reform: Refocusing the conversation* (pp. 84-93). New York: Teachers College Press.

Montague, M. (1997). Cognitive strategy instruction in mathematics for students with learning disabilities. *Journal of Learning Disabilities, 30,* 164-177.

Montague, M., & Applegate, B. (1993). Mathematical problem-solving characteristics of middle school students with learning disabilities. *The Journal of Special Education, 27,* 175-201.

Montague, M., Applegate, B., & Marquard, K. (1993). Cognitive strategy instruction and mathematical problem solving performance of students with learning disabilities. *Learning Disabilities Research and Practice, 8,* 223-232.

National Center for History in the Schools (1992). *Lessons from history: Essential understandings and historical perspectives students should acquire.* Los Angeles: Author.

National Commission on Social Studies in the Schools (1989). *Charting a course: Social studies for the 21st century.* Washington, DC: Author.

National Council of Teachers of Mathematics (NCTM) (1989). *Curriculum and evaluation standards for school mathematics.* Reston, VA: Author.

National Council of Teachers of Mathematics (NCTM) (1991). *Professional standards for teaching mathematics.* Reston, VA: Author.

Nieto, S. (1996). *Affirming diversity* (2nd ed.). White Plains, NY: Longman.

Owens, D.T. (Ed.) (1993). *Research ideas for the classroom: Middle grades mathematics.* New York: Macmillan.

Pressley, M., & McCormick, C.B. (1995). *Cognition, teaching, and assessment.* New York: Harper Collins.

Pressley, M., Forrest-Pressley, D., Elliott-Faust, D.L., & Miller, G. E. (1985). Children's use of cognitive strategies, how to teach strategies, and what to do if they can't be taught. In M. Pressley & C.J. Brainerd (Eds.), *Cognitive learning and memory in children* (pp. 1-47). New York: Springer-Verlag.

Pugach, M.C., & Warger, C.L. (1993). Curriculum considerations. In J.L. Goodlad & T.C. Lovitt (Eds.), *Integrating general and special education* (pp. 135-148). New York: Merrill.

Pugach, M.C., & Warger, C.L. (1996a). Treating curriculum as a target of reform: Can special and general education learn from each other? In M.C. Pugach & C.L. Warger (Eds.), *Curriculum trends, special education, and reform: Refocusing the conversation* (pp. 1-22). New York: Teachers College Press.

Pugach, M.C., & Warger, C.L. (1996b). Challenges for the special education-curriculum reform partnership. In M.C. Pugach & C.L. Warger (Eds.), *Curriculum trends, special education, and reform: Refocusing the conversation* (pp. 227-252). New York: Teachers College Press.

Scruggs, T.E., & Mastropieri, M.A. (1996). Teacher perceptions of mainstreaming/inclusion, 1958-1995: A research synthesis. *Exceptional Children, 63,* 59-74.

Schunk, D.H. (1996). Goal and self-evaluative influences during children's cognitive skill learning. *American Educational Research Journal, 33,* 359-382.

Spector, J.E. (1992). Predicting progress in beginning reading: Dynamic assessment of phonemic awareness. *Journal of Educational Psychology, 84,* 353-363.

U.S. Department of Education (1994). *Sixteenth annual report to Congress on the implementation of the Individuals with Disabilities Act.* Washington, DC: Author.

Vaughn, S., Schumm, J.S., Jallad, B., Slusher, B., & Saumell, L. (1996). Teachers' views of inclusion. *Learning Disabilities and Practice, 11,* 96-106.

Villa, R. A., Thousand, J.S., Meyers, H., & Nevin, A. (1996). Teacher and administrator perceptions of heterogeneous education. *Exceptional Children, 63,* 29-45.

Vygotsky, L. (1986). *Thought and language.* Cambridge, MA: MIT Press.

Warger, C.L., & Pugach, M.C. (1996). Forming partnerships around curriculum. *Educational Leadership, 53,* 62-65.

Webb, N.L., & Welsch, C. (1993). Assessment and evaluation for middle grades. In D.T. Owens (Ed.), *Research ideas for the classroom: Middle grades mathematics* (pp. 299-316). New York: Macmillan.

Woodward, J., & Baxter, J. (1995). *The informed instruction project: Preliminary findings and implications for future research in mathematics for students with learning disabilities.* Unpublished manuscript.

Woodward, J., & Baxter, J. (1997). The effects of an innovative approach to mathematics on academically low achieving students in mainstreamed settings. *Exceptional Children, 63,* 373-388.

Woodward, J., Baxter, J., & Scheel, C. (in press). It's what you take for granted when you take nothing for granted: The problems with general principles of instructional design. In T. Scruggs & M. Mastropieri (Eds.), *Advances in learning and behavioral disorders* (Vol. 11), pp. 199-234. New York: JAI Press.

CHAPTER SIX

Strategies for Teaching English-Language Learners

RUSSELL GERSTEN, Ph.D., SCOTT K. BAKER, Ph.D.,
& SUSAN UNOK MARKS, Ph.D., Eugene Research Institute

This chapter focuses on issues related to *productive instructional strategies* and approaches for English-language learners. Our goal is to reveal principles that underlie quality instruction for these students, regardless of the official label used to help define their educational needs.

The suggestions we provide are examples of tools teachers can use. The principles we present, and the strategies we discuss to illustrate them, will be recognizable even to teachers with little experience working with English-language learners. We believe that effective instruction may not have as much to do with using unique teaching strategies and approaches as it does with using familiar strategies and approaches in ways that meet the language and learning needs of English-language learners.

One of our explicit assumptions is that schools should make a major effort to provide high-quality instruction to English-language learners. Much previous research with these students has focused on issues of assessment and program eligibility. As a result, inadequate

This research was supported in part by Grant Number H023E50013 from the Office of Special Education Programs of the U.S. Department of Education.

attention has been devoted to the coherent curriculum framework necessary to ensure that English-language learners considered at risk of learning difficulties actually learn important content. Although we recognize the importance of developing more accurate assessment practices to determine student eligibility for special educational and other programs, we will not attempt to address assessment issues in a comprehensive way.

Rather than providing a list of step-by-step instructional procedures and materials, we believe it is more useful to present a cohesive framework of the underlying learning, language, and cultural principles on which a vast array of specific and appropriate instructional procedures may rest. In this way, greater flexibility can be achieved in teaching a broad range of English-language learners in public school. This flexibility is especially important because there is considerable variability among English-language learners in their previous experiences with English and with learning in structured contexts such as schools. This variability cuts across student age, grade level, and subject area.

Although the principles we present cut across grade levels and subjects, they are especially appropriate for English-language learners in kindergarten through eighth grade. The examples offered come from materials used in research studies, from classrooms observed by our research team, and from the experiences of expert teachers.

KEY CONCEPTS IN EFFECTIVE INSTRUCTION FOR ENGLISH-LANGUAGE LEARNERS

Many educators are baffled about how to provide high-quality instruction to English-language learners when they are unable to speak the native language. Actually, there are many effective strategies and procedures for providing high-quality instructional opportunities for English-language learners, *even when the teacher does not speak the student's native language.*

Current federal policy requires that districts teaching English-language learners must provide them with two major types of instruction. The first, and more easily understood requirement, is that districts must provide some instruction that promotes English-language acquisition. As will be seen, there are numerous means of providing English instruction to speakers of other languages.

The second, more complex, and less easily understood requirement is that schools need to provide English-language learners with *meaningful access to the school's curriculum.* In essence, this means that students are entitled to instruction that deals with grade-appropriate content, concepts, and skills.

The law provides for great flexibility in how this second goal is met. It intentionally does not specify the language of instruction that should be used to achieve this goal; students can be taught key concepts either in English or in their native languages. This complex requirement essentially means that academic subjects must be taught in a way that ensures that students receive *comprehensible input.*

Comprehensible Input

The requirement of comprehensible input is intended to ensure that students are able to understand the essence of what is being said or presented to them. This does not mean, however, that teachers must use only words that students understand. Krashen (1982) posits that students learn a new language best when they receive input that is just a bit more difficult than they can easily understand—when they can understand most, but not all, of the words the teacher is using. By using context or visual cues, or by asking for clarification, students enhance their knowledge of English. When "input" is comprehensible, students can understand most aspects of what is required for learning, and the learning experience pushes them to further understanding.

One way teachers can assure that material is sufficiently comprehensible is to provide relevant background knowledge or ask questions that link new content to what students currently know. Yates and Ortiz (1991) stress the importance of background knowledge in comprehension:

> It is difficult for [English-language learners] to respond appropriately when discussions revolve around leprechauns, blarney stones and the joys of eating corned beef and cabbage if they have no prior experience with these topics. The principle of comprehensible input ... is violated when teachers use topics, materials and tasks that are linguistically, experientially and culturally unrelated to students' backgrounds. (pp. 15-16)

Note that according to Yates and Ortiz (1991), comprehensible input is related to more than just language development and curriculum content; appropriate context is crucial. One way for teachers to be sensitive to the linguistic and cultural backgrounds of their English-language learners is to provide instruction that draws on the experiences of their students. Teachers need not be "experts" in their students' cultures, but they do have to understand how effective it can be to connect students' learning to their past experiences.

Many other techniques can be used to increase the likelihood that students will understand what is being said to them; these include using consistent language, using many visuals, providing frequent opportunities for students to express their ideas, and numerous other strategies described later in this chapter. During instructional dialogues, the focus should primarily be on accuracy of content, not on rigid requirements associated with correct language use.

In order to continually modulate and clarify the language of instruction, teaching must also be highly interactive. Teachers must constantly involve students, ask many questions, and encourage students to express their ideas and thoughts in English. The principle of comprehensible instruction requires that teachers carefully control their vocabulary and use graphic organizers, concrete objects, and gestures when possible to enhance understanding.

Comprehensible input is as much an ideal as it is an achievable reality. In teaching English-language learners, we can attempt to reach this "ideal" level of support and challenge, but in the context of complex and fast-paced classroom interactions, it may rarely be achieved to the level we would like. Nonetheless, this is a critical concept to remember when developing a program for each English-language learner.

Meaningful Access to the Curriculum

As mentioned earlier, the purpose of providing comprehensible input to English-language learners is to ensure that they have meaningful access to the curriculum; these students are entitled to instruction that deals with grade-appropriate content, concepts, and skills. In determining how to provide meaningful curriculum access, it is first important to understand what meaningful curriculum access is *not.* Providing meaningful access is *not* allowing a student who knows virtually no English to sit through a lesson that she does not comprehend at all. Nor is it providing fifth-grade students with a first-grade curriculum because their English-language standardized tests place them at a first-grade reading level in English. Nor is it placing these students in special education.

What, then, is meaningful curriculum access for an English-language learner? A few examples may help clarify.[1]

- If students in a particular district are learning about the weather in grade 4, then English-language learners in grade 4 should be learning the key concepts about the weather. This may or may not mean that these students use the typical fourth-grade science text. It does mean that these students receive "something extra" to ensure that they learn the key principles in that unit of fourth-grade science.
- If learning about character clues and character motivation in a novel is a major district objective for grade 6, then English-language learners in grade 6 should be reading novels, should

---

[1]   These examples were developed in the course of a National Association of State Directors of Special Education Forum with input from the Office of Civil Rights (OCR).

be taught how to detect character clues, and should be given opportunities to write about character clues. The novel may be at a lower than sixth-grade readability level, if this fits the students' current English-language reading ability. It could also be written in the student's native language. However, the novel should contain engaging characters with interesting motives and clues as to reasons for the decisions they make. The teacher's responsibility is to require the English-language learners to learn the analytical skills related to character clues and character motivation.

The most common obstacle to providing meaningful access to the curriculum has been the view of English-language learners as simply low-performing native English speakers (Baca & Almanza, 1991; Yates & Ortiz, 1991). It is critical that teachers avoid this reaction when confronted with students who do not use English proficiently. In thinking about curriculum access, the important goal is that students understand the critical concepts being presented—not that they know the correct English label for these concepts. Although English-language learners often lack fluency in oral expression, they have ideas to contribute and will do so in an accepting classroom environment. Participation in activities that require higher-order thinking skills, where the focus is on content rather than on grammar, is an important element of meaningful curriculum access.

One teacher we saw read *Wilfred Gordon McDonald Partridge*—an Australian story about a woman losing her memory—to her fourth-grade class. In discussing the story afterwards, when asked what the story was about, a student answered "it was kind of sad." The teacher asked the class "How do you know?" and one boy, whom the teacher described earlier as a student with learning difficulties, said, "Because old people." Although the response is very brief and has grammatical problems, a perceptive teacher will recognize that this student has thought about the story in an intelligent and serious way. In many contexts, however, these kinds of responses by English-language learners are interpreted to be evidence of limited intelligence and limited learning potential. Typically, it is extremely difficult for teachers to assess the academic capabilities of English-language learners because of the language barrier between students and teachers, and because of the uneven progress associated with learning content and a second language simultaneously.

One educator described what it was like to come to the US with very little English and suddenly change from perceiving herself as a "smart" person to perceiving herself as someone with lots of academic problems. Her feelings of inadequacy remained very private, because there was no opportunity for her to share them with anyone else. She believes it would have been enormously helpful to hear from other students about these same kinds of feelings—to understand that these feelings were normal, and that the difficulties were understandable reactions to learning in a new language and environment.

The consequence of viewing English-language learners as having limited ability is the disastrous tendency to merely adopt watered-down versions of the standard curriculum, which is in clear conflict with curriculum access. A second-rate curriculum denies English-language learners access to quality instruction and, ultimately, to real academic opportunity. In thinking about potential solutions and remedies, it is important to remember there is no one right way, and currently, there are no experts who have precise remedies. Nevertheless, we are making rapid advances in this area, and promising practices are emerging. At the heart of these practices is clear recognition that English-language learners face unique learning challenges that demand innovative practices.

The point is that it is essential to teach all students, including English-language learners, how to read and understand basic academic principles and to build academic reasoning skills. Although not all of an English-language learner's time has to be spent on grade-level material, access to the key grade-level concepts in the curriculum is essential to meeting the guidelines of current federal policy.

Conversational vs. Academic Language

The distinction between conversational and academic language is a critical one for classroom teachers working with English-language learners. Successful educators of English-language learners understand that demonstrating language proficiency depends heavily on contextual factors. Hakuta and Snow make the point this way: "Language is not a unified skill but a complex configuration of abilities. Language used for conversational purposes is quite different from language used for school learning" (cited in Crawford, 1989, p. 89). Conversational English is often called *basic interpersonal communication*. The formal language used in academic dialogue is referred to as *cognitive/academic language.*

Basic interpersonal communication can be thought of as the language of the playground, the language for talking to friends. It is heavily dependent on clues, gestures, conversational responses, and short, partially grammatical phrases. It is thus very different from the formal language used in academic contexts such as explaining scientific concepts and articulating themes in novels. Many have found these distinctions, first articulated by Cummins (1981), important in understanding why students who seem to speak English fairly well in their conversations with peers still struggle with reading textbooks or sophisticated novels in English.

For English-language learners, success in school will depend on their ability to successfully learn the types of language skills involved in cognitive/academic language proficiency (CALP) development. Many argue that teaching CALP is a necessary objective of schooling for English-language learners (Collier, 1995; Cummins, 1981). There is an emerging knowledge base on how to perform this instructional goal. Development of CALP is a major theme of this chapter. One way to help develop CALP is by reinforcing verbal exchanges with written words. Numerous examples of how to do this are presented throughout the chapter.

PROVIDING MEANINGFUL ACCESS TO THE CURRICULUM

Initial Steps

As teachers begin to develop instructional strategies that increase students' access to curriculum concepts, a few initial steps can help immensely in preparing the right kind of instructional environment. These initial steps are easily overlooked, but if used correctly, they provide an excellent starting point for meeting the learning needs of English-language learners.

When students first arrive in school, it is helpful to provide them with a list of common school vocabulary and concepts. This will help orient new students to the school setting and give them a concrete way of independently checking and learning the meaning of important concepts. This list would include names of important people and places in the school, common verbs, and ways to ask for help.

Other useful introductory activities that have been implemented in schools include the following (Echevarria & Graves, in press):

- In one middle school, English-language learners are paired with bilingual students. Together they study critical vocabulary and prepare an interview. This interview is conducted in English with a member of the school community. The information gained through the interview is then shared by the two students with the other students.
- In another program, elementary school students tour the school with a teacher when they first arrive. Throughout the tour, the teacher takes Polaroid photos of important areas of the school and of school personnel (i.e., office, cafeteria, school nurse, secretary, etc.). These photos are used to create a map of the school which is labeled with words and the photos. The final product is displayed in the office for visitors to see.

- In one secondary school, English-language learners are paired with a "host" student for the first day of school. The host student introduces the English-language learner to school procedures, shows the location of important areas, and helps the English-language learner understand what life is like in the new school.

Teachers can help students feel comfortable in a new school setting by incorporating students' native languages in the materials and instructional strategies selected. For example, having some native-language books available that students can read, allowing students to use their native languages to respond to questions or to demonstrate and express what they know, and allowing students to work in small groups using their native language can significantly increase English-language learners' opportunities for meaningful access to curriculum concepts.

One teacher captured well the importance of language in social interactions: "There is that certain click of understanding and interest that happens when you do speak their native language. But when I don't, then I make sure that ... the environment is social enough and safe enough that children get what they need from each other, and not always just from me."

Teachers who take the time to learn and use at least a few words in a student's native language usually appreciate the investment. These (frequently humbling) encounters with learning a second language, even if at a very basic level, demonstrate teacher interest and respect for the language and cultural background of the English-language learner.

One of the teachers we with spoke put it this way: "There were ... teachers in my team who learned some Spanish in order to be able to teach a class and get their point across. They are not native speakers of the language. They have a different culture, different cultural background. The connection takes a little bit longer to be established, but the effort was well worth it."

For teachers new to working with English-language learners, it can be extremely beneficial to observe others who are successful with these students or who have been trained to work with them. This is an excellent investment of district resources and emerged as a strong recommendation from our focus group discussions. Videos featuring experienced teachers and guides can also be useful, particularly when new teachers have a chance to discuss the content.

One school district provides a mentoring program in which experienced English as a second language teachers are paired with new English as a second language or general education teachers. They spend one year sharing concerns, ideas, and suggestions, and coach each other on specific teaching tasks in real classroom settings. The program also includes structured opportunities for English-language learners to share with teachers their thoughts about learning English, including what they found most helpful and what they found most difficult or confusing.

Overview of Key Instructional Principles

Eight key instructional principles for teaching English-language learners, described briefly here, will be addressed and exemplified in the remainder of this chapter.

1. *Vocabulary instruction* is crucial for English-language development, and can serve as a cornerstone for content-area learning. By vocabulary instruction, we do not mean memorizing the definitions of 20 new vocabulary terms each lesson. Rather, we refer to a range of instructional strategies that can be used to help English-language learners acquire vocabulary. Such strategies include learning vocabulary in the context of understanding new concepts through literature discussions, student talking, writing, cooperative group activities, and semantic maps.

2. *Visual organizers* are excellent tools for helping English-language learners process information. The double demands

of learning content and a second language are significant. Because the spoken word is fleeting, visual aids such as graphic organizers, concept and story maps, and word banks are useful in helping students to process, reflect on, and integrate information.

3. *Modeling* activities and strategies gives students a clear sense of what is expected of them. Teachers can assist students by presenting multiple examples of concepts or of finished assignments, by using "think-alouds," or by assessing students' abilities to repeat or model instructions. For English-language learners, it is essential to perform step-by-step modeling of what needs to be done and to present examples of completed assignments or projects.

4. *Concrete examples and experiences* can also help students better understand the concepts being presented, by making a presentation more meaningful. These additions to classroom instruction can enhance and give students a variety of ways for understanding the information being presented, rather than always receiving the information via lecture and verbal explanations.

5. *Ongoing assessment* of the effectiveness of instructional activities in producing student learning helps instructors ensure that their teaching methods are effective. Curriculum-based assessments and informal assessments show teachers clearly what is being learned, and thus guide them in providing responsive feedback and adjusting teaching tactics.

6. *Consistent language use* is very important, especially early in second language learning. For English-language learners, listening to explanations or lectures can be confusing if the teacher uses many idioms, synonyms, or metaphors. Many words and phrases may not be familiar to these students, and using a range of similar words to convey the same essential concept can make learning difficult. Teachers should also monitor their language pace. As students learn more English, the pace can increase, but this depends on the complexity of

the content and other factors.

7. A *balance between cognitive and language demands* needs to be struck, so that students can effectively learn both English and grade-level content-area information. Effective teachers intentionally and carefully reduce the cognitive demands on students when the primary goal is to encourage English-language expression (either written or oral). When the cognitive task is inherently demanding (e.g., a new science concept or complex literary content, such as character clues), effective teachers allow and encourage students to use a variety of supports. Use of students' native languages can be an excellent means to help students learn challenging concepts, even if the teacher does not speak the languages.

8. *Peer tutoring and collaboration* are potentially useful approaches for increasing access to the curriculum. In collaborative learning, English-language learners can work on important learning objectives in small groups. In a sense, students can "pool" their language skills to describe concepts, define words, and provide examples to each other. Similarly, use of a tutor who speaks the child's native language to explain key concepts and clarify any difficult points can increase an English-language learner's access to important content-area information.

STRATEGIES FOR IMPLEMENTING THE CORE INSTRUCTIONAL PRINCIPLES

Essentially, teaching strategies to increase access to curriculum concepts for English-language learners involve (a) providing comprehensible input to students and (b) giving frequent opportunities for English-language learners to use language during instruction. In this section, we expand on the strategies outlined above, illustrating how they meet these goals.

Strategies for Vocabulary Instruction

The number of new vocabulary terms introduced to English-language learners at any one time should be limited. A list of 20 new vocabulary words that students are expected to learn at one time is not an effective way to help English-language learners develop vocabulary. Teachers from our discussion groups recommended using lists of seven or fewer words that students work on over several days. It is important that teachers have criteria for selecting words—selecting, for example, words that convey key concepts, words that are of high utility, words that are relevant to the rest of the specific content being learned, and words that have meaning in the lives of students.

Using such selection criteria helps ensure that students learn word meanings at a deep level of understanding. For example, one teacher had her entire class analyze words that represented complex ideas—adjectives like *anxious, generous,* and *suspicious,* and nouns like *memory*—words that English-language learners are likely to need help with. Later, this teacher had the students—both native English speakers and English-language learners—read a story and look for evidence that certain events pertained to these vocabulary words in relation to a particular character or incident. For instance, students had to use three sources of information in the story to explain why they thought a character was anxious.

These vocabulary words were effective target words for instruction because they are tied to human motivation and are critical for literary analysis. Words such as *anxious, memory,* and *persevere* have the ability to serve as important curriculum anchors for language and content learning. On the surface, some of these vocabulary words may seem too easy for fourth- or fifth-grade native English speakers. Yet the words are critical for second-language learners, and discussion of their meanings can go well beyond standard dictionary definitions. The words were also of high utility and had the potential to link to language learning and literature activities, and to resonate with issues in students' lives.

In contrast, another teacher we encountered in our research

assigned a word list that presented significant problems to students. At first glance, the teacher's motivation made sense: she wanted to create a list of words that students often confused, and that prevented them from understanding content. She provided a word list consisting of the following:

then • this • that • which • weather • the

Students were asked to use these words to write a story, with an interesting story starter: "The most terrible thing about the storm was …" Yet students struggled with the assignment.

The problem with this word list is twofold. First, too many words that can be easily confused are taught at once, so students' frustration levels are likely to be high. A second problem is that too many abstract words are introduced at once. Note that except for "weather," none of the words are evocative. Short, abstract words in English, presented in isolation, may be confusing for beginning students for one reason or another. For example, the English words *in* and *on* both translate to the Spanish word *en*.

In our 3-year study on effective instructional practices (Jiménez, Gersten, & Rivera, 1995), we encountered one fourth-grade teacher who used a very productive vocabulary activity. The teacher, very experienced in working with English-language learners, frequently asked her students to write brief essays or poems using *word banks*, places where key vocabulary is stored and posted for students' reference. The purpose of these activities is twofold: to improve vocabulary, and to develop proficiency in writing.

In this particular lesson, composing *cinquains*—five-line stanzas—helped build students' vocabulary and fostered meaningful access to curriculum content for the English-language learners in the classroom. The activity consisted of three components. The teacher began by describing to students her reactions to a rainy day. She asked the students to describe similar feelings and to name related vocabulary. The class created a word bank of potential English vocabulary to use in their poems. These words included *rain, wet, cold, drops, thunder,* and *scare.* Next, the teacher gave students a format for writing a cinquain and explained its parts to them. She also modeled her own approach to writing a cinquain. She wrote the format on the board as follows:

_____ (topic)

_____ _____ (two adjectives)

_____ _____ _____ (three verbs)

_____ (a sentence showing feelings)

_____ (a synonym for the topic)

Finally, students were directed to write a cinquain. Examples of some of the student cinquains are presented below in Figure 6-1.

Students were learning how to write poetry—an important and age-appropriate language arts-skill—while they were building and solidifying their command of the English language. The activity provided a clear framework for what the students were to do. Although the amount of English the students needed to understand and use was confined to a defined framework, the range of potential involvement students could have with the language was limitless. The

Figure 6-1. Examples of student cinquains developed by English-language learners.

Rain
wet, cold
drops, scares, crying
It makes me feel sad
Water

Rain
Cool, Clear
Crazy, kick, hits
It makes me feel wild
Wet

Rain
Wet, water
pretty, cool, crystal
You are so fun when you sprinkle
Wild Thunder

activity had something for students who knew very little English, as well as for students who were fully proficient in English. Finally, not only did the teacher provide the format students were to use in their poetry compositions, but she also gave them an explicit model for how to do it.

Of course, the success of this activity lies in how the students responded to it and what they learned from it. This particular teacher had a great deal of experience working with English-language learners and drew on that experience in presenting this lesson. It seemed to work for all the students in her class. Even teachers new to working with English-language learners can use this technique successfully and can extract from it important instructional principles. Note that this exercise is a form of vocabulary instruction, but an interesting and engaging one.

Important principles for teaching vocabulary include the following:

- *Present multiple exposures.* Research has shown that students require multiple exposures to a new vocabulary term to develop a basic understanding of the word's meaning. Additional exposures to the word in a variety of contexts are required for students to develop a deeper understanding of the word's meaning and have the word available as part of their "expressive" vocabulary.
- *Give practice with new words.* Another important strategy for teaching vocabulary is to let students practice using new words. One example we observed was the use of the word *audience* in "Mr. Popper's Penguins." After discussing the story and the use of *audience,* students discussed other kinds of audiences, such as an audience at a rock concert, an audience at a movie, and an audience at a sporting event.

     English-language learners experiencing academic difficulties frequently have difficulty with retention of new words and concepts. In second-language acquisition, it takes a long time and many opportunities for students to progress from having a rudimentary understanding of a word's meaning to being able to use that word appropriately in academic conversations. Teachers often confuse such stages of second language acquisition with learning concerns.

- *Use explicit organizers.* As students learn new vocabulary words, these should be added to a word bank. The term *word bank* is commonly used to indicate a place where vocabulary is posted for students' reference for a particular activity (as in the cinquain example above) or for an extended period of time. The creation of word banks can be a group activity involving the contribution of many students, and can be the source of lesson content over time. Words in the word bank should be important words, ones critical to the concepts students are learning.

Visually displayed word banks can be created on an ongoing basis. For example, as evocative vocabulary is introduced, word meanings and key content attributes can be written on butcher paper and posted around the room. These word banks become reference points for students to remember definitions and relationships between terms, and serve as guides for correct spelling. Word banks can be dynamic. As students learn more about words and how they are used, this new information can be added to existing definitions.

To help teachers select words for compiling word banks, Nagy (1985) presented a simple but useful set of criteria. Also, some reading series and some state and local curriculum departments provide word lists to go along with novels commonly used in schools. Remember, however, that judicious use of these word lists is critical. As mentioned earlier and articulated by Nagy (1985), it is important that criteria for word selection be based on utility, relevance for understanding key concepts, and relevance for students' lives. For example, in reading a short story, explaining what a *salt cellar* is may not be as essential as explaining what a *refugee* is. English-language learners are not likely to benefit much from knowing what a salt cellar is; understanding the word *refugee* is likely to have more direct relevance for students' experiences and may help them engage in academic conversations and understand current events.

- *Focus on a small number of critical words.* Teachers who are effective with English-language learners do not drill students on lengthy word lists, even though districts or publishers usually provide such lists. Rather, they focus on several critical words at a time and emphasize these for several days. When possible, teachers can also use short stories, below-grade-level books, and personal writing projects to amplify understanding of the concepts surrounding the vocabulary terms. These types of activities help establish the semantic networks that are critical to deep vocabulary learning, and that are the cornerstones of pioneering research on vocabulary instruction.

- *Introduce new words before they are encountered in reading.* The time-tested practice of introducing new vocabulary prior to the reading of new stories can be especially helpful to English-language learners (Rousseau, Tam, & Ramnarain, 1993).

- *Focus on idioms.* Idioms can also play an important role in language and content learning for English-language learners. Teachers can effectively use idioms to focus on differences between standard and contextual definitions of words, as well as to sharply increase student comprehension. Some caution is warranted, however; the use of idioms with English-language learners can easily cause problems, because the meaning of idioms is typically quite different from the sum of the meanings of the individual words in the expression.

Visual Organizers

Visual organizers can help English-language learners understand and "see" the connections between language and curriculum content. A recurrent refrain among teachers and researchers, and in the emerging literature on effective instruction (Reyes & Bos, in press; Echevarria, in press; Chamot & O'Malley, 1996; Fitzgerald, 1996), is the importance of using visuals and visual organizers as teaching tools. Teachers may not be aware that many of the teaching tools that they use successfully with native English-speaking students (such as se-mantic maps and story maps) will also work with English-language learners—provided they are modulated so that input is comprehen-sible. These tools can help students access concepts in a new language that they could not grasp if instruction were solely verbal.

We will present four of the many types of visual organizers that help English-language learners learn important curriculum content: *semantic maps* to enhance understanding of vocabulary concepts, *story maps* for comprehension and writing, *text structures* to serve as a basis for writing, and *KWL maps* for accessing funds of knowledge. Teachers are invariably more effective when they integrate only one or two visual organizers into their teaching repertoire than when they are learning and using a wide array of organizers. Each technique requires time for both students and teachers to feel comfortable with it and use it effectively (Kline, Deshler, & Schumaker, 1992).

Semantic maps. Semantic maps can be used to help students learn important vocabulary, verbalize relationships, provide examples, and learn from examples provided by others. One frequently used tactic is to list common objects by classification category (e.g. types of vehicles, types of foods) and discuss the concept or "label" that applies. More abstract concepts can also be categorized for English-language learners. For example, lists of adjectives can be categorized as "words that describe" and then discussed.

Semantic maps, or webs, are graphic depictions of main ideas and concepts in a story or article, and of the relationships of these ideas to each other and to more minor themes or concepts. These depictions help students to organize information and to see the interrelation-ships between key concepts. Two models for teaching students to use a semantic map are presented in Figures 6-2a and 6-2b (from Reyes & Bos, in press).

Anderson and Roit (in press) provide a model of how to use visual organizers to help the vocabulary development of English-language

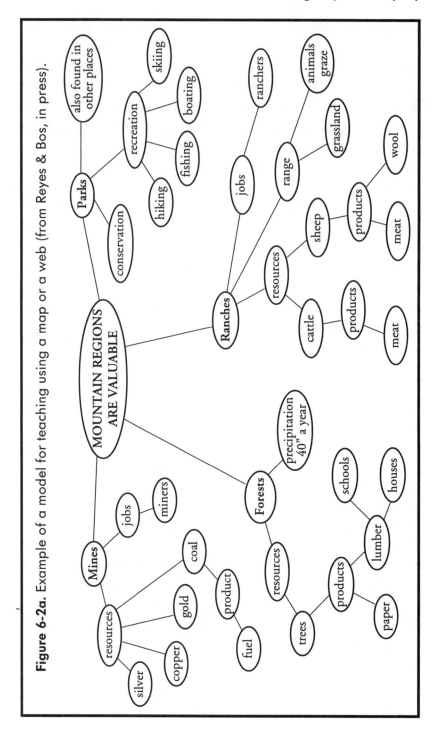

Figure 6-2a. Example of a model for teaching using a map or a web (from Reyes & Bos, in press).

Figure 6-2b. Example of a model for teaching using a relationship chart (from Reyes & Bos, in press).

KEY − = related ? = Undecided LEYENDA − = relacionado ¿ = No puedo decidir		MOUNTAIN REGIONS ARE VALUABLE El Valor de los Regiones Montañosas			
		Important Places / Lugaros Importantos			
Important Ideas **Ideas Importantes**		Mines Minas	Forests Bosques	Ranches Ranchos	Parks Parques
resources recursos	coal carbon				
	gold oro				
	silver plata				
	trees arboles				
	fish pesces				
	cattle ganado				
	sheep ovejas				
product producto	meat carne				
	wool lana				
	lumber madera				
	fuel combustible				
recreation recreacion	hiking cominatas				
	skiing esquiar				
	fishing pescar				
jobs ocupaciones	miners mineros				
	ranchers rancheros				

learners. They note that semantic map activities are often carried out as one-shot collective activities to which students do not return, or are done too infrequently to provide the consistency needed for English-language learners (Campbell, Gersten, & Kolar, 1993). In contrast, Anderson and Roit's *vocabulary networking* model focuses on helping students develop and retain the understanding of word meanings and the relationships between words and concepts necessary for deep vocabulary knowledge (Beck, McKeown, & McCaslin, 1983). This model includes three similar techniques.

One recommendation is that a variety of vocabulary networks be kept on separate sheets in a reference notebook, learning log, display area, or central file, so that all students can return to them, add to them, and share them over time. It is critical that the teacher either frequently allow time or set a regular time for students to work with these vocabulary networks, so that learning is reinforced. Vocabulary learning for all students depends on frequent exposures to words and their use in context. New words for networks should be added regularly. Introducing too many words simultaneously, however, can cause confusion.

The second activity is best used with words that Short (1994) refers to as transition markers—abstract words such as *some, during, however,* and *except* that tend to heavily influence the meaning of content. These words may be relatively simple for native English speakers but can be problematic for English-language learners. Text-books are filled with these transition markers. The following excerpt from *Exploring American History* illustrates the importance of these words to the meaning of the content:

> Parliament passed a tax law called the Stamp Act ... *However* ... Parliament passed the Declaratory Act ... *Because* the British government still needed money, Parliament in 1767 passed the Township Acts ... The Townshend Acts caused more and more colonists to protest. (O'Connor, 1991, pp. 186-187, italics added)

The transition marker words, *however* and *because*, reinforce the concept that the colonists reacted to British actions in the hope of changing the situation. Short and others (e.g., O'Connor, 1991) have suggested that because these types of words can be difficult, it is helpful when English-language learners are *"explicitly taught to recognize them and understand their functions* [italics added]" (Short, 1994, p. 7).

One way for students to enhance and retain their understanding of these transition marker words is through the technique suggested by Anderson and Roit. In this technique, students write these words at the top of blank sheets of paper. Under each word, students organize meanings, examples, relationships, text references, and impressions for each word, drawing from their experiences, conversations, and readings throughout the year. This networking strategy is designed to help English-language learners understand these words and remember that they convey critical, yet subtle information. Developing these networks and sharing their ideas about words in this way both increases students' understanding of particularly difficult words and provides a functional source of vocabulary ideas for writing.

In the third technique, students create maps of related words that cut across texts in a particular domain, such as the American West or species survival. This helps increase awareness of how frequently words are used, which is beneficial to learning word meanings. Students can also color-code words that are frequently repeated across texts, and that are crucial to a certain domain. This activity not only increases vocabulary knowledge, but also fosters the intertextual awareness that is so characteristic of good readers (Hartman, 1995).

Story grammar and story maps. Most stories are structured in such a way that they are easily depicted with visual aids. Almost 10 years ago, Idol (1987) noted the potential of providing concrete representations of story structures for students with academic difficulties:

> The reader is instructed about interrelated components or parts of a story, which provide a basic framework that draws the reader's

attention to the common elements among narrative stories. This increases the possibility of the reader searching his or her mind for possible information, searching the text for such information, and using the story map as a framework for drawing the two information sources together. (p. 197)

Typically, Western story grammar consists of five major elements—character, goal, obstacle, outcome, and theme. Story maps are the visual representations of this story grammar. The story grammar elements listed vary slightly from source to source, but the basic components are very similar. A slightly different variation of this story grammar is presented in the map developed by Beck (1991) and presented in Figure 6-3.

It is important to note that students typically use a story map such as this one as an organizer prior to reading, and then again after reading to fill in information and search the text for important information they did not get while reading the story. During the actual reading of the story, however, the story maps typically are not used, so that the flow of reading the story is not broken. After reading the story, as students complete their story maps, they will hopefully begin to understand that successful "reading" involves much more than merely reading something through one time.

Text structures. The term *text structure* refers to the way in which a person organizes ideas in a text to develop arguments and defend positions. Text structure can be usefully depicted through visual organizers to help English-language learners "see" ideas and the connections between concepts, and to document important recurring content themes. Text structures can also be used when acquiring new knowledge. Common text structures include *comparison/contrast* and *problem-solution-effect.*

The comparison/contrast organizer has been used effectively with native English speakers as well as English-language learners. An example of this type of text structure organizer is presented in Figure 6-4. This example, from Englert, Raphael, and Anderson (1992),

Figure 6-3. Story Map example from Beck (1991).

Purpose: To provide literary essentials such as the main characters, the setting, the problem, the major events, the problem solution, and the theme for a story.
Grade Levels: Regular and less prepared students in grades K–8.
Description: A Story Map helps students glean essential data from a story. In this activity, students complete the Story Map as a whole class or reading group in the primary grades, writing the required information in the space provided. Middle and upper grade students can fill in the outline on their own. Less prepared students may need assistance with ideas and procedures. Some guidance in deciding the main events of the story may be necessary, or students may include too many facts. Students need to learn to combine like events, give them a broader title, then proceed. In completing the Story Map, students should first listen to the entire story, if it is being read aloud. If they are reading the story or a book in parts or segments, they should complete the assigned portion prior to filling in the Story Map. Otherwise, they will lose the thread of the story or interrupt its flow by stopping to insert data in the Story Map. The completed Story Map provides much material for discussion or writing, whichever is most appropriate for the literary selection being used.

SAMPLE STORY MAP FOR *MOLLY'S PILGRIM* BY BARBARA COHEN

Setting/Main Characters		Home and school. Molly, Mama, Miss Stickley, Elizabeth.
Statement of the problem		The other children laugh at and make fun of Molly.
	Event 1	The children tease Molly.
	Event 2	The class has to make Pilgrim clothespin dolls.
	Event 3	Mama makes Molly's doll look like herself.
	Event 4	The children laugh at Molly's doll because it doesn't look like a Pilgrim.
	Event 5	The teacher tells about modern Pilgrims and the Jewish holiday that inspired Thanksgiving.
Statement of the solution		The children understand about Molly and decide to be friends with her.
Story theme ("What is this story really about?")		People are different, but when you get to know them, you often like them.

Figure 6-4. An example of a text structure organizer from
Englert et al. (1992)

COMPARISON / CONTRAST ORGANIZATION FORM				
What is being compared/contrasted?	Dad and me			
	On what?	Size and looks		
		Alike?	Have brown eyes Brown hair	Different? Dad is big and I am short
	On what?	Day		
		Alike?	Work	Different? Dad at office I work at school
	On what?	Food		
		Alike?	Both like pizza	Different? Dad likes fish patties

---

shows how one student used the comparison/contrast format as a first step in preparing a story she was writing. What makes such an organizer potentially very useful for English-language learners is that it does not require complex reading strategies to understand, the content is important and grade appropriate, and students can actually use the organizer to write or speak from. Notice that in using the organizer, spelling, grammar, and other writing conventions are not emphasized. The focus is on organizing text for understanding and composing.

Another popular and versatile text structure is problem-solution-effect. This text structure is used extensively in subjects like history that deal with sequences of events and social interactions. For example, issues associated with the Great Depression or the rise of Nazism lend themselves to problem-solution-effect maps. These maps are excellent ways to help English-language learners and other students see problems from a variety of perspectives. For example, they can view the American Revolution from both a British and a colonist's perspective, view the New Deal from the position of an unemployed worker and a bank president, and view the current peace process in Israel from an Arab and a Jewish perspective.

In Figure 6-5, we present an example of a problem-solution-effect map that might be used to help students understand the causes of the American Revolution. Note how the structure provides some support for the students so they can complete the map. As students read their

Figure 6-5. An example of a Problem-Attempted Solution-Effect Concept Map and Phrase Bank.

PROBLEM	ATTEMPTED SOLUTION	EFFECT
Colonists' Problem	Colonists' Attempted Solutions	Effects on Colonists
I am a colonist. I do not want to pay taxes to the British government because... 1. 2. 3.		
British Problem	British Attempted Solutions	Effects on British
I am a British citizen. The colonists should pay taxes to the British government because... 1. 2. 3.		

PHRASE / IDEA BANK
I am not represented in the British government.
The money from the taxes does not benefit the colonists.
The British government needs money to maintain the navy.
The British government needs money to maintain the country.
The Stamp Act
The Intolerable Acts
The Boston Tea Party

textbooks and try to understand what they read, they should be able to develop this map to depict the revolution from both the colonists' and the British perspectives.

In the second half of Figure 6-5, we present an *idea bank* that can be developed in conjunction with the problem-solution-effect map. Generating an idea bank may be useful with students who have difficulty accessing information; it gives them a structure for developing a list of important ideas with which they can attempt to reason out their positions. Idea banks are especially useful with English-language learners because reducing the extent to which students have to rely on their memory of information and event details gives them a better opportunity to reason out a position, explain their choices, and explain the overall effects of the historical period.

KWL maps. English-language learners come to school with a range of experiences and knowledge that they can share in the school context. When these sources of information are incorporated into instruction, students are able to personalize new information within familiar topics. This lowers the anxiety level often associated with language learning and increases comprehensible input, because students are able to relate the new concepts to their own personal experiences and interests.

A visual organizer that can be used to access what the students already know in the service of new learning is the Know-Want-to-know-Learned (KWL) map. In the three-part sequence of developing a KWL, students:

- list what they know about a topic,
- list what else they would like to know about a topic, and
- after reading, list what they learned about a topic.

The KWL map promotes language use by giving students an opportunity to verbally identify what they know about a topic and what they would like to know. It motivates students to draw on their background knowledge when they encounter new information, and it helps them assume responsibility for their own learning, which should increase their motivation to learn. Finally, because of the diversity of the individual sheets, many different ideas will be available to promote interesting classroom discussions. Discussions will be lively because students have a great deal of choice of what to focus on, which increases their interest in discussing the topic with their peers.

In fact, the main purpose of the KWL activity is to give students the opportunity to tap into what they already know (and so reduce their anxiety about learning new material), share their knowledge with their peers, and ask questions. These questions help focus the students as they explore topics related to the core concept. The students' questions build commitment and a sense of ownership that guide learning (Ogle, 1986). In addition, tapping prior knowledge and using student generated questions as key activities increases students' conceptual knowledge.

A good way to begin using the KWL visual organizer is as a group activity. The teacher introduces the main concept by writing it on the board, on an overhead, or on butcher paper. Students begin by sharing information they know or think they know about the topic. The teacher records this information so that students can see it. To encourage participation, the teacher does not evaluate students' statements, and all responses are recorded—regardless of accuracy.

After all ideas have been recorded in the Know column, the teacher asks the students what they want to know or find out about the topic. To stimulate participation, he or she models questions that will help students formulate their own questions. All questions are recorded in the Want to Know column.

Next, the teacher explains that the students will confirm or amend information in the Know column of the KWL grid and answer questions from the Want to Know column as they progress through the unit of study. This is an interactive, recursive process in which students draw information from the textbook, supplemental readings, guest speakers, and films. Periodically, answers to the students' questions are recorded in the "Learned" column of the KWL grid. Students can then use the map or chart as a study tool and as a guide for writing summaries of the content.

In summary, visuals can help encourage English-language learners to take risks, try out expressions, express complex thoughts in a
new language, and ask questions. Even short phrases and expressions
can represent higher-order thinking. Maps and other visual organizers not only help English-language learners express these complex
thoughts and ideas; they also provide some of the support needed for
native English speakers to understand what English-language learners
are expressing, and thus promote the effective engagement of interactive dialogues. These types of dialogues are at the heart of efforts to
promote cognitive/academic language proficiency.

Modeling

Teachers should model activities and strategies carefully and check
frequently for comprehension. Demonstrating the activities and the
strategies being taught provides students with a model for completing
assignments or applying strategies. Some ways teachers can provide
this support are:

- Present numerous examples of the concepts being taught.
- Show visual examples of a finished assignment as you verbally
  explain the steps for completing it. (Use the overhead projector or chalkboard to keep everyone together.)
- Use "think-alouds." Talk out your strategy for tackling the
  instructional task (e.g., "I'll read the paragraph first. Then I'll
  reread it to look for the answer to the first question … I'll
  underline where I think the answer is, etc."). Label the
  learning strategy, explain why this particular strategy was
  chosen, and tell students why the strategy might be helpful to
  them. Also encourage students to use "think-alouds."
- Check for understanding by asking students to repeat or
  model the instructions and steps presented, before having
  them independently complete the assignment. At first, ask

simple, yes/no questions to check for understanding. As language acquisition progresses, more complicated instructions and questions (including "who, what, why, when, and how") can be interspersed. Even though these types of questions are more difficult, because they tend to be more thought provoking than questions that have short, factual answers, they should be included in these instructional dialogues—even if the English-language learner is just beginning to develop English proficiency. It is important to remember that a lack of English fluency does not mean that English-language learners cannot participate in tasks requiring complex thinking skills.

Concrete Examples and Experiences

Concrete examples and experiences can make input more comprehensible. These include visuals, films, field trips, science experiments, and cooperative learning activities that make a presentation more meaningful. These additions to classroom instruction give students a variety of ways to understand the information being presented, rather than always receiving the information via lecture and verbal explanations. Three issues to keep in mind are:

- Use materials and subject matter that relate to the students' background experiences and interests.
- Allow students to share information and personal experiences in their native language.
- Support the oral presentation of lessons (i.e., lectures) with a variety of visuals, and intersperse these with opportunities for students to participate in hands-on activities.

Ongoing Assessment

Teachers should frequently assess the effects of instructional activities for all students through an array of measures. Ongoing, curriculum-based assessment is a widely advocated approach to measuring both English-language development and academic/cognitive growth. Such measures can be administered in the students' native languages and/ or in English, depending on the purpose of the assessment. Informal instructional assessment during class time is also an excellent way to probe and track, in multiple ways, what students are getting out of lessons, discussions, practice, independent work, partner learning, or cooperative groups. These assessments can guide teachers in adjusting their teaching methods and providing responsive feedback.

The need to provide feedback and correction varies with the development and age of students. In the beginning stages of English-language learning, it's important for the teacher to model correct usage and to provide feedback on concepts and ideas, rather than always correcting student use of grammar. During later stages of English-language learning, however, it is important that the teacher identify grammatical errors and provide specific feedback to students.

Consistent Language Use

Teachers should be particularly thoughtful and consistent in the way they use language in the classroom. For example, synonyms, metaphors, similes, and idioms should be used carefully and purposefully. The adage that if someone does not understand what you are saying, you should try a different example, may not be helpful with English-language learners. Even though the new example may be an excellent one, students may not understand the words in the new language; repetition of the first example can be much more helpful.

Remember that using clear, consistent language does not mean using "childish" language. We have seen teachers effectively use quite sophisticated terms such as "character clue" and "migration" with English-language learners. However, these terms were clearly defined, with relevant examples provided.

Teachers should also monitor their language pace. For example, many fourth-grade teachers of native English speakers may see their role as providing models of the richness of the English language, and therefore use many synonyms and metaphors as a means of demonstrating that richness. This approach can be disastrous for English-language learners, depending on their level of English proficiency.

The main point for teachers is to be aware of their language use. Of course, the use of idioms, synonyms, and metaphors is part of dynamic, rich instruction, and should be included as long as students are given adequate explanations for these words. In using these words, it is important for the teacher to be aware of the language levels of the students in the classroom. In addition, it is important to be aware of appropriate times to use these types of words. One general rule of thumb that evolved in our discussions with researchers, teachers, and administrators is to be extremely careful and consistent in language use when presenting a new concept, and to use synonyms, similes, and metaphors primarily when expanding on or reviewing a concept.

It is common for many students with academic difficulties to receive services from a variety of support programs—making consistency even more crucial. For example, it is not uncommon for students with disabilities to receive language and academic support in regular education programs such as English as a second language, Title I, and Migrant Tutorial, and once they are in special education, to be included in other programs for students with learning disabilities or speech and language impairments. Unless there is a high degree of coordination between these programs, the issue of consistent language use may be compromised, and instruction may in fact be less comprehensible than it would be in any single program.

Balance of Cognitive and Language Demands

A balance needs to be struck between language and cognitive demands. Effective teachers reduce the cognitive demands on students when the primary goal is to encourage English-language expression, and encourage students to use a variety of supports, including the native language, when the cognitive task is inherently demanding. In addition to English-language acquisition and English use in content areas, it is important for teachers to encourage some use of native languages in the content areas; skillful use of both English-language and native-language resources is critical.

English-language use. Adequate instructional time for English-language learning should be established. This does not necessarily mean there needs to be a separate time for English-language instruction; English-language learning can be integrated into content areas. However, some of the teachers and administrators we have spoken with note that attempts to merge ESL instruction with content-area instruction sometimes run the risk of focusing so much time on content learning that English-language learning is compromised. They feel that teachers need to have clear, focused times when the goal for students is to build English-language skills.

There's a need to set aside time for English-language acquisition, as well as for English-language learning. Acquisition involves opportunities for English-language learners to practice speaking in the new language to develop fluency and proficiency. It is sometimes thought of as the subconscious process of learning language, mimicking the process we go through when acquiring our first language. In contrast, English-language *learning* implies learning new English-language skills. This is the more conscious process, which has to do with "knowing about the language" (Krashen, 1982). English-language learning can be done through academic content; acquisition can be done through opportunities to engage in conversations, interactions, and discussions. Writers' Workshop can provide good opportunities for language acquisition.

It is important to ensure that students have sufficient opportunities to actively use *academic* language, especially in oral discourse. Learning environments should be structured so that students have many opportunities to use language beyond single-word answers and short phrases. For example, rather than answering questions that have correct and incorrect answers, English-language learners should be given opportunities to explain information in their own words, summarize the meaning of new information, explain why they believe certain content is important, and talk about what they liked best or found most interesting about a particular lesson. Class-wide peer tutoring activities seem to provide an excellent framework for helping students actively participate in structured academic discussions.

Native-language use. Use of students' native languages can be an excellent means to help student learn new concepts. Native language use can be respected and fostered through the availability of books and other materials in the students' native languages, and through the availability of other individuals who speak the students' native languages—including teaching assistants, parents, local high school or university students, and, of course, classroom peers. In an effort to "speed up" the process of learning English, some teachers and administrators do not allow students to use the native language when working with other students of the same language background. Administrators also frequently separate these students during instruction. This is often not advisable.

One effective technique for English-language learners is to preview information and the core vocabulary in the native language. After the English presentation and practice activities, reviewing and checking for comprehension in English and the native language helps determine levels of learning and retention. This intentional balance may be one of the most essential instructional practices for English-language learners experiencing academic difficulties.

Some understanding of varying cultural norms regarding language and communication is also critical. A "one size fits all" approach to classroom discussions will not work; each culture has its own conventions. These conventions can relate to the amount of talking that is considered appropriate during a lesson, the meaning of direct eye contact, and the volume of speech—to name just three of many potentially important examples. Basic material about key cultural conventions can and should be accessed from conversations with parents and other members of the community. Teachers should not stereotype students—assuming, for example, that all Russian students act in a particular fashion. Respect for individual differences is crucial.

Peer Tutoring and Collaboration

Language minority students must be given opportunities to move from learning and producing limited word translations and fragmented concepts to using longer sentences and expressing more complex ideas and feelings (Barrera, 1984). The task of encouraging students to express their ideas in a new language, and in increasingly complex forms, presents a significant challenge for general education teachers working with English-language learners. A more natural, fluid learning environment is necessary for language development. English-language learners need frequent opportunities to use language to obtain what they want or to express their thoughts, feelings, and ideas (Fradd, 1987). The teacher's role in these activities is to create a classroom atmosphere where students are encouraged to express what they are thinking and how they are doing.

Two promising strategies for providing opportunities to use language during instruction are cooperative learning groups and class-wide peer tutoring (Arreaga-Meyer, in press). Small cooperative groups allow students to interact with peers while working on schoolwork assignments, and give them a chance to share their knowledge and language skills. Peers can often be excellent mediators in helping to bridge language gaps between classroom teachers and English-language learners. Peers, in essence, can serve as unofficial "teacher assistants" for English-language learners. A paid paraprofessional, a parent volunteer, a community member, or an older student could also serve as a tutor.

Teachers and administrators we spoke with noted the benefits of using cooperative learning and class-wide peer tutoring strategies, especially for English-language learners. Use of cooperative learning groups with English-language learners provides many potential benefits, such as:

- creating opportunities to use language in a meaningful and nonthreatening fashion (Baca & Cervantes, 1989; McGroarty, 1989);

- drawing on primary-language skills while developing second-language skills, especially if other English-language learners work together (McGroarty, 1989);
- promoting higher-order cognitive and linguistic discourse (Garcia, 1992); and
- fostering peer modeling and peer feedback rather than formal and often embarrassing error-correction procedures.

It is important to note, however, that adequate structure and purpose is necessary for students to benefit from these kinds of activities. In fact, the experiences of teachers suggested that it takes at least one academic year to learn to organize and manage cooperative learning groups efficiently and effectively. Many times, students needed a great deal of assistance in developing the organizational skills necessary to run cooperative groups efficiently. It is also important for teachers to spend a good deal of front-end time explaining and modeling expectations for how students are to tutor or work cooperatively. While students work in cooperative groups or peer tutoring teams, teachers need to institute processes to ensure that students keep focused on the purpose of the activities.

Instructional options that include tutors and paraprofessionals should not replace teacher-student interactions and instruction. Teachers inexperienced in working with English-language learners frequently turn over the bulk of instructional responsibilities to others and provide insufficient monitoring of the learning that takes place. It is always the classroom teacher's responsibility to ensure that high-quality instruction is provided to English-language learners and that they are learning appropriate curriculum objectives. Teachers are responsible for ensuring that the learning goals they set with English-language learners are in concert with key school, district, and state objectives.

SUMMARY AND CONCLUSIONS

This chapter presented a range of strategies that have been highlighted in discussions with researchers and teachers, and in our own reading of the research. Although what is viewed as effective instruction for English-language learners continues to be refined, the strategies presented here have much promise for increasing the academic performance of many English-language learners. We recognize that although the strategies presented in this chapter appear to be simple in theory, they are not necessarily easy to implement. In our experience, we have found that it is critical for teachers working with this diverse student population to collaborate and share ideas.

In addition to communication between teachers, teachers stressed the importance of including parents and community members in efforts to improve instructional practices. Creating school settings in which parents feel encouraged to participate (posting bilingual signs, sending home notices in the home language, etc.) and setting up strategies to encourage parental involvement with students' homework can help to bridge the often observed gap between home and school. One educator noted how assigning homework that can be completed in either English or the home language, or that requires students to talk with their parents (such as interviewing parents for their experiences or thoughts), can increase parental involvement. Students can also be encouraged to read books in English to their parents, regardless of the English-proficiency levels of the parents.

Teachers and administrators also noted the importance of long-range planning for this group of students. One theme that has recurred frequently in our discussions with teachers and administrators is the lack of long-range planning for English-language learners. Even in districts with experience working with English-language learners, there is often a tendency to deal with each problematic situation by "putting out the fire." We believe it is critically important for districts and schools that are going to work with English-language learners to clearly think through what they hope to accomplish over the long term, and how they believe they can best get there.

Sitting down and establishing where teachers and other professionals at a school would like to see each student be in a 2- or 3-year period can be an extremely worthwhile experience. It can help prioritize instructional focus areas and goals, and it can solicit parental input in determining what instructional programs are best for their child. Also, long-range planning gives schools the opportunity to learn about variations in the rates of student cognitive growth over time. In particular, it is important for teachers and school personnel to understand that the pace of growth will differ between students. Even with each individual student, academic growth is not necessarily a consistent, linear process. However, meaningful growth should occur for every student, and effective long-range planning must include procedures to determine whether sufficient progress is taking place.

Improving the learning experiences of English-language learners requires the integration of a range of teaching strategies, active parental involvement, and sufficient planning. We believe that this chapter highlights what is currently known about practices that can best support both the language and academic needs of English-language learners.

REFERENCES

Anderson, V., & Roit, M. (in press). Reading as a gateway to language proficiency for language minority students in the primary grades. In R. Gersten & R. Jiménez (Eds.), *Promoting learning for culturally and linguistically diverse students: Classroom applications from contemporary research.* Atlanta, GA: Wadsworth.

Anderson, V., & Roit, M. (1996). Linking reading comprehension instruction to language development for language-minority students. *Elementary School Journal, 96*(3), 295-310.

Arreaga-Meyer, C. (in press). Language sensitive peer mediated instruction for culturally and linguistically diverse learners in the intermediate elementary grades. In R. Gersten & R. Jiménez (Eds.), *Promoting learning for culturally and linguistically diverse students: Classroom applications from contemporary research.* Atlanta, GA: Wadsworth.

Baca, L., & Almanza, E. (1991). *Language minority students with disabilities.* Reston, VA: Council for Exceptional Children.

Baca, L., & Cervantes, H.T. (1989). *The bilingual special education interface* (2nd ed.). Columbus, OH: Merrill.

Barrera, R. (1984). Bilingual reading in the primary grades: Some questions about questionable views and practices. In T.H. Escobar (Ed.), *Early childhood bilingual education* (pp. 164-183). New York: Teachers College Press.

Beck, I. (1991). Story map. In J.M. Macon., D. Bewell, & M.E. Vogt (Eds.), *Response to literature.* Newark, DE: International Reading Association, Inc.

Beck, I.L., McKeown, M.G., & McCaslin, E.S. (1983). Vocabulary development: All contexts are not created equal. *Elementary School Journal, 83*(3), 177-181.

Campbell, J., Gersten, R., & Kolar, C. (1993). *The perplexities of providing quality instruction to language minority students with learning disabilities: Five findings from micro-ethnographies.* (Tech. Rep. No. 93-5). Eugene, OR: Eugene Research Institute.

Chamot, A.U., & O'Malley, J.M. (1996). The Cognitive Academic Language Learning Approach (CALLA): A model for linguistically diverse classrooms. *Elementary School Journal, 96*(3), 259-274.

Collier, V. (1995). Acquiring a second language for school. *Directions in Language and Education National Clearinghouse for Bilingual Education, 1*(4).

Crawford, J. (1989). *Bilingual education: History, politics, theory, and practice.* Trenton, NJ: Crane Publishing Company, Inc.

Cummins, J. (1981). The role of primary language development in promoting educational success for language minority students. In *Schooling and language minority students: A theoretical framework.* Los Angeles, CA: Office of Bilingual Bicultural Education.

Echevarria, J. (in press). Preparing text and classroom materials for English-language learners: curriculum adaptations in secondary school settings. In R. Gersten & R. Jiménez (Eds.), *Promoting learning for culturally and linguistically diverse students: Classroom applications from contemporary research.* Atlanta, GA: Wadsworth.

Echevarria, J. & Graves, A. (in press). *Sheltered content instruction: Teaching English-language learners with diverse abilities.* Des Moines, IA: Allyn & Bacon.

Englert, C.S., Raphael, T.E., & Anderson, L.M. (1992). Socially-mediated instruction: Improving students' knowledge and talk about writing. *Elementary School Journal, 92*(4), 411-449.

Fitzgerald, J. (1995). English-as-a-second-language learners' cognitive reading processes: A review of research in the United States. *Review of Educational Research, 65*(2), 145-190.

Fradd, S.H. (1987). Accommodating the needs of limited English proficient students in regular classrooms. In S. Fradd & W. Tikunoff (Eds.), *Bilingual education and special education: A guide for administrators* (pp. 133 - 182). Boston: Little, Brown.

Garcia, E. (1992). Analysis of literacy enhancement for middle school Hispanic students through curriculum integration. *The Journal of Educational Issues of Language Minority Students, 10,* 131-145.

Hartman, D.K. (1995). Eight readers reading: The intertextual links of proficient readers reading multiple passages. *Reading Research Quarterly, 30,* 520-561.

Idol, L. (1987). Group story mapping: A comprehension strategy for both skilled and unskilled readers. *Journal of Learning Disabilities, 20* (4), 196-205.

Jiménez, R., Gersten, R., & Rivera, A. (1996). Conversations with a Chicana teacher: Supporting students' transition from native-to-English-language instruction. *Elementary School Journal, 96*(3), 333-342.

Kline, F.M., Deshler, D.D., & Schumaker, J.B. (1992). Implementing learning strategy instruction in class settings: A research perspective. In M. Pressley, K.R. Harris, & J.T. Guthrie (Eds.), *Promoting academic competence and literacy in school* (361-406). San Diego: Academic Press.

Krashen, S. (1982). *Principles and practice in second language acquisition.* New York: Pergamon.

McGroarty, M. (1989). The benefits of cooperative learning arrangements in second language acquisition. *NABE Journal, 13*(2), 127-143.

Moll, L.C. (1992). Bilingual classroom studies and community analysis: Some recent trends. *Educational Researcher, 21*(2), 20-24.

Nagy, W.E. (1988). *Vocabulary instruction and reading comprehension* (Tech. Rep. No. 431). Champaign, IL: Center for the Study of Reading, University of Illinois.

O'Connor, J.R. (1991). *Exploring American history.* Englewood, NJ: Globe.

Ogle, D.M. (1986). K-W-L: A teaching model that develops active reading of expository text. *The Reading Teacher, 39*(6), 564-570.

Reyes, E., & Bos, C. (in press). Interactive semantic mapping and charting: enhancing content area learning for language minority students. In R. Gersten & R. Jiménez (Eds.), *Promoting learning for culturally and linguistically diverse students: Classroom applications from contemporary research.* Atlanta, GA: Wadsworth.

Rousseau, M.K., Tam, B.K.Y, & Ramnarain, R. (1993). Increasing reading proficiency of language-minority students with speech and language impairments. *Education and Treatments of Children, 16*(3), 254-271.

Short, D. (1994). Expanding middle school horizons: Integrating language, culture, and social studies. *TESOL Quarterly, 28,* 581-608.

Yates, J.R., & Ortiz, A.A. (1991). Professional development needs of teachers who serve exceptional language minorities in today's schools. *Teacher Education and Special Education, 14*(1), 11-18.

INDEX